Presidential Campaigning
in the Internet Age

Oxford Studies in Digital Politics

Series Editor: Andrew Chadwick, Royal Holloway, University of London

Presidential Campaigning in the Internet Age

JENNIFER STROMER-GALLEY

OXFORD
UNIVERSITY PRESS

Oxford University Press is a department of the University of Oxford.
It furthers the University's objective of excellence in research, scholarship,
and education by publishing worldwide.

Oxford   New York
Auckland   Cape Town   Dar es Salaam   Hong Kong   Karachi
Kuala Lumpur   Madrid   Melbourne   Mexico City   Nairobi
New Delhi   Shanghai   Taipei   Toronto

With offices in
Argentina   Austria   Brazil   Chile   Czech Republic   France   Greece
Guatemala   Hungary   Italy   Japan   Poland   Portugal   Singapore
South Korea   Switzerland   Thailand   Turkey   Ukraine   Vietnam

Oxford is a registered trademark of Oxford University Press
in the UK and certain other countries.

Published in the United States of America by
Oxford University Press
198 Madison Avenue, New York, NY 10016

Library of Congress Cataloging-in-Publication Data

Stromer-Galley, Jennifer.
Presidential campaigning in the Internet age / Jennifer Stromer-Galley.
pages cm
ISBN 978–0–19–973193–0 (hardcover : alk. paper) — ISBN 978–0–19–973194–7 (pbk. : alk. paper)
1. Internet in political campaigns—United States.   2. Digital communications—United States.
3. Presidential candidates—United States.   I. Title.
JK2281.S78 2014
324.7'3—dc23
2013024870

9 8 7 6 5 4 3 2 1
Printed in the United States of America
on acid-free paper

To my dad, Merlin Stromer,
for teaching me to "work first, then play."

Contents

List of Figures

Acknowledgments

Although I have studied presidential campaigns and their use of the Internet since my masters thesis on Bob Dole's website back in 1997, this book would not have come into being without Andy Chadwick, editor of this series on Digital Politics. It was his suggestion back in 2008 at a conference at Royal Holloway University that sparked the kernel of an idea that eventually became this book. It was his belief in my ideas that helped transform this book into a reality. For his thoughtfulness and care in cultivating scholarship on digital politics, I am grateful. A sincere thank you to Angela Chnapko, my acquisition editor, and to the rest of the publishing team at Oxford for deftly guiding me through the process and helping make this work shiny.

I am indebted to many people who helped me construct this book. Three of my students helped me collect news and academic articles: Chris Flowers, Ian Sheinheit, and Xiaoai Ren. Chris and Ian further digested the articles on presidential campaigning online, giving me a handy resource while I wrote. Several people read and provided vital feedback on drafts of chapters, identifying where I was off course and reassuring me when I was on track. They include Camilo Aggio, Jaime Banks, Jim Bonville, Philip N. Howard, Daniel Kreiss, Brian McKernan, Marina Marcou O'Malley, Michael Rancourt, and Jingsi Christina Wu. Emily Gould brainstormed with me the role of the Dean for America blog in facilitating parasocial interaction. Andrea Baker helped me analyze the Dean blog. Taewoo Nam had the insight to explore the relationship between social media use and political communication and participation in the 2008 election using Pew Internet & American Life data. Micah Sifry and Michael Turk opened up their address books to help me track down campaign staff. Sarah Beth Evans diligently helped me get my citations into order. Cathy Hannabach did the magical work of indexing the book. Richard Isomaki was my judicious copy editor who saved me from total embarrassment in a few places. The flaws that remain in these chapters are solely my own.

xii *Acknowledgments*

This book would be incomplete without the insight provided by the nineteen campaign staff I interviewed, who provided me background and important details about the campaigns. I have been conducting interviews with campaign staff since 1998, and thus many of the interviews were conducted with staff who had recently completed their campaigns. On occasion, I needed to collect additional information while I was writing this book, and was able to track people down to get their recollections of events. The following campaign staff were generous with their time and insights: Rob Arena (Dole '96); Peter Daou (Kerry '04 and Clinton '08); Max Fose (McCain '00); Sam Graham-Feisten (Obama '08); Ben Green (Gore '00); Katie Harbath (Giuliani '08); Vincent R. Harris (Huckabee '08); John Hlinko (Clark '04); Rosy Kalfus (Obama '08); Justine Lam (Paul '08); Lynn Reid (Bradley '00); Josh Ross (Kerry '04 and Clinton '08); Patrick Ruffini (Pawlenty '12); Mike Shannon (Bush '00 and '04); Lynn Siegel (Clinton '96); Mark SooHoo (McCain '08); Andy Sohn (Clinton '96); Tim Tagaris (Dodd '08); Michael Turk (Bush '04 and Thompson '08). I also attended several conferences over the years that featured campaign staff dishing what worked and did not, and much of what I heard is in these pages. These conferences include the Personal Democracy Forum, Campaigns & Elections Campaign Tech, and George Washington University's Institute for Politics, Democracy and the Internet conferences.

This book's foundation rests upon groundwork laid through the variety of records that exist about presidential campaigns in the Internet age. The journalists' and commentators' reports helped inform this historical account of campaigns' practices. I would have been lost without the website www.4president. org for the 1996 and 2000 website screen captures that are provided. I thank the site's creator, Mike Dec, for making available the historical archive of campaign sites for the public. The Pew Internet & American Life Project and its head, Lee Rainie, provide an important record of the reach and impact of digital communication technologies in the United States. Finally, the Internet Archive (web. archive.org) is the source of many of the images included here. I am grateful that such an archive of the Internet exists.

I received support to work on this book from a University at Albany, SUNY Faculty Research Activity Program Award, and with a semester-length sabbatical. I also received support from the School of Information Studies at Syracuse University to complete the final touches on the manuscript.

Several people have served as inspiration to me and have provided mentoring and counsel that helped hone my scholarship. They include Bruce Bimber, Karlyn Kohrs Campbell, Richard Davis, Kirsten Foot, Theresa Harrison, Ron N. Jacobs, Kathleen Hall Jamieson, Nick Jankowski, W. Russell Neuman, Anita Pomerantz, Vince Price, Robert E. Sanders, Ed Schiappa, and Tomek Strzalkowski.

Finally, the people I share my daily life with give me inspiration and joy. A sincere thank you to Rosa Mikeal Martey for her friendship. I must express my gratitude to my au pairs—Sabrina Konig, Elena Lichtscheidel, Tuija Hillner, Frauke Adams, and Natasha Makrukha—who have so carefully and kindly helped watch my daughters while I worked. Isabel arrived the year before I started this book, Audrey and Bridget arrived the year after, and they taught me that I could do my best writing at 5 a.m. To Jon, words fail to express my gratitude. The spouse who is willing to help me sort out the arguments in this book while also carrying the burden of domestic life especially during the last months of manuscript preparation is one who deserves to sleep in more often.

1

Introduction: The Paradox of Digital Campaigning in a Democracy

> A lot of people on the Net have given up on traditional politics precisely because it was about television and the ballot box, and they had no way to shout back. What we've given people is a way to shout back, and we listen—they don't have to shout anymore.
> —2004 presidential candidate Howard Dean[1]

In the United States, scholars, pundits, and political watchers have rejoiced over the opportunities that digital communication technologies (DCTs) seemingly bring to electoral politics,[2] opening up political campaigns at the presidential level to greater involvement by ordinary citizens. The interactive capacity of DCTs—the Internet and the many software applications that run through it via computer or smartphone—offers symbolic and practical opportunities for two-way communication to occur between campaigns and their supporters. Such two-way communication can make traditionally hierarchical and controlled political campaigns more decentered, genuinely involving ordinary citizens in the work of campaigning.

Barack Obama's presidential victory in 2008 is held up as a model campaign that embraced and listened to its supporters. The campaign directly involved people in the work of campaigning, generating excitement and spreading information about the candidate, which in turn seemed to contribute to his remarkable victory. Obama's re-election campaign in 2012 further cemented the sense that he had found the magic ingredient of direct inclusion of supporters in the campaign through digital media that helped propel him to victory.

Elements of this thinking are right. Obama established his strength as a contender through his ability to invest a large number of supporters in the campaign enough to contribute small amounts of money online. In this way, he was able to draw attention to his nascent candidacy in early 2007 against an established, formidable opponent in Hillary Clinton.

Yet the premise that DCTs have been used by political campaigns in truly democratic ways is largely incorrect. Democracy in the truest sense is about broad participation by the citizenry, with all voices equal. Instead, paradoxically, political campaigns in a democracy (especially at the presidential level) are undemocratic affairs. DCTs, channeled through the Internet but increasingly over smartphones and tablets, have affordances or characteristics with the potential to involve and directly connect people. Campaigns, however, do not use them ultimately that way. Indeed, the purpose of a presidential campaign is not to genuinely engage citizens as coequal actors. Instead, *citizen involvement in the campaign historically has been and continues to be a means to an end*: winning the election for the candidate.

This symbolic reality has always been the case in the United States, but the affordances of DCTs magnify that reality, rendering it visible. It is not all affordances, either, but the specific affordance of *interactivity* that reveals the imperative of political campaigns to craft strategic messaging that motivate segments of the electorate to mobilize for one candidate or against the other. Interactivity, as a concept, can be thought of as a property of the communication channel that makes feedback possible, either feedback with the computer system or application, or feedback between people channeled through the Internet.[3] That distinct, simple property reveals the ways that presidential campaigns aim typically to circumvent interaction when it gives supporters greater genuine participatory voice in the campaign, and promote it when it serves strategic aims and goals.

To understand presidential campaign practices as they adapt to and adopt DCTs, I conducted nineteen interviews with political campaign staff, several of whom were interviewed immediately following their campaigns. I immersed myself in the news and events during each of the past five election cycles, and recently reread and combed news coverage of the political campaigns for key events, actors, and public and elite perceptions. I also observed campaigns' practices, from websites to speeches to tweets, since 1996.

This immersion in political campaigns of the last five presidential election cycles leads me to conclude that the decidedly undemocratic view of *controlled interactivity* is how most campaigns operate.[4] Campaigns have historically used affordances of medium or system interactivity,[5] in which people can interact with tools, click on polls, watch videos, and forward messages from campaigns to others. Opportunities for human interaction through the Internet, with candidates and campaign staff and with each other, were restricted. In the past three election cycles, a shift happened that increased opportunities for interaction among supporters and with the broader electorate, but interaction with campaign staff online remains restricted. There is little strategic advantage for campaigns to enable rich dialogue with citizens about campaign strategy or about policy positions of candidates. The purpose of a campaign is to raise enough money to build an adequate organization to target the right kinds of voters that will turn out to vote for the candidate on Election Day. Efforts that attack opponents and make their supporters feel less interested in turning out to vote do not hurt either.

Thus, the argument of this book continues in a vein of scholarship about politics online that goes back to Margolis and Resnick's book, *Politics as Usual*, which argued back in 2000 that there would be no cyberspace "revolution." Instead, elite political actors who were most active and involved in the mass-media era would also be the ones to benefit in the digital media era. They argued that for all the hope that the Internet would open up new degrees and kinds of political involvement, the reality is that the same advantages and disadvantages that exist politically offline would manifest online. My argument is that the ways that politicians and their staff use DCTs ultimately are meant to benefit the candidate; greater genuine democratization is not on their agenda.[6]

In addition to providing evidence for that argument, this book details the strategies by presidential campaigns as DCTs were adopted. Several books have been published over the past decade and a half that provide snapshots of election cycles and the ways digital media were used and affected campaigns' and voter behavior. Selnow and Davis each examined the 1996 election cycle as part of their books highlighting how digital media might change politics and who would most likely be affected.[7] Bimber and Davis looked in detail at the 2000 election, focusing on content of campaign websites and examining voting effects as campaigns expanded their strategic messaging to the Internet.[8] The edited collection by Williams and Tedesco examined multiple dimensions of the 2004 election online.[9] Kreiss conducted rich ethnographies of the Howard Dean 2004 campaign and the 2008 Obama campaign, illuminating their organizational practices around new media.[10] Foot and Schneider examined presidential and congressional web practices in the 2000, 2002, and 2004 election cycles, noting how web campaigning changed.[11] Each of these books offers important insight into presidential campaigning online, and I draw on that work here.

Arguably, though, presidential campaigning through the Internet has reached a state of maturity. Given its development, there is a need for a book that looks across campaign cycles. Thus, this book contributes to historical understanding about the shifting practices of presidential campaigns. Popular and academic claims are made that Obama's 2008 campaign was the first to truly harness the Internet. Based on a long view of presidential campaigns, as well as a look at "also-rans" (those candidates who ran but did not win), it is evident that Obama's campaign got the calculus correct with regard to deploying digital media in the campaign, but his campaign was in no way the first to experiment. As far back as

Bob Dole's website in 1996, in each campaign cycle creative breakthroughs, bold acts born of necessity, and clear-eyed recognition of affordances of DCTs moved the practices of digital campaigning in important directions. Thus, a mission of this book is to help scholars of political communication and digital media contextualize and better understand the shifting practices by campaigns long before Barack Obama was a household name.[12] After five presidential election cycles, a book that details the history of presidential campaigns in the Internet age is warranted.

To that end, this book takes an approach similar to Jamieson's in her analysis of the practical and symbolic image construction in television advertisements by presidential campaigns from 1952 to 1992.[13] In the chapters ahead, I examine the presidential campaigns in the United States from 1996, when the World Wide Web was first used for presidential campaigning, through 2012, when practices were being tuned to perfection using data analytics for targeting and mobilizing particular voter segments for the purpose of winning the election. I highlight some of the technological and legal shifts that campaigns have adapted to while also looking at the ways in which they harness DCTs to channel citizen involvement in their campaigns, construct their organization, and craft their political image. The term *campaigns* in this book refers to the many individuals who comprise the organization that work on behalf of the candidate as well as the practices and technologies they deploy in the work of campaigning.[14]

This chapter situates my argument by providing a brief explanation of the philosophical underpinnings of this book, then frames an understanding of DCTs relative to the prior mass-media era, and examines why DCT uses today can be better understood in relation to the era of broadcast and cable. Then, because this book aims to provide detail and analysis of campaign strategizing, I unpack a logic for thinking about presidential campaign practices borrowed from political communication scholar Robert Denton, which I further expand on to reflect the realities of the contemporary campaign environment.[15] Then I provide a brief examination of the theoretical scholarship that has underscored our contemporary worries about an unfettered, fully interactive electorate. Last, I walk readers through a brief outline of the book, underscoring the shifting campaign practices that occurred between 1996 and 2012.

Philosophical Underpinnings

The philosophical orientation of this book aligns with the normative vision set forth by Benjamin Barber in *Strong Democracy*, while noting that symbolically the actual work of campaigns continue to be as problematic as Murray Edelman observed of mass-mediated politics in *Constructing the Political Spectacle*.

Benjamin Barber advocated a "strong democracy," what he describes as "politics in the participatory mode when conflict is resolved in the absence of an independent ground through a participatory process of ongoing, proximate self-legislation and the creation of a political community capable of transforming dependent, private individuals into free citizens and partial and private interests into public good."[16] In a strong democratic system, citizens are active in governance, monitoring and informing the work of their representatives. They talk with each other about political and social issues and about political processes as part of their daily lives. They are amateurs, not elites; they have no particular specialty and engage each other without what Barber calls the "intermediary of expertise." Barber sees communication technology as key to enabling strong democracy because it promotes genuine interactivity across distance, bringing diverse groups of people together to discuss and reason and come to collective judgment about what is right and just in society in the spirit of working toward a common good.

Although much hope still pervades popular and academic thinking about digital technologies (especially the communication technologies captured by the phrase *social media*), the reality is that political campaigns do not use DCTs to genuinely engage citizens and supporters. Instead, when we examine campaigns for their symbolic behaviors, in the spirit of Edelman, much of what is offered as interactivity is a simulacrum,[17] a show. The rhetoric of participation and the presence of interactive gadgets, blogs, or Facebook profiles create merely a spectacle of interactivity. DCTs have characteristics, or affordances, that facilitate genuine engagement in a strong democratic sense: the perspectives and aspirations of the citizens are seriously heard, contemplated, and incorporated in political campaign practices, serving to inform policy as well as campaign strategy. Yet the realities of presidential campaigns are such that DCTs are used to direct and control citizen-supporters to work in concert to achieve campaign goals.[18]

Some might argue that campaigns are not the right venue for a strong democracy program, and that the right place for citizen engagement is policy matters during the legislative process. This view, however, ignores that political campaigns are sites of political renewal in democratic society. Elections in particular are important rituals that enact our common ideal of democracy and celebrate citizens' role in it.[19] Presidential campaigns are exactly the opportunity for a strong democracy to emerge, especially in the contemporary communications environment in which DCTs enable networked interaction across the electorate.

Thus, one might hope a strong democracy would emerge in the context of a presidential campaign, especially in light of the contemporary digital media environment that enables genuine interactivity. The practical realities, however, suggest otherwise. Activism and involvement by citizens in the political process might happen through the work of advocacy organizations,[20] but that is not what political campaigns currently see as their purpose, nor will DCTs on their own genuinely open up campaigns to true democratic participation in which citizens are coequal participants in the process of campaigning.[21] Thus, the rhetoric of empowerment produced by candidate Howard Dean in the epigraph to this chapter suggests a campaign that is genuinely open to the views of supporters. When one looks closely at the practices of his campaign, however, it becomes evident that such rhetoric is largely symbolic and that genuine dialogue and interaction with supporters was generally absent.[22] This is the symbolic and practical reality we face.

The Digital Communication Environment

To understand the contemporary communication environment that presidential campaigns are utilizing and why interactivity is a key affordance that might lead to conclusions of empowerment and expanded participation by the electorate, it is important to understand how the Internet came to be and why its uses actualize its affordances.

The infrastructure of the Internet was designed for uninterrupted flow of communication between humans or between humans and computer systems. The Internet was designed to solve a concrete problem in the 1950s: how to keep communication flowing in the United States with government and military commanders after a nuclear attack by the Soviet Union.[23] Paul Baran conceived the idea of a communications network that would packet information into small chunks with a "to" and "from" encoded in them that could go from one node to another in a network until they reached their destination. No central node would be responsible for ensuring the packet reached its destination.[24] "Packet-switching" of information, as it is called, is a key digital innovation that made the Internet as we know it today possible.

Although many other breakthroughs helped build the Internet of today, one particular set of innovations stand out. In 1992 Tim Berners-Lee created HyperText Markup Language (HTML).[25] It and the related HyperText Transfer Protocol (HTTP) connected information through *hyperlinks*, using tags to format text and pictures to provide layout and design, such as italics or colors, and also eventually to channel images, movies, and music. By 1994, when the company Netscape, which created the first commercial World Wide Web browser, had its initial public offering (IPO) the public began to take notice of this nascent communication infrastructure.[26] By 1996 major telecommunication companies such as AT&T purchased the primary infrastructure from the government, and regulations allowed commerce to grow online.

A report by the Pew Research Center in the summer of 1995 found that about 24 million Americans were going online regularly, a twofold increase from the prior year.[27] About half of Internet users in 1995 subscribed to an online service, such as America Online, but interest and dependency on the technology was "soft."[28] Only one-third of survey respondents said they would miss going online "a lot" if they could not do so. As one social commentator characterized the Internet in the by-gone era:

> It's 1996, and you're bored. What do you do? If you're one of the lucky people with an AOL account, you probably do the same thing you'd do in 2009: Go online. Crank up your modem, wait 20 seconds as you log in, and there you are—"Welcome." You check your mail, then spend a few minutes chatting with your AOL buddies about which of you has the funniest screen name (you win, pimpodayear94).[29]

There was not much else to do; there was no Facebook, YouTube, or Google. During the 1996 presidential campaign, only about 10% of American adults said they got some political news or information from the Internet.[30]

In contrast, by 2012 over 80% of American adults were online, according to the Pew Internet & American Life Project.[31] Over 90% of Internet users read e-mail or used a search engine to find information. Just over 70% watched a video on a site like YouTube, and 66% used a social networking site like Facebook. In August 2011, 60% of Americans read political information online, and during the 2012 presidential campaign, 60% of Americans used social media to express their thoughts about politics and to read the political views of others.[32] By way of comparison, 55% of adult Americans surveyed in September 2012 reported watching broadcast or cable news, and only 33% reported reading a print newspaper.[33] Digital communication today is ubiquitous in the personal and political life of Americans.

Channeling human interaction is a core function of the Internet—from its earliest conception through to today's social media applications. In the Internet's earliest days, when computers were the size of classrooms, users queued to use them. Even though the purpose of those computers was to analyze numbers, users programmed applications so that they could leave messages for each other. Ray Tomlinson, an engineer at BBN Corporation in Boston, designed the first e-mail program in 1971 to work over the Internet.[34] Leonard Kleinrock, who worked at Stanford and conducted network analysis for ARPANET, noted that e-mail soon consumed two-thirds of the bandwidth on the fledgling Internet, competing with file transfers and remote connections with networked computers.[35] Thus, the purpose of computers and the Internet as designed by their creators was to channel and analyze information. Yet what became an equally important function for the users of these systems was interaction, and e-mail was the killer app. Today, those killer apps extend beyond e-mail to include Facebook, Twitter, and video-sharing sites such as YouTube. Network traffic on the Internet still predominately is communication between people.

Thus, the Internet and interactivity are connected concepts. The Internet, as a dynamic, distributed communication system, advanced interactivity as a technological affordance. *Interactivity*, at its definitional core, is about feedback, either feedback indicated in a communication message between people or responsiveness in a communication system. Cybernetics theories back in the 1940s called attention to system interaction,[36] highlighting the ways in which a digital system that channels pulses of light could increase responsiveness within the system itself, reacting to input in appropriate, tailored ways. That responsiveness in the system has been referred to as system or network interactivity and medium interactivity.[37] The core idea is that technological systems can be designed to enable human input and receive a response from the system, such as showing the front page of the *New York Times* website, giving the results of a click poll about who will win the next reality contest, or playing new episodes of *Arrested Development* on Netflix.

That responsiveness also manifests in the form of human interaction. Rafaeli's definition of human interactivity I find particularly helpful in articulating the concept. He defines it as "an expression of the extent that in a given series of communication exchanges, any third (or later) transmission (or message) is related to the degree to which previous exchanges referred to an even earlier transmission."[38] The core idea is that when two people speak, they are interacting with each other when subsequent messages respond to prior messages. Rote expressions, such as the exchange "How are you today?" "Fine, thanks" are not interaction in Rafaeli's sense, because they are following a rehearsed social script. If instead, Lynn asked how Samira is doing today, and Samira responded by explaining that her day has been lousy because her car died on the way to work, now they are no longer following the social script. If Lynn replied by offering to give Samira a ride home from work, that would constitute an interaction. Communication with computer or software systems, called system interactivity or medium interactivity, is a lesser degree of interaction than that between humans through the Internet because humans have less agency when interacting with a system. The system's responsiveness is often preprogrammed for a specific response or set of responses, whereas interacting with another human typically means getting any range of responses, some predictable, some unpredictable.

Yet even system interactivity is more dynamic and user-empowering than the era of broadcast media of television, radio, and print. The broadcast model of communication is typically one-to-many, whereas the Internet can be one-to-one, one-to-many, many-to-many, and even many-to-one. With broadcast media, the content creators, producers, and distributors of that content are elites, sending their messages to a mass audience who passively receive that content. Online, audience feedback or user-generated content is not only possible but has become a norm of digital media application development.[39] The boundaries between author and reader blur in the Internet age, flattening longstanding hierarchies between content producers and content consumers.[40]

Communication Environments and Political Campaigning

Just as digital media affordances have shifted the relationship between author and audience, so to have they shifted the relationship between campaign and citizen. Thus, it is helpful to understand campaigns in the contemporary digital communications environment by contextualizing them within political campaigns of past eras. If we look back at prior campaigns and media systems, it becomes evident how interrelated the practices of campaigns are with the communication channels available to them.

The first presidential elections had little that we might call campaigning. Supporters and surrogates declared their support or opposition to candidates in the form of handbills and other print publications. As transportation became easier, a shift began in the 1820s as candidates more actively submitted themselves before the public. Budding political organizations would host barbeques in the South or clam bakes in the Northeast where candidates and other political officials would speak before the assembled potential voters.

The rapidly developing transportation infrastructure, combined with a change in the Electoral College and the growth of the political party, made the 1824 campaign closer to the mass campaigns of more contemporary times. Friends of the three candidates, John Quincy Adams, Henry Clay, and Andrew Jackson, traveled across the eastern and southern states stumping for their man through speeches and public meetings.[41] Voters knew when casting their ballots that they were voting for electors who were committed to voting for a given candidate; thus, the general public was voting more directly for candidates, engaging voters more directly in the national political process than had previously been the case.[42]

The penny press in the United States between the 1830s and 1840s, so-named because these newspapers cost a penny rather than the typical six cents for older papers, was tailored to appeal to a broader audience and included descriptions of social affairs, state and world events and crime, and political events.[43] These papers included editorials on social and political issues and had well-known affiliations with the political parties or political beliefs of the time.[44] Between 1800 and 1850 the country went from having about 250 papers to over 2,000 papers, with a quarter of those in 1850 being dailies.[45]

The broader dissemination of printed newspapers and handbills through the postal service made truly political *mass communication* possible. By 1840 there was a post office for every thousand people.[46] The infrastructure of the postal system enabled interested citizens from anywhere in the growing country to gain access to news about political events. According to Bimber, the combination of the post and the press "constituted a new political communication system in the United States"[47] wherein citizens could become informed about government and about citizens' opinions in other states. In turn, political elites could learn the opinions of citizens, theoretically creating interactivity, but at a macroscopic level.

The 1840 election between incumbent Martin van Buren and challenger William Henry Harrison is viewed by political campaign scholars as the first true political campaign.[48] The political parties established a stronger grassroots organizational structure that worked to mobilize eligible voters, which grew as suffrage rights expanded. Moreover, the political parties harnessed the mass media of the penny press and inexpensive steam printing for handbills and fliers to disseminate their candidate's message. The Whig Party made effective use of symbols to efficiently communicate a persona of Harrison as a war hero and a common man, by highlighting his role in the battle of Tippecanoe and deploying an image of a rural log cabin to manufacture Harrison as a man of humble origins, rather than the more accurate picture of him as son of a governor and the owner of a stately brick home. Jamieson describes the campaign as "a form of national jamboree replete with orchestrated parades, banners, torches, transparencies, and flags, omnipresent log cabins and hard cider, and coonskin caps."[49]

Over the next sixty years, political campaigns continued in this vein. Campaigning was more of a circus show than a serious airing of competing ideas and the genuine engagement of potential voters. Although the Lincoln-Douglas debates of 1858 for the Illinois Senate seat have been glorified as exhibiting the kind of carefully crafted arguments on significant policy matters to an audience of engaged and knowledgeable voters, Schudson casts doubt on such a narrative.[50] The debaters engaged in ad hominem attacks and made baseless arguments. Lincoln spun a tale of conspiracy suggesting Douglas and several other Democrats wanted to expand slavery. It is true that the audiences were large, numbering in the thousands, but they likely were not engaged, since they could not hear the debaters. Those who showed were there for the entertainment, the debates more akin to a boxing match than a reasoned series of argumentations. Audience members, as Douglas spoke, yelled out "hit him again" and "he can't dodge you."[51] Political parties organized large parades in towns that the presidential candidates would come through, and glee clubs were organized to sing patriotic tunes. In short, political campaigns were meant to entertain, not enlighten.

In the handbills and parade era of presidential campaigning, the political candidate was a central character in a drama to which the public was audience. The ultimate role the public played was in turning out to vote on Election Day. The political party had the critical job of energizing the public for the cause of the party, for which the candidate was the figurehead. The candidate was someone on display, to be watched, but not to be interacted with by the general public.

Broadcast technologies—radio around 1920 and television around 1950—are typically what we think of as mass media, and they created more opportunities for political communication to reach an increasing number of Americans. The diffusion of mass media meant that more Americans were receiving at least a little exposure to political news.[52] The three TV broadcast channels through the early 1980s aired the news at the same time each evening, and as a result a majority of Americans could not escape the news completely. Presidential campaigns purchased air time during the nightly news as well and the most popular programs in order to capitalize on the high likelihood that many potential voters would see the ad.[53]

The mass-media environment of the second half of the twentieth century shaped in specific ways the communication produced by candidates to reach ordinary citizens. Speeches were increasingly tailored to be carried broadly to the public through the filtered and framed messages of journalists in carefully constructed sound bites meant to be replayed on the nightly news or quoted in a news article.[54] Advertisements on TV and radio were crafted to produce maximum effect in shaping the attitudes of voters.[55]

Of great importance to understanding political campaign practices is that until recently the communication was one-way: candidates to voters. There were limited opportunities for citizens directly to participate in the political campaign, unless they were deeply involved in the organized labor movement.[56] Involvement for most citizens centered on watching those carefully constructed TV ads or reading political news articles and watching the nightly news to gain enough information as framed by candidates and journalists.

The channels of communication in the age of digital networks enable more associations to occur between political actors than were possible in the era of mass media. The ability of a campaign to mass-disseminate its message was combined with the demise of the strong political party, which in its heyday helped shepherd voters via political bosses and ward or precinct captains. The decline of the political party organization meant that citizens were more likely to be free agents in the political process. Indeed by 2012, one-third of registered voters were unaffiliated with the two major political parties.

Add to that the more communitarian values in the engineering of digital media and we see a distinct ethos emerge as compared with the broadcast media environment. Ryan refers to this changing ethos as a centrifugal, as opposed to centripetal, force: Digital technologies, in the way they were designed, push outward, enabling independence of users, rather than drawing inward, enabling dependence, as in the broadcast era.[57] Those who worked to create the core technologies that gave rise to the Internet developed a system that was to some degree *self-organizing*, where the algorithms channeled digital bits equally regardless of where or what they came from or where or to whom they were going. Moreover, the standards established to channel bits were defined in an egalitarian fashion, in which the protocols or rules would change as better ideas came along, while maintaining a basic standard of compatibility between hardware and software across the network. Indeed, the Web 2.0 Internet further pushes against hierarchy and control, aiming for a greater user-centered environment.[58] This design has important effects on presidential campaigning, potentially enabling greater citizen participation in political campaigns: citizens producing messages of their own as much as consuming messages from the campaign.

Presidential Campaigns and Their Purpose

Although the technological infrastructure of the Internet affords greater citizen involvement, presidential campaigns have a stake in keeping campaigns hierarchical and candidate-centered. To do so, they use the communication channels available to them to inform and persuade the electorate. Because of this, political campaigns are sensitive to the communication environment, and their strategies have changed along with the communication environment.

Since political campaigns are inherently communication campaigns,[59] the means of communication dictate the tactics they deploy to achieve their primary objective, which is winning. In the prebroadcast era, political campaigns relied on public spectacles—parades and picnics—to bring people in a community together, meet the candidate, identify strong supporters who could serve as local organizers once the campaign moved on to another town, and use them to get the less involved to turn out to vote on Election Day. In the broadcast era of television and cable, the focus shifted to carefully scripted messages on TV to sway as much of the electorate as possible. Campaigns still needed a field campaign and local organizers to contact people interpersonally, but the money and energy of presidential campaigns were heavily brought to bear on mass messaging.

The shift to a digital communication environment has opened up new tactics to meet the campaign's goals of winning the election. Strategists have started to think of citizens and their role in the campaign differently, neither as passive receivers of messages nor as coequal participants in the campaign's practices, but as *instruments* that can be harnessed in new ways to work on behalf of the campaign. Although the terminology we use has shifted from passive *viewers* in the broadcast era to active *users* in the digital era, such a shift does not necessarily mean that citizens have become full-blown actors in the work of campaigns, coequal in their strategizing and policy-making for the candidate.

In examining presidential campaigns as they have adapted to this changing communication paradigm, I find Robert Denton's typology helpful to conceptualize their essential strategic elements.[60] These elements will be used in the next chapters to illuminate the interrelationship between campaigns' imperatives and their uses of digital communication to meet those imperatives: *strategic environment, organization, finance, public opinion polling, media,* and the candidate's *image*. One component that Denton did not include is *citizen involvement.* This oversight underscores how little agency scholarship in the mass-media era considered ordinary citizens to have in the campaign process. Yet they are included in this book because the complex communication environment of the Internet age has opened up new opportunities for citizens to be more directly harnessed by political campaigns. Each of Denton's components is described in what follows.

For Denton, the *strategic environment* constrains campaign messaging.[61] It includes the current economic situation, domestic issues and events, and international events, such as wars. The mood of the electorate, the communication technologies and the state of the laws restricting campaigns also are part of that environment. These components are not something that campaigns can directly change, but instead shape campaigns and the sorts of tactics they deploy to win. Over the past two decades, campaigns have grappled with how to understand and effectively use digital communication channeled through the Internet, and increasingly over smartphones and tablets, to meet their objectives.

The *organization* of the campaign can be thought of as the nuts and bolts essentials: who has been hired to manage the campaign, how many field offices have been established, who are the consultants.[62] A key part of a political campaign is creating and managing an organization that can deal effectively with incredibly tight time constraints and an ever-changing messaging environment. The strategy and underlying tactics established at the start of the campaign need to shift to respond to what the opponent is doing and saying. An effective organization can do that for a candidate.

Money is the lifeblood of a campaign, explains Denton.[63] Without it, the organization and communication engine seizes, and the campaign is over. Campaigns need money to hire staff and consulting firms for polling, strategy, and communication, rent offices and equipment, create television ads and buy airtime, pay for direct marketing through the mail, and pay to crisscross the country for fundraisers and other campaign events.

The construction of the candidate—that is, the efforts to shape how the electorate thinks of the candidate—is a core component of presidential campaigning.[64] The candidate's *image* comprises many factors, including the candidate's personality, leadership abilities, character, lifestyle, and values. Effective image construction requires conveying strength, integrity, and empathy, which are especially important candidate characteristics for voters.[65] Candidates hire professional campaign staff and consultants to carefully construct and tailor messages to convey a particular image. Once that message is crafted, mass media are the primary vehicles to convey that message, through news stories by journalists in the form of "earned" media or as TV advertising or other "paid" media.[66]

Denton explains that *public opinion polls and the news media* are also critical elements that shape a presidential campaign.[67] A candidate who gains little traction in public opinion polls has difficulty raising contributions and getting media coverage. A campaign that gains traction in the polls is able to raise new money and get earned news media coverage. One that can show strong fundraising numbers at the end of a quarterly reporting cycle, especially if they are surprising, can generate earned media, which in turn often gives the candidate a boost in the polls.

In the context of DCTs, campaigns can contemplate new ways to bring citizens more directly into organizing, messaging, fundraising, and mobilizing efforts. Presidential campaigns since 1996 have had on their websites ways for supporters to "get involved" with the campaign, whether it is signing up to volunteer, registering to vote, or, more recently, getting telephone numbers and a script to make calls to identify supporters or remind people to vote on Election Day. *Citizen involvement* thus manifests in a variety of ways for campaigns.

The challenge for campaigns is in determining how best to engage citizens to help the campaign win, while not getting drowned out or sidetracked by those citizens. Campaigns have been leery of giving citizen supporters too much control over the messaging and events held on behalf of the campaign.[68] Yet they also recognize that in the digital era, motivating their most energized supporters to reach out to less-involved friends and family is a factor for winning. Thus, the old paradigm of information dissemination and persuasion via the mass media has shifted to a new paradigm of controlled interactivity via digital media.

Indeed, the theory of two-step flow described by Katz and Lazarsfeld is still highly relevant in contemporary digital times.[69] Two-step flow emerged out of research to understand the greatest influences on housewives in consumer behavior as well as public affairs, in order to understand the effect of the mass media on opinions and behavior. Researchers interviewed housewives and learned that the sources they valued most and had the most influence were not broadcast or print advertisements but word of mouth from knowledgeable and trusted people in their social network. Thus, the core idea of two-step flow is that advertisers or others who wish to persuade should identify opinion leaders and target them with persuasive messages; those opinion leaders, in turn, spread the word to others, within their family and social networks.

The principle of two-step flow was mostly lost to campaigns in the mass media era but has returned in the age of the Internet. With the diffusion of television, campaigns shifted their attention to the power of mass communication, buying into the idea that K Street consultants with Madison Avenue production firms could help them move vast audiences through carefully tailored advertisements. In the digital age, with its network logic, campaigns have returned to the idea encapsulated in two-step flow, using digital technologies to identify and empower supporters to persuade others in their own social network through word of mouth online or offline.[70] The technological affordance of networking, that centripetal force, which both encourages independence of users while also nurturing interconnections between them, makes two-step flow easier to actualize. Thus, for campaigns, the shift from mass media to networked media is a powerful one that enables a greater role for citizens in the service of the campaign, if campaigns can find the best way to control and structure that role.

Enduring Attitudes about Citizens

Having provided some context for contemplating the key elements of presidential campaigns and the ways that the communication environment structures them, I should emphasize that the impulse of presidential campaigns to enact controlled interactivity in the service of winning the campaign, rather than truly engaged, democratic interactivity, is not in any way new. Historically, there has been frank concern about the role of ordinary people in governance. Most theorists are skeptical of the strong democracy argument advanced by Barber.[71] Indeed, ancient theories of governance expressed caution about the ability of ordinary people to participate in their own governance. In the enlightenment era, we see a shift and a new optimism about what ordinary citizens by right and obligation ought to do on behalf of their own governance. Yet, even over the past century, in democratic countries like the United States, we see enduring unease about the role of citizens in governance.

Of primary concern is the relationship between *those that govern*—elected officials, government bureaucrats, groups that harness their collective energy to exert influence (e.g. activist groups, corporate lobbyists), political pundits[72]—and the *governed*—ordinary citizens. The concern is power: who has power to exercise decision-making over whom? Much of the history of political thought has focused on this problem, with many theorists arguing that the masses, unlike elites, lack the necessary faculties and opportunities to contribute to governance. Such views were articulated by the ancient Greeks, especially in Plato's influential Socratic dialogue *The Republic*. In it, he advocates for a philosopher-king, someone with the mental faculty to govern through reason and with justice. He expressed trepidation with democratic forms of government, arguing that democracy emerged out of oligarchy. In his view, the tensions between the classes in the oligarchic society, with the rich plotting against the poor, would eventually lead to a democratic uprising of the poor against the rich. The poor would elect someone with great appeal to the masses but without the sense of justice to guide rightly, and thus would turn eventually to a despot who rules with absolute control.

Such concerns are echoed by subsequent philosophers, including Thomas Hobbes, who declared in *Leviathan* that all are equal in their potential to be killed by other people, and that all are in competition with everyone else, since we all pursue the same thing and are in constant danger from each other. This "state of nature," as Hobbes characterized it, necessitates a strong supreme ruler to wield power and enforce what he called "the social contract"; an agreement between people must be made to give up some rights (such as to kill others for their property) and assume some obligations. The social contract, however, can only work when there is a strong sovereign, such as a king, to control the state of nature, work as a civilizing force against it, and enforce the social contract. Hobbes also characterized inalienable rights, which no sovereign can infringe upon, including life, liberty, and happiness—rights that made their way into the American colonists' Declaration of Independence from King George III and the Crown of England.

Subsequent philosophers were more optimistic about the state of nature and the ability and necessity of a broader swath of people in a society to participate in governance. John Locke is perhaps Western democracy's most influential thinker about political participation. His *Two Treatises of Government* sets forth theories of reason, property rights, and democratic governance that significantly influenced the British political system in the seventeenth century, and in turn framed and honed the perspectives of many of the writers of the Declaration of Independence and the US Constitution. Locke, much like Hobbes, viewed all people as having inalienable rights, including life and liberty, which no one ought encroach on, but he disagreed that our state of nature is chaos or war in the service of self-interest. For him the state of nature was one in which everyone is equal to others and, more importantly, has the faculty of *reason* to govern behavior. Like Hobbes, Locke argued for the necessity of the social contract; yet he viewed the people, not the king, as sovereign. That is, Locke held that the government enforces the social contract, but if those that govern fail, the people ultimately have the right to reject their leaders. The people ultimately hold the power; the government's power is only possible by consent of the people.

Concerns about citizen participation in democratic governance continue in modern times. Delli Carpini and Keeter identify three factors that shape the likelihood of citizen participation in government: ability, opportunity, and motivation.[73] Scholars have highlighted the generally low levels of knowledge the public has about current events, political actors, foreign affairs, and even the workings of government.[74] One cause for this weak knowledge is that most citizens lack opportunity or motivation to follow politics, preferring to consume entertainment over news and current events.[75] An additional concern is the ability of citizens to process information pertinent to governance logically and rationally. Page and Shapiro find in their analysis of fifty years of public opinion data that in the aggregate a coherent and relatively stable set of attitudes emerges that is in the publics' fundamental interest, though they lack deep understanding of specific policies,[76] while Zaller's research finds that the public's attitudes tend to reflect elite messaging on policy issues, suggesting that public opinion is easily swayed.[77] Schudson contends that citizens are cognitive misers who pay attention when problems arise that require their attention.[78] Neuroscience research further supports this idea.[79]

A wealth of scholarship has been published in the past two decades that examines the potential for digital communications to democratize. Early scholarship identified great potential for citizens to be more involved in the political process through ease of opportunity to follow current events and participate more actively in democratic governance.[80] Others, most notably Margolis and Resnick, urged caution about the potential of the Internet to democratize politics.[81] They advanced a normalization hypothesis, which predicted the same inequalities in political participation that occur offline would manifest online. Others, particularly Sunstein,[82] expressed concern that there would be increased fragmentation of the public sphere, meaning that those involved would have even greater opportunity to participate, but those less interested would be further marginalized and excluded. Indeed, as the scholarship on the democratic potentials of the Internet has evolved from theorizing and speculation to empirical examination, notions of revolutionary change in political participation and involvement from those historically underrepresented appear to be unfounded; the participation divide continues.[83]

Having moved into a transitional and destabilizing moment, as the communication environment has shifted with increased usage of digital communication technologies (DCTs), we can see attitudes about the role of citizens in the political process in stark relief. As Bruno Latour, one of the progenitors of actor network theory (ANT), highlights, we need close examination of *how* actors build relationships between each other to construct the social.[84] Such assemblages are often easiest to see when there is some controversy, to borrow Carolyn Marvin's words, some "drama in which existing groups perpetually negotiate power, authority, representation, and knowledge with whatever resources are available."[85] The ANT lens is especially helpful when examining the relationships between groups, since it posits that objects like communication technologies also have agency in enabling and constraining social relationships. Marvin's own scholarship on electricity and telephones is a case in point. She examines how "new media [i.e., the telephone] intrude on these negotiations [between actors] by providing new platforms on which old groups confront one another."[86] As these groups work out their station relative to other groups—which has been disturbed by emergent channels of communication—one can see their definitional boundaries come into relief. We can also observe the fluid, negotiated, and sometimes contested nature of those boundaries, in this case with regard to the role of citizens in democratically organized societies.

The symbolic relationship between political campaigns and citizens comes into stark relief when we examine the affordances of DCTs, and their interactive potentiality. It is helpful to take a page out of Edelman's analytic playbook to see this relationship.[87] Edelman examines the language and messaging of political actors, describing the power dynamics at work that ultimately situate the public as spectators in their democracy. His approach, which examines the symbolic nature of public policy debates, can also be used to examine the ways political actors symbolically use media.

What I see using Edelman's approach when examining presidential campaigns' practices over five election cycles is that, for political campaigns, citizens are like pawns on a chessboard: whom to move when to get the most strategic effect. The power dynamic between campaigns and citizens, ultimately, is still hierarchical: candidates and their voices are valued over those of citizens. Presidential campaign staffs, such as those of Democratic candidate Howard Dean in 2004 and Republican candidate Ron Paul in 2008, learned that unfettered citizen interactivity was unproductive for the campaigns. The truly democratic self-organizing by supporters through DCTs did not ultimately help the candidate win. Subsequent campaigns have learned from this and have worked to craft opportunities for interactivity that better *controls and manages* the enthusiasm of supporters for greatest advantage—not of citizens but of the candidate.

Plan of the Book

The next chapters examine how campaigns have come to win while involving and mobilizing supporters to work on behalf of the campaign in a controlled way. Chapter 2 examines the 1996 presidential campaign, in which senator and World War II veteran Robert Dole tried to unseat a popular but scandal-plagued president, William Clinton. This presidential election, the first in which the World

Wide Web and related DCTs were used in the campaign, highlights the practices of campaigns still squarely in the mass-media paradigm, with limited interactivity used to engage and mobilize supporters. Ironically, however, it was the elder statesman Dole who had the more cutting-edge campaign website, while the hip, young president's web presence was decidedly conventional. Chapter 3 looks at the 2000 presidential election, when Vice President Albert Gore Jr. and George W. Bush ran one of the most competitive campaigns in history, the final results so close that ultimately the contest had to be settled by the US Supreme Court. Both campaigns had as a resource the prior presidential cycle to improve upon and expand the uses of DCTs. Yet they too relied primarily on the mass-media model of campaigning, making their websites ancillary rather than integral components of their campaigns. What is noteworthy are the uses of DCTs by challengers. Indeed, in 2000 innovations came from the challenger's campaign. John McCain discovered the power of small-donor giving with his insurgency after a surprise New Hampshire win vaulted his candidacy ahead of the other contenders and drove supporters to contribute via his website.

Political watchers undoubtedly hold the 2004 campaign of Howard Dean as the harbinger of the shift in practices as campaigns began to better recognize the interactive affordances of DCTs. Certainly that is correct, but what is less well known is the equally intriguing case of the movement to draft Wesley Clark, which demonstrated in stark relief the joys and sorrows of interactivity for both Dean's and Clark's political campaigns. The 2004 campaign also shines light on the beginning of another vital practice for presidential campaigns in the Internet age: data analytics. The Kerry campaign did careful A/B testing (i.e., controlled online experiments) of its website, experimenting with, for example, the placement, labeling, and colors of the contribute button, as well as message testing of e-mail. The Bush campaign built what was at the time the most impressive voter database to engage in careful analysis and segmentation of the electorate to target particular voters of interest to the campaign.

The 2008 and the 2012 campaigns exhibit the campaigns' shift toward controlled interactivity and deeper embodiment of networked campaigning. Not only the Obama campaign, but the Ron Paul, Hillary Clinton, and Mike Huckabee campaigns in 2008 put into practice carefully constructed interactivity, though to different degrees. It was the Obama campaign that combined a rhetorical stance that constructed the role of the citizen as an empowered actor in the political process with digital affordances of campaign-tailored self-organizing. That winning combination served as illustration of what appeared to be a perfect balance that empowered but controlled a movement of citizen-supporters for his candidacy. The 2012 campaign extended that approach, although both Romney's and Obama's campaigns had to more actively massage enthusiasm out of their supporters via social media. More powerfully, both campaigns pushed data analytics to a new level, crafting carefully tailored messaging to targeted voters. The targets were not the "usual suspects" of already moderately engaged voters; both campaigns reached beyond their usual support profiles to rustle up new voters, extending a process started by Howard Dean in 2004.

The book concludes by examining implications of this shift in campaigning as the practices of candidates have moved from the mass-mediated paradigm to the networked paradigm of campaigning, arguing that the ways that campaigns have shifted to adapt to the new affordances of DCTs. In turn have changed other aspects of campaigns, from fundraising to organizing. The chapter reflects on the changed communication environment, arguing that, even with the increased interactivity affordances of DCTs, citizens are harnessed in the service of the campaign; yet challenges emerge in new ways as campaigns attempt to control and anticipate the messaging environment in the increasingly complex hybrid media environment, which, as Chadwick explains, has emerged as digital and traditional media interact and reverberate in unanticipated ways.[88] The chapter also examines fragmentation in this complex media environment, arguing that siloed, isolated issue and interest publics, which Sunstein and others worry digital media create, will not be necessarily perpetuated.[89]

Political campaigning in the Internet age reveals the nature of political power in the United States. Although candidates offer a rhetoric of emancipation in light of the interactive affordances of DCTs, where ordinary citizens are fully empowered in the work of the campaign—as Howard Dean once so passionately declared—there is really only a simulacrum of empowerment.

2

1996: Mass-Mediated Campaigning in the Nascent Internet Age

World War II veteran Robert Dole faced an uphill climb in his attempt to unseat popular but scandal-plagued incumbent President William Clinton. Dole had a bruising primary season, defeating several challengers in the Republican primaries, including Patrick Buchanan, a libertarian conservative with a firebrand message of populism, former Tennessee governor Lamar Alexander, Senator Phil Gramm of Texas, Senator Richard Lugar of Indiana, and two businessmen, Steven Forbes and Morry Taylor. One small component of Dole's overall effort to win the White House was the most innovative political campaign website of its day. The creator, a volunteer turned staff member named Robert Arena, crafted a forward-thinking blueprint of digital strategies that detailed the opportunities that DCTs offered campaigns. Ironically, it was the seventy-three-year-old senator who had the hip, innovative website, while Bill Clinton—the young, saxophone-playing president—had a website with a cautious style.

The 1996 campaigns had no previous presidential examples to learn from about using the Internet. Thus, the design and tool building done by these innovators created the groundwork of the genre of the presidential campaign website: introducing the candidate, serving as a repository for speeches, campaign ads, and detailed position papers, and offering a set of features to engage supporters.[1] It also demonstrated nascent approaches to encouraging supporters to contact their friends to support the candidate—the first efforts to promote the theory of two-step flow digitally, in which supporters were encouraged to promote the candidate in their online and offline social networks.[2] More importantly, if we look at these practices through the lens of actor network theory,[3] we observe that the old mass-mediated practices of campaigning ran up against the affordances of digital communication, and the resulting tension reveals the underlying attitudes typical campaigns held toward citizens: they are to be managed and controlled, persuaded but not empowered except in the most limited sense.

Background and Strategic Environment

THE STATE OF THE INTERNET

Digital life in 1996 looked quite different than digital life presently. Today, nearly 80% of Americans access the Internet through a range of devices. In 1996, only about 20% of adults did, and gained access through their personal computer. In 1996, Internet users had "dial-up" access through a telephone line and a modem with a 56 kilobytes per second (kbps) data-transfer speed. By comparison, today's smartphones can download data anywhere from 14% to 30% faster than computers did in 1996. High-speed Internet through DSL or cable fiber-optic networks today is even faster.

In 1995 the Internet was just beginning to diffuse through the US population. Between 16 and 20 million American adults were online.[4] Many Americans experienced the Internet through e-mail and the walled gardens of America Online and CompuServe. These online communities created specialized content for their subscribers. There was no Google. Yahoo's indexing of websites was the newest, most cutting-edge search technology people could use, providing only limited results of available information and sites. No one downloaded movies or watched TV shows through the Internet; streaming short thirty-second advertisements was novel. The World Wide Web for citizens, candidates, and the press felt much like an uncharted frontier, what Vice President Al Gore called the *information superhighway*, and its possibilities were only being imagined.

Despite the still relatively limited reach of the Internet into the lives of ordinary US citizens, D'Alessio found in a study of political campaign use in 1996 that all of the major-party and 80% of the minor-party presidential candidates had websites, while 66% of the major-party and 36% of the minor-party senatorial candidates, and 22% of the major-party and 7% of the minor-party congressional candidates had a site.[5] He also found tentative evidence that having a website increased the probability that candidates won their electoral contest, though the reasons for that may have been the cash advantage candidates with websites had—with the websites indicating superior financial resources rather than providing a strategic advantage to the campaign.

There was great hope about digital technologies in 1996, although it was largely unfulfilled. Ed McCracken, CEO of a now-defunct computer company called Silicon Graphics, noted, "I can envision a [candidate's] Web environment that has videos of every speech a candidate wants people to see. It would be a real video and audio archive of the entire campaign. People could really get a feeling for a candidate's personality, far beyond television news or the printed page."[6] Indeed, both Dole and Clinton sites provided audio and video of some television advertisements their campaigns had created, and Gore recorded an audio file that welcomed visitors to the Clinton-Gore campaign site. Yet text and pictures were the dominant modes of expression, because McCracken's full vision was not yet a capability of the Internet.

URLS

In 1996, URLs (uniform resource locators), the Web address people type into their browser's address bar to go to a web page, were indicative of the state of campaign websites; they represented indeterminate practices. By this, I mean there was not a clear convention yet about the best way to name a site. Given that the practice of domain naming was in a state of flux, it reveals the state of thinking by campaign staff about the purpose and practice of digital campaigning.

For a political campaign, the name of the candidate is a most valuable asset. The name of the candidate is always prominently displayed at events, on literature, and in advertising, and in the surfacing stage of the campaign developing name recognition is a core goal. Symbolically, URLs can serve as an important extension of a campaign's brand. The URL is the name and identity of the site, and it can be added to flyers, to podiums at campaign events where the candidate speaks, and in TV advertising. Today, the convention is that the URL is the candidate's name: www.JaneGonzalez.com.

With one exception, presidential campaigns in 1996 did not follow the practice of naming their site with the candidate's name. Two Republican primary candidates did not even have their name in the main URL but as part of a subdomain. Lamar Alexander's URL was http://www.Nashville.net/~lamar. Richard Lugar's website was www.iquest.net/lugar/lugar.html. Two campaigns, that of Bob Dole and of Steven Forbes, featured the candidate's name in the URL and also included the campaign year '96. Dole's primary campaign domain name was www.dole96.com, and Forbes's was www.forbes96.com. Putting the year into the domain effectively restricts the utility of that domain name to the 1996 election cycle. Only Pat Buchanan's domain name, www.buchanan.org, was timeless, and could have been (and was) used in successive presidential campaigns.

Buchanan's URL highlights another practice in flux: the use of the.org domain rather than the .com domain. Some presidential campaigns used the .com domain, which signifies that the owner of the domain name is a business. Others used the .org domain, which signifies that the owner is a nonprofit organization. Of note, Dole's presidential campaign URL in the general election after his vice presidential running mate was switched to www.dolekemp96.org.

All of the aforementioned URLs included the candidate's name somewhere. The URL for presidential incumbent Bill Clinton and his vice president, Al Gore, was especially unconventional; it was www.cg96.org. Like other campaigns' sites, the year is in the title, suggesting that the staff was focusing on a platform that would be relevant only in the 1996 campaign. Puzzling is the lack of the presidential candidate's name (Clinton) in the URL, and the equally odd CG, which stood for Clinton-Gore. This acronym and domain name would be impenetrable for the politically uninvolved and generally uninterested, especially given that typically less than half of Americans know the name of the vice president.

The lack of a domain name convention nicely reveals the state of presidential campaigning online. Just as campaigns had no established practice to work from in deciding what information to put up on their websites or tools and widgets to help supporters connect with other supporters or work on behalf of the campaign, there was no agreement on how to name the campaign website. In hindsight it would seem logical that a campaign would pay for a domain with the candidate's name, but campaigns were not yet thinking about their web page as a resource that might endure past the election cycle, or even thinking of their website as a key resource in the first place. Indeed, campaign staff choices of domain names reveal that for them the function of the website was still unclear.

FINDING POLITICAL INFORMATION ONLINE

Not using the simple candidate-name-as-URL practice, combined with the limited search capabilities of the Web in 1996, meant that for ordinary Americans it was hard to find political campaign sites; they were relatively "invisible."[7] Search tools in 1996 were unsophisticated, so searching by or browsing an index for a candidate's name might not always pull up a useful set of results, especially when the candidate's name was not in the URL or part of a subdomain. Moreover, campaigns did not yet have at their disposal targeted banner advertisements on news portals and popular websites to drive traffic to a site. Yahoo's index of the World Wide Web captured only about 10% of the existing websites, and it was cumbersome to use (See Figure 2.1).

Good government groups and enterprising individuals tried to fill the need by providing a repository of political links and created websites or portals of those links. Vote Smart was one such effort developed by the Center for National Independence in Politics to provide nonpartisan election information. It featured information from the candidates on specific policy issues as well as links to campaign and government websites.[8] The League of Women Voters also created a site for voter-relevant information and links. Other sites for election

- **Arts** - - *Humanities. Photography. Architecture. ...*
- **Business and Economy [Xtra!]** - - *Directory. Investments. Classifieds. ...*
- **Computers and Internet [Xtra!]** - - *Internet. WWW. Software. Multimedia. ...*
- **Education** - - *Universities. K-12. Courses. ...*
- **Entertainment [Xtra!]** - - *TV, Movies. Music. Magazines. ...*
- **Government** - - *Politics [Xtra!]. Agencies. Law. Military. ...*
- **Health [Xtra!]** - - *Medicines. Drugs. Diseases. Fitness. ...*
- **News [Xtra!]** - - *World [Xtra!]. Daily. Current Events. ...*
- **Recreation and Sports [Xtra!]** - - *Sports. Games. Travel. Autos. Outdoors. ...*
- **Reference** - - *Libraries. Dictionaries. Phone Numbers. ...*
- **Regional** - - *Countries. Regions. U.S.States. ...*
- **Science** - - *CS. Biology. Astronomy. Engineering. ...*
- **Social Science** - - *Anthropology. Sociology. Economics. ...*
- **Society and Culture** - - *People. Environment. Religion. ...*

Figure 2.1 The Yahoo! search engine index from 1996

information were campaign.96.com, publis.net, and www.politicsnow.com. A website called The Skeleton Closet and hosted by Real People for Real Change provided (and still provides) a website with a synopsis of the metaphorical skeletons in political candidates' closets.

In addition to portal-type sites, several news organizations created websites devoted to election news. C-Span's Road to the White House and CNN's AllPolitics sites went online that year, and continue today. Several news organizations banded together to offer election-related news content. ABC News, the *Washington Post*, and *Newsweek* created a site called ElectionLine. It included information on the dates of primaries and caucuses, campaign schedules, links to campaign websites, and political news.[9] The *New York Times* in partnership with National Public Radio also provided news on the political campaign.

In addition to these portal and news sites, campaign staff tried to pull people to their content. They did so by urging their communications staff, speechwriters, and the campaign manager to get the URL of the campaign website plastered onto podiums and campaign literature, referenced explicitly by the candidate in the standard stump speech, and featured as a tagline on TV ads. The World Wide Web, before social media, was primarily a "pull" medium—meaning that content providers had to find ways to pull people to the content—rather than a "push" medium—which, like television, pushes content at viewers. As such, the most effective way for campaigns to spread the word of their website was not by counting on people using a search engine but by putting the URL on other material that was already getting in front of potential supporters.

POLITICAL BACKGROUND

In addition to the challenges campaigns faced spreading their message digitally, they had all of the usual contextual factors to contend with. This campaign was an uphill battle for Republican senator Bob Dole. He faced a popular incumbent, President Bill Clinton, and what seemed an unprecedented apathy in the electorate. Drew and Weaver surveyed Indiana residents and found a 48% drop in being "very interested" in the 1996 political election as compared with 1992.[10] Viewership of the two presidential debates was only 41 million Americans, compared with 66 million who watched the 1992 debates and 70 million who watched the 1984 debates.

The nation was politically apathetic perhaps because it was enjoying a sense of peace and prosperity. Internationally, the world seemed relatively calm from American eyes. In late 2005, a peace deal was brokered to end the war in the former Yugoslavia, between Bosnians, Serbs, and Croatians, and US military forces that had been deployed to the region began to come home. Domestically, the economy was on the rebound. Bill Clinton took office in 1993 at the end of a short recession that started in 1990 and ended in 1991. In his first term, Clinton practiced a politics of "triangulation" in which he found issues that the political Right had been pushing and advanced them as his own agenda,[11] including being "tough on crime," a traditionally Republican stance, by giving states and large municipalities increased federal contributions for police, and reforming welfare with bipartisan support. He also enjoyed a growing economy as the dot-com boom began its meteoric rise.

That boom meant that the Internet channeled a variety of applications and software (i.e., websites, e-mail, discussion forums) and was gaining public and corporate legitimacy. In turn, presidential campaign staff were curious to find ways to use these communication channels as another tactic of campaigning. The challenge for staff of presidential campaigns in 1996 was the following: because there was little precedent and thus no clear and tested techniques for how to use digital media for the purpose of campaigning, they were trying to determine if there was anything about these channels that could give them a competitive advantage in the campaign.

Not only was it confusing what the messaging, features, or uses of digital media might be, it was also unclear who among the potential voting public would make use of digital channels to learn about or get involved with a presidential campaign. Laura Segal, a staffer who worked on the Clinton-Gore '96 website, noted that the campaign puzzled over the value relative to the cost of an untested and unknown medium.[12] Although websites were cheap, especially compared to TV ads, they still carried costs: to rent server space to host the website, pay for contractors to design and build the site, and hire staff to oversee it. All of this, she explained, carried "cost for a medium that is untested, with no clear value at present." Yet, having said that, she also described the website as "integral" and "an important component to conveying the campaign's messages and providing information to the electorate." A research study confirmed what Segal suggested: campaigns used their websites in 1996 primarily as information repositories containing the text and images that had been produced elsewhere (such as speeches and press releases) and then also made available online.[13] This practice led to the truism that political campaign websites in 1996 were primarily "brochure ware."

Digital Media's Minor Role in the Campaigns' Organization

One factor that helps illuminate presidential campaign processes and objectives of digital communication is campaign organization. As noted in the introductory chapter, Denton's typology of factors that affect the success of a campaign includes the vision of the candidate and the organization he or she creates.[14]

Dole was a micromanager with little appreciation for what the Internet could offer his campaign. He made decisions without consulting his staff, keeping senior members in the dark about the strategies of the campaign as it unfolded. For example, he decided to step down as senator in the early summer of 1996 so that he could campaign full time. Such a decision could have been capitalized upon to promote the candidate both on- and offline, but instead was met with confusion and internal struggle within the campaign. As a result, the overall messaging from the campaign to the electorate was muddy and unfocused.

Clinton, on the other hand, ran a tightly organized and disciplined campaign. He faced no primary challengers, a freedom he took advantage of by running ads against Dole in the late spring of 1996, using his significant financial advantage. After Dole began claiming that he would be a better advocate and protector of children than Clinton, for example, the Clinton campaign ran contrastive ads against Dole that critiqued his legislative record on children's issues.

In 1996, the organizational positioning of digital media staff was muddled. The communication director or the media director might supervise the website, which was often an afterthought for those directors who were focused on TV ads, strategic ad buys, finely honed messaging for microtargeted direct mail, scripted campaign events and fundraisers, and managing the news media.

The Dole website was designed and managed by Robert Arena, a Dole volunteer supporter who eventually became a paid staff member.[15] He worked with a web design company in Arizona to build and design the site. He explained that there was no clear structure within the organization for including the website or paying for it. The Dole campaign had adopted the same spending plan as George H. W. Bush, who in 1992 had no line item for the Internet. Eventually, Arena was folded into the communication staff of the campaign, which approved the content he created. The cost of hosting and designing the website came out of the media budget, costing the campaign 0.1% of the total revenue for the campaign. Dole knew about the website but had no input into it.

The Clinton campaign had a more advanced organizational chart. Adam Sohn was hired as director of technology, having worked on the 1992 campaign and for the Democratic National Committee on technology and strategy.[16] He reported to the staff responsible for organization, which included information technology acquisitions and management, and not through the communications or media departments. There was one paid staff member, and a handful of interns who did much of the digital media work. They worked with an external firm, KPE Enterprises, to design and host the site. Laura Segal, who worked under Sohn, explained that KPE provided no original content, and that she oversaw and ensured that the text and photos aligned with the messaging and themes of the campaign more broadly.[17] Anything that KPE produced was reviewed by campaign staff before being uploaded to web servers and made public. The Clinton campaign website cost about $200,000.[18]

Political Fundraising at the Dawn of the Internet Age

Until 2008 major-party presidential campaigns took advantage of federal matching money to help fund their campaigns. The Federal Election Campaign Act passed in 1974 by Congress restricted eligible matching contributions to personal checks written by supporters. Credit card contributions were excluded. Because of this, in 1996, there was little incentive to encourage supporters to contribute money to a campaign via credit card, since it would not be matched from the fund.

Nevertheless, campaigns did invite contributions online. Both presidential campaigns during the general election as well as the Republican candidates in the primaries provided a downloadable web form that a supporter could print out, fill in, and then mail back with a check or money order to the campaign's headquarters. Arena explained that the campaign received contributions that way, more than enough to pay for the campaign's website but not enough to pay his salary.[19] From a strategic messaging perspective, he explained that he did not want the website to be perceived as focusing only on raising money. He wanted visitors to see the website as a source for information about Dole's policy positions, history, and background, and as a way for visitors to get involved with the campaign. Fundraising simply was not a strategic focus for the digital campaign.

Constructing Image through Digital Communication Technologies

Just as political TV ads and direct mail aim to craft an image of the candidate as well as to provide a contrast with opponents, so too were websites used for this purpose. The presidential campaigns in 1996 used them to promote their candidates, increase their visibility with potential supporters, give journalists background materials on policy positions and the candidate's biography, and do the symbolic work of image construction.

A noteworthy example of how campaigns used digital media to construct and reinforce the candidate's image was that of Republican primary candidate Lamar Alexander. His digital tactics illustrated two images he was trying to craft: one of him as an ordinary guy, and the other of him as an innovator. The former was promoted by the background image of his website, his trademark red and black plaid lumberjack shirt (See Figure 2.2). A large image at the top of his biography page declared, "Lamar!," highlighting his first name as a way to construct familiarity between himself and his visitors. Klinenberg and Perrin describe the symbolism on the website as that of a "populist, back-country" organizer.[20] At the same time, the public relations work of his campaign was meant to establish him as an innovator. On May 23, 1995, the former Tennessee governor was the first presidential candidate to announce he was running for president on America Online. The campaign's press release highlighted Alexander's image as an entrepreneur, noting that he had started a satellite-only TV network, with monthly broadcasts highlighting Republican issues.

Both major-party candidates naturally used their websites to advance their image. Ironically, although the Clinton campaign slogan highlighted a foreword-thinking agenda, "Building a bridge to the 21st Century," the campaign website did not exemplify that bridge. Instead, Bob Dole, the seventy-three-year-old "hatchet man" from Kansas, had a more cutting-edge website that paved the way of campaign sites of the twenty-first century. Yet his virtual image clashed with his candidate self.

The image of Clinton coming into the 1996 campaign was tarnished. He was involved in what seemed a never-ending series of scandals. There were allegations of sexual affairs during the 1992 presidential primaries that nearly derailed

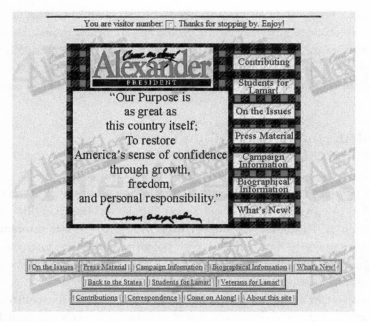

Figure 2.2 The front page of Lamar Alexander's website

his campaign; once he was in office, rumors continued, as did a string of investigations by independent counsel Kenneth Starr. He initially investigated the suicide of the deputy White House counsel and close friend of the Clintons, Vincent Foster, then expanded his investigation into the potentially inappropriate firing of White House Travel Office staff, the misuse of FBI records, and a lawsuit by Paula Jones, who alleged sexual misconduct against Clinton when he was governor of Arkansas. In sum, Clinton had a character problem coming into his reelection campaign.

Dole emphasized Clinton's character problem while trying to repair his own image. Senator Dole was seventy-three by the time of the general election in 1996, having served in the US Senate since 1969. He had built up a reputation as a "hatchet man" during his early career when he worked for President Richard Nixon and when he chaired the Republican National Committee. He also had an acerbic wit that tended to get in the way when he was irritated. The nation had witnessed his sharp tongue during prior unsuccessful runs at higher offices.[21]

The Dole campaign worked to soften his image in several ways. They commissioned a biographical film of Dole's life and used the website to provide intimate details about his military service, war wounds, and events that led him to a career in public service. Dole had rarely talked about his injuries and remarkable recovery when he campaigned for his prior offices, but his website provided intimate detail of a time in his life he seldom discussed. His biography featured pictures of him as a young, proud solider, then as an injured veteran wrapped head to toe in bandages on a bed, and later of him with a shriveled right arm, but standing upright, working to regain what he had lost. The accompanying biographical narrative told a compelling story of a man who nearly died, spent two years in casts, was told he would never walk or use his right arm again, but through intestinal fortitude and a remarkable tolerance for pain made himself walk again, taught himself to write with his left hand, and found a purpose in running for political office in Kansas.

The website was, in comparison to the other websites from 1996, the trend setter in features that established the genre of campaigns to come. The website design was clean but dense, similar to portal and news sites in the years to come, with a heavy reliance on tables to help organize the content on the screen into columns. The site also used icons, uncommon for political websites, with short textual descriptions to indicate to visitors what was behind the link (See Figure 2.3). An "About the Team" link showed a small picture of Dole and his running mate, Jack Kemp. The words "Dole Interactive: Games, trivia, posters, and postcards" was centered under a small picture of a monitor on a desktop PC with an image of Dole waving to a crowd.

The campaign found ways to draw users to the site and keep them there with "sticky" interactive features. A Dole trivia game foretold future efforts to "gamify" political content. Dole's signature campaign issue, a 15% tax cut, was featured on the front page of the campaign website, in the form of a tax calculator in which visitors could enter their income and learn their tax savings under a Dole presidency. Such a feature would be used in future elections, with campaigns hoping to concretely exemplify how their economic policies would shape the lives of Americans while keeping visitors on the site. They also used cookies, which allowed visitors to customize the site.[22]

So Dole's website, through its gee-whiz features and cutting-edge design, portrayed him as a playful, savvy, digital campaigner, someone who at the advanced age of seventy-three was at the forefront of a digital revolution. That digital image clashed with the real Bob Dole.

This was best exemplified during the closing statement of the first debate with Clinton. Dole spoke directly to young people, asked them to get involved in his campaign, to not use or stop using drugs, and encouraged them to "tap into my home page, www.dolekemp.org." Commentators and journalists declared Dole's reciting of his URL as "bizarre"[23] and "flat."[24] A reporter quoted a college student saying that when Dole asked young people to visit his website, "I was picturing my grandfather using a computer."[25] The preachy and stodgy nature of his address to young people to not use drugs and to "tap into my home page" was a stark contrast with the cutting-edge, youthful design of his website.

Figure 2.3 The home page of Bob Dole's website

To make matters worse, the URL Dole delivered was incorrect. Dole's URL was www.dolekemp96.org. As a sign of troubles to come for future campaigns, The dolekemp.org domain was owned by Ron Fitzherbert, a web designer. He had approached Dole after the Republican National Convention to see if the campaign wanted to buy the domain or pay him for help designing the Dole site. The campaign refused, so Fitzherbert put up a simple page with the words, "You've tried to access the old way. Please choose the new way instead." Two arrows showed on the screen. If the left or back arrow was clicked, a message popped up that said "Nope, you cannot go back now," and if the forward button was clicked, the browser redirected to the Clinton-Gore campaign site. Peter Jennings, anchor for ABC's *World News Tonight*, declared it "dirty tricks on the Internet," and then the next night issued a correction, noting that Dole had given the wrong URL during the debate. "It wasn't hackers. It was a prankster," he explained. The URL fiasco served to generate negative news coverage and was a bit of embarrassment for the Dole campaign.[26] The cutting-edge website could not overcome the staid Bob Dole.

The Clinton campaign used the official WhiteHouse.gov website until early in the general election campaign season. While Bob Dole was competing for the nomination against his Republican rivals, the White House website served as Clinton's presentation of self, reinforcing his incumbency and giving him symbolic identification with the office he sought to keep.

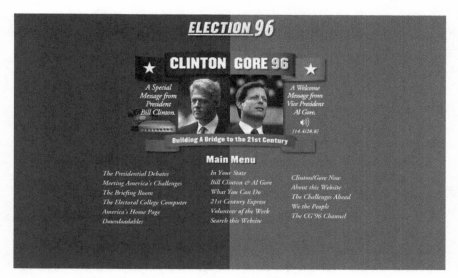

Figure 2.4 The Clinton-Gore campaign website

Once the official campaign website launched in July 1996, a red and blue background supported several pictures, including profile photographs of the president and vice president, which were located in the center of the page. Below the photos read a banner containing the campaign slogan: "Building a bridge to the 21st Century." Below that a "Main Menu" of eighteen links ranging from "Meeting America's Challenges" to "Volunteer of the Week" to "Clinton/Gore Now" was displayed (See Figure 2.4).

During the press event to announce the launch of the website on July 10, Vice President Al Gore, in a somewhat rambling speech, described the site as featuring two cutting-edge features: a news-style ticker along the bottom, and a slide show of pictures on the home page: "It's not very common to have this kind of ticker with a changing message at the bottom constantly moving or to have a server pushing new pictures onto the page with regularity right to your own computer." Thus, the website, according to Gore, exemplified the latest technological wizardry. Yet the site loaded slowly because of the rotating images and ticker along the bottom. Rob Arena believed that Clinton's website was not heavily investigated beyond the home page because of this technical flaw.[27]

Continuing a common practice of incumbent campaigns whenever confronted with new communications media, the Clinton campaign approached the Internet, with its unclear legal status and untested symbolic properties, cautiously. Segal explained that there were challenges with the campaign website.[28] Because Clinton was the incumbent president and faced intense scrutiny from the independent counsel, the campaign took care with the images and activities featured on the campaign site. Anything that might have been paid for by public money could not be included. There was no precedent for linking practices (i.e., creating a hyperlink from the campaign website to a third-party site) in political campaigns, and there were legal questions about what the implications might be of linking, for example, to an advocacy or a corporate group. Staff members were unsure whether the FEC would interpret this practice as engaging in illegal communication activities, so they erred on the side of caution and linked to no outside groups or individuals.

The campaign had good reason to be cautious. News stories of the time suggested that political actors and news reporters generally lacked digital literacy. For example, a news story reported on a controversy that was being generated by the opponent of Virginia Democratic gubernatorial candidate Mark Warner. The article explained that he was under attack for linking to MTV, the youth-oriented music television cable station, from his campaign website.[29] His opponent attacked Warner because "through Mark Warner's home page, the children of Virginia who may have been surfing the Net were brought face to face with very offensive messages," according to his opponent's spokesman. He charged that Warner was advocating "lesbian sexual fantasies" and "encouraging young people to disobey authority figures." His opponent suggested that the mere fact of the link revealed that Warner advocated the messages on MTV's site. That it became a prominent news story highlighted the perils for candidates in the untested digital media context of 1996.

Nearly Nonexistent Citizen Involvement

Campaign staff had ideas but not much clarity with regard to how to use the communication affordances of the Internet to engage and mobilize supporters. As inherently cautious organizations, campaigns tend to use proven tactics. Only insurgency campaigns with little to lose are likely to experiment. Dole, who was behind in the polls in the early part of the general election, had the strategic opportunity to engage in innovations in presidential campaign tactics: through a design that would presage today's icon-driven smartphone interface; gamification efforts that make sticky content similar to online games; and, as I will describe here further, efforts to encourage two-step flow.

Rob Arena, who created Dole's web presence, drafted a "New Media Blueprint," a document that described his vision of a web strategy for the general election campaign. The document's target audience was the campaign manager, whom Arena hoped to persuade to devote resources to the Internet. It described the web audience, highlighting the desirability of being able to reach Internet users, who at the time were more affluent, more professional, and more engaged than average. It detailed the plan for types of content and their purposes. Of significant note, Arena argued that a central purpose of the website was mobilizing potential supporters to be effective in *influencing those in their social network who were less politically involved.* The document stressed the advantage of being able to communicate directly to supporters without the filtering of mainstream media, in part by e-mailing supporters weekly. To address the challenge of drawing visitors to the website, Arena stressed marketing the site broadly by including the URL on all campaign literature and having the candidate mention it to help drive traffic to the site—at the time a novel idea. Envisioning campaign practices to come, it also recommended creating an attack site: "peoplelast.com/ realclinton.com" (which the campaign did not adopt). In many ways, Arena's vision became *the* blueprint for digital media strategy for political campaigns.

In addition to the visioning document, Arena implemented a number of features on the website to encourage supporters to appeal to their less politically involved friends (See Figure 2.5). In the "Get Involved" section, supporters could send an electronic form to the campaign indicating their interests in volunteering for particular campaign activities.[30] Over 15,000 volunteers signed up that way.[31] In the "Dole Interactive" section visitors could make a button, do a crossword puzzle, or answer trivia questions. They also were invited to create a postcard to e-mail to friends, allowing the sender to configure the postcard by choosing from different images of Dole and the background to put the

Figure 2.5 The Dole-Kemp website interactive page

selected image onto, including an American flag or Mount Rushmore. The widget also included prescripted notes to send to the friend. Other tools invited users to print out signs to put in their windows or give to friends, and download screen savers and background images for their computer monitors to show their support for Bob Dole. These media-interactive features were meant to engage supporters, especially those who were under forty, a group Dole was having difficulty reaching.

Arena explained that the purpose of these media-interactive features was to give the "hard-core," Dole's most ardent supporters, a way to involve themselves more deeply in the campaign.[32] The electronic postcard, he explained, was meant to get them to send it to ten of their friends, thereby starting a conversation about Dole, and putting into practice the idea of opinion leaders shaping the voting preferences of their social network, especially the undecided.

The Clinton campaign's focus for its website was on the practice of informing, providing information to visitors about the candidates and their positions.[33] A website "provides a much more widely accessible source for the public to go to for more detailed and in-depth information," Segal explained. "We considered this one of the most central and important functions of the site—to provide a place where people [could] get the full text of a speech the President made or to get more detailed information about the President's position and accomplishments on any particular issue."[34] Thus, using digital communication to encourage supporters to reach out and personally appeal to their friends and family was not one of the primary considerations of Clinton campaign staff.

The Clinton campaign discussed having a message board where supporters could interact with each other. A message board functions as its name suggests: people can post messages for others to read and respond. Commenting on blogs or YouTube videos is akin to message boards. Segal explained that the concerns and risks outweighed the potential opportunities.[35] Specifically, they had concerns about security and integrity. With regard to the security, they were concerned about hackers, and they saw the message board potentially opening them up to security attacks. As for integrity, the campaign was concerned about the implications of an unfiltered, unscripted measure board for the campaign. The strategists worried that negative messages about the candidate would appear on the message board, or messages inconsistent with the rest of the website.

The Clinton campaign, unlike the Dole campaign, had no vision for the function of digital media in the campaign, and had no inclination to use digital media for two-step flow. In my interview with Segal, she noted that the campaign website presented no clear value, and so the candidate did not devote any time to an online event. Efforts were focused on getting Clinton in front of people in the traditional ways of campaigns, through speeches, fundraisers, and on TV. The Clinton site invited people to e-mail the campaign through "America's Home

Page." Instead of two-step flow mobilization efforts, the Clinton campaign posted favorable comments e-mailed to the campaign, a kind of testimonials page featuring praise for the candidate, and carefully controlled to put him in the best light.

Rob Arena voiced similar concerns about the added value of featuring an area where supporters could coordinate or talk in a public way. Arena explained that people "are there to learn about the candidate, not discuss the issues." He likened it to a campaign rally: people are there to see the candidate, not chat with the people standing next to them about tax policy.[36] Arena also shared Segal's concerns about the "uncontrolled" nature of an online public forum. From a cost-benefit perspective, there was little reason to open up the campaign website as a place for people to talk about politics. Nor was there any expectation that the campaign should be inviting feedback or ideas from people. Arena noted that a political candidate is a leader; as such, "if a candidate is using the website to listen to the people, in an effort to shape direction of leadership, that's fine. But four months out, the candidate needs to be leading, not listening."[37]

Of the presidential candidates, it was Patrick Buchanan, a conservative populist running an insurgency campaign, who engaged in the greatest effort to empower his supporters through digital media. The campaign website prominently featured opportunities for citizens to mobilize and engage each other. Buchanan's site emphasized "The Buchanan Brigade," and the message board forum on the site presented the ideas and opinions of Buchanan's supporters. Writers to the message board forum submitted their post and Linda Muller, Buchanan's website designer, reviewed and excerpted comments for the site. The forum spanned dozens of pages. It was not a free-ranging conversation among supporters and visitors to the site, but instead served as evidence that Buchanan was a populist candidate prominently featuring the voices of his supporters. His campaign, as an insurgency, had even more freedom to experiment in involving supporters than did Dole and especially the incumbent, Clinton.

Although e-mail lists are today the workhorse of digital media communication strategy, in 1996 campaigns were still trying to figure whether and how to use them. The Dole website allowed people to subscribe to a distribution list, and it collected over 1,000 e-mail addresses, though the e-mail list was unused until after the Republican convention.[38] The Republican National Committee and the Democratic National Committee as well as Ross Perot's United We Stand America did use e-mail lists. The parties e-mailed press releases, notices about political events, newsletters, and updates and information on major policies to subscribers.

Just one of the challenges for campaigns in using e-mail lists was trying to make it easy for people to subscribe. In 1996 signing up was not as easy as filling out a textbox on a website and clicking the "subscribe" button. Interested people had to send a request typically by e-mail to a Majordomo e-mail server. A news article in the *Washington Post* detailed the instructions: "To subscribe to any of the Republican lists, send an e-mail message to majordomornc.org and leave the subject line blank. In the message area type: subscribe [list name] (e.g. subscribe goptvlist)."[39] This set of steps meant that only the most motivated were likely to subscribe.

Another concern was ensuring that campaign e-mail was not considered junk mail. Unwanted e-mail from weight-loss pill dealers and Nigerian scam artists, called spam, was and continues to be a source of aggravation for e-mail users. Campaign staff worried that their e-mail might be considered spam, which could irritate the people they were trying to court. Although they were tempted to buy e-mail addresses in the same way they bought postal addresses to send target messages, a popular story circulated among campaign staff of a statewide campaign that did so and then faced intense backlash from recipients that leaked into the news media, giving the campaign a reputation akin to that of a Nigerian scammer. Buying e-mail addresses thus became taboo nearly from the start of online campaigning. If campaigns were going to get e-mail addresses, they were going to have to find ways to lure people into giving them. In 1996, such lures were untested by campaigns.

Establishing Practices

The 1996 presidential campaign was historic in establishing the genre of the campaign website.[40] The major-party candidates in the primaries and in the general election visualized their campaign websites as information repositories where people could learn more about the candidate's biography and issue positions through postings of speeches, press releases, and policy reports. They could also learn how to get more involved in the campaign through finding campaign events, by mailing in a check, or by signing up as a volunteer.

The information function of the campaign website was obvious to campaigns, especially unfiltered by the news media. Deborah Steelman, a Dole campaign advisor, highlighted in an interview on the *CBS Evening News* the advantages of websites, which had no time constraints and could offer depth of information for voters: "This segment's—What?—a minute long? It's going to be a lot easier to get into our website, spend as much time as you want than through watching this shot. So it will be a lot easier to get deeper into things you care about."[41] The ability to draw in users and keep them on the site by offering lengthy issue statements or news releases had appeal, and personalizing that information seemed especially desirable in those early days, especially if it allowed the candidate to speak more directly and at length to the interested visitor than the filtering and framing of the news media, which, especially for Republicans, were suspect because of perceptions of liberal bias.

Other types of practices, such as getting supporters involved through digital means, giving them greater voice, or linking to other websites were met with much more caution by campaigns. There was no obvious payoff to the campaign in opening up greater citizen voice and involvement. Instead, they feared losing control of their message and their organization by supporters or by being hijacked by hackers and miscreants aiming only to cause trouble.

Campaigns wanted their websites to be informational cul-de-sacs, where people came but there was no outlet to leave. They also were concerned about the social and legal implications of linking. If a campaign linked to another political website, was that an in-kind contribution? The legal rules of communication were unclear and untested, and the campaigns' risk-averse ways meant they were unwilling to push communication boundaries. Moreover, the symbolic practice of linking was unclear. What does a link to another website say about the candidate? In Mark Warner's case, he got attacked for linking to MTV, and attacks are something that campaigns typically try to avoid.

Strategically, the Web was an untested medium with unknown value. The campaign websites' URLs reflected this general lack of clarity about what use the website had for the overall goals of the campaign. Including "96" in the domain name, burying the candidate's name in a subdomain, or using unclear acronyms suggested that campaigns did not see the value yet in branding the website with the most important currency a candidate has: his or her name. It also suggested they did not see the website as a potential ongoing resource or asset for the candidate if elected, nor did they see the value in a domain as a resource if they were to try again at a political campaign in the future.

Conclusion

Although the Internet was mostly a side note to the traditional mass media strategies of the 1990s, the campaign website genre was established and shaped expectations of the core components of presidential campaign sites. Bob Dole had the more sophisticated website in 1996. The senior senator from Kansas experimented with iconic representations of content, rather than the more typical list of menu items described in text; elementary gamification techniques to make the site sticky and engaging to visitors; and widgets to help supporters reach out to their social network to generate new support for the candidate. Rob Arena's blueprint for the strategic value of the website conceptualized the merit of the

Web and digital communication more generally for presidential campaigns. By contrast, the young, popular (though scandal-plagued) sitting president produced a more cautious and conservative website that relied on informing visitors, but little more. Dole's website was more of a "Bridge to the 21st Century" than was Clinton's. Thus, in a twist of irony, the hip President Clinton campaign was not thinking about using digital media for citizen involvement, but the campaign of the World War II veteran was, though in a limited way.

Interactivity through digital media was limited in 1996. The interactive components to websites were focused on medium or system interactivity, such as Gore's audio greeting or Dole's e-mail postcards. There were no applications to help supporters to interact with others and self-organize, nor did either campaign provide an opportunity to interact directly with the campaign through the medium and thereby promote human interactivity.[42]

What does become evident is that who the candidate is and who directs the campaign matters in terms of digital media experimentation. A candidate or an enlightened staff member, such as Arena on Dole's campaign, can push the envelope with digital campaign tactics to find the competitive advantage. The 2000 election bears this out more clearly.

3

2000: Experimentation in the Internet Age

The 2000 presidential election is most remembered for the historic ballot recounts, court rulings, and final US Supreme Court decision of *Bush v. Gore.* That court decision ultimately led to George W. Bush becoming the forty-third president of the United States. More historic events occurred in 2000 than just hanging chads, however, in how campaigns used the Internet in bold, creative ways.

The theme of digital media strategies in the 2000 campaign was *experimentation.* There is an old saying that necessity is the mother of invention, and the saying is especially true for presidential campaigns. Insurgent campaigns, those with little or nothing to lose, experimented in 2000 with digital technology in new ways with the hope that the experiment, risky as untested methods are for campaigns, might bring unexpected assistance in the form of money, supporters, or earned media. Front-runner campaigns, by contrast, had more to lose and so took the less risky path, building on the apparently effective digital tactics from the 1996 election.

In 1999, when the campaign season began, digital communication technologies (DCTs) and their uses seemed fluid; they did not have the tried-and-true practices that had solidified over dozens of campaign cycles, as was the case with television advertisements and direct mail. Political campaign staff were thus unsure how to strategically deploy websites and other digital channels, but they knew they had to be online, and many explored different practices to see what would help advance the campaign's objectives. Democrat John Kasich's website, for example, invited people to write essays on their heroes. All of the campaigns began collecting e-mail addresses of potential supporters. They all experimented with ways to drive money to their campaign coffers. Benjamin L. Ginsberg, a Bush campaign lawyer, captured the attitude of campaigners: "It's a brave new world out there. We're on the cusp, just as we were in 1952 and TV had just taken over as something different."[1]

Optimists viewed the digital communication channels on the Internet as making possible a two- or three-point swing for a candidate, which would make a difference in tight elections. Rick Segal, candidate Steven Forbes's Internet strategy advisor, explained "It used to be said the candidates had to have a good message, a good ground game and enough money to wage a good air game on TV. This is the first cycle that it can be proven that a candidate needs to have a good on-line game as well."[2] It was clear by 2000 the Internet was here to stay and even might be a factor in a political campaign's success, and would certainly be so in the future.

In the pages that follow, I examine the political and digital environment that shaped messaging and strategy for the presidential campaigns. I then examine more closely several key campaigns, describing their organizational structures, their fundraising efforts, and their image construction through digital media. This chapter closes with a look at how campaigns aimed to use rudimentary levels of interactivity to mobilize supporters and also describes how campaigns used DCTs to build databases of potential supporters to micro-target.

Background and Strategic Environment

POLITICAL BACKGROUND

In the months leading up to the 2000 presidential election, the optimism and energy of the booming 1990s seemed to flag. Concerns grew that the dot-com bubble, the engine of growth for the US economy from information and communication technologies, might burst. International terrorism—with attacks in Kenya and against a US naval vessel, USS Cole—further suggested that the stability and prosperity of the last decade might not be so easily sustained in the first decade of the twenty-first century.

The sour economic mood was coupled with a bitter political landscape. In December 1998 President Bill Clinton was formally impeached by the House of Representatives for perjury and obstruction of justice related to testimony involving a lawsuit filed by a former mistress and an affair with a White House intern. In February 1999 he was acquitted of the charges in the Senate. The drawn-out investigations of the Clintons by the independent counsel, Kenneth Starr, which ranged from landholdings to firings of travel agents to misuse of FBI files, had generated a highly partisan political climate. Although Americans overwhelmingly approved of President Clinton through the impeachment process, opinions declined about Congress, and the nation experienced Clinton fatigue as candidates began to emerge for the 2000 election.

A number of Republican candidates surfaced in 1999, including billionaire business entrepreneur and publisher Steve Forbes, Texas governor George W. Bush (and son of President George Herbert Walker Bush), Arizona senator John McCain, Tennessee senator Lamar Alexander, former vice president Dan Quayle, and former Transportation secretary and president of the Red Cross Elizabeth Dole, who also was wife of Senator Bob Dole, the Republican presidential nominee in 1996. These candidates and others campaigned on a strong reform message, highlighting the infidelities, ethical breaches, and policy failures of the Clinton White House.

The heir apparent on the Democratic side was Vice President Albert Gore Jr. Gore, who had distanced himself from the president during his impeachment, campaigned on the strong economy of the past seven years, and argued for new policies to help the middle class and to promote technology. He was challenged by former Knicks basketball player and New Jersey senator Bill Bradley, who campaigned on a reform platform. Dick Gephardt, Iowa's senior senator, also appeared early in the surfacing stage, but in the end chose not to run. Gore had a rocky start to his campaign, with weak, sometimes trailing poll numbers behind George W. Bush. Gore struggled to separate himself from Clinton, who in turn hurt Gore through offhand comments early in the campaign that highlighted Gore's weak organization and standings in the polls.

STATE OF THE INTERNET

Between 1996 and the 2000 presidential campaign, much changed on the digital landscape. In the United States, access to the Internet continued to expand, and software applications advanced. In addition to advances in HTML design that structured web pages, instant message (IM) programs, such as AOL and Yahoo's Instant Messenger programs, were heavily adopted by younger Internet users. Mobile phones continued to diffuse through the population, and Research in Motion's Blackberry, which brought e-mail and IM programs into the hands of millions of users, foretold a future when the mobile phone would become a central way people communicated by voice and text over the cellular network. The number of households with Internet access more than doubled between 1996 and 2000 to 44 million.[3]

Over a dozen search engines had cropped up by the time of the 2000 campaign. In addition to Yahoo! and the growing ascendency of Google, other search engines were developed, including Ask Jeeves, Lycos, and AltaVista. Thus, finding political information about the campaigns in 2000 was easier than in 1996. An organization called Search Engine Watch found that Bradley and McCain sites were the easiest to find, coming up on fifteen of eighteen search engines. Bush and Gore were found only on eleven and ten respectively.[4] Traffic to campaign websites was modest, however. According to Nielsen/Net Ratings, Gore had 232,000 and Bush 285,000 visitors the week before the general election. This put them on par with the US Navy and United Airlines websites.[5] Bimber and Davis found in their surveys of the voting public in 2000 that only about one US adult in ten visited any of the presidential candidate websites in the primaries.[6] Those who did tended to be more affluent and younger than the rest of the voting population and were significantly more likely to be male (62% male to 38% female).[7] Campaigns tried to drive traffic to their sites through banner advertisements and other forms of online advertising. The general view, however, was that online ads were ineffective.

Political watchers of the 2000 election were intrigued by a much-vaunted campaign of a former World Wrestling Federation wrestler named Jesse Ventura, who ran for governor of Minnesota on the Reform Party platform in 1998. Much to everyone's amazement, Ventura won against two household names in Minnesota politics. Bill Hillsman, who worked on Ventura's campaign, told Judy Woodruff on CNN's *Inside Politics* that the Internet "can be very important, especially for insurgent candidates" (March 9, 1999). He also noted that the Internet was just another tool in the kitbag of political campaigns, but

> in Jesse Ventura's campaign, what I don't think people realize is the magnitude of what was accomplished there. It was done without any polling. It was done without any direct mail. It was done without any telemarketing. It was done without any real organized field operation or get-out-the-vote effort. What the Internet can do is it allows people to sort of self-organize, and it fills in for some of those deficiencies.

Although, the Internet was still dominated by younger, wealthier white men, Hillsman noted that was changing, and with expanding demographics grew expanding possibilities for campaigns to experiment. Ventura had done so and won, suggesting that those who were willing to take the risk might also reap the rewards.

Political watchers were beginning to realize, in the vivid words of Phil Noble, president of Politics Online, one of the first political Internet strategy companies: "Some snot-nosed kid with an attitude can organize a political force."[8] Dick Morris, who was Clinton's campaign manager for his 1996 run, declared in an interview with Larry King on CNN that the Internet was the future home of campaigning. He mused that the broadcast audience was declining and that eventually "it costs more and more to reach few and fewer people on television. And after a while it is going to get so expensive to reach so few people that candidates will basically stop" (June 28, 1999). Later in the year, he predicted on *CNN Morning News* that the Internet would affect the 2000 election, comparing it to the 1960 election when the TV debate between Kennedy and Nixon marked the increased influence of the TV medium in the presidential campaign (December 8, 1999). Although Morris was wrong on both predictions, his enthusiasm and prognostications of the power of digital media for campaigning were in sync with many in the political professional industry.

Organization

In the 2000 election, the staff devoted to digital strategy was more integrated in the campaign hierarchy than in 1996. The campaigns of challengers had greater integration than the campaigns with front-runner status. Those with the most active Internet presence were the ones with the greatest integration.

Both Max Fose, who was the Internet director for the McCain campaign, and Lynn Reed, Bill Bradley's Internet campaign strategist, were directly involved in major planning and strategy meetings. Their integration enabled the campaigns to capitalize on momentum from external events as well as to generate volunteers and money when it most mattered for the campaigns. Fose, for example, explained that his campaigns' strategists viewed their website as a "virtual headquarters." Fose carefully built the site to help support other components of the campaign, such as collecting information about supporters to in turn call them to action when needed.[9]

The digital media directors of the Gore and the Bush campaigns reported through the communications arm of the campaign. Ben Green, Gore's Internet director, explained that for the first six months the Internet component was organizationally under information technology—the part of the campaign involved in acquiring and managing computers, databases, and establishing a network between local and state field offices and the national field office. As the campaign progressed, however, "it became evident that this was not just a function of information technology. It was message delivery, it was fundraising, it was organizing. It cut across."[10] As the senior leadership of the campaign recognized this pattern, they shifted Green and his subordinates to report through the communications director, Chris Lehane.

The Internet team was hierarchically organized within the communications team in the Bush campaign, although e-mail was under the control of the strategy team. The campaign's digital operation was overseen by a physician, Dr. William Rice. His qualifications were not that he knew about digital communication but that he had helpful ties to executives and elites in Silicon Valley, the home of high technology companies. As Mike Shannon, a strategist for Bush in 2000, explained, "Nobody at the senior level knew what to make of the Internet.... It wasn't like we'd go and hire someone from Yahoo." Having someone with Silicon Valley ties and an interest in digital communication was enough.[11] With two more web-savvy staff involved in the day-to-day design and function of the website, Rice's job was primarily to build further bridges to potential revenue sources and campaign supporters among California's technology elite.

Exploring Ways to Tip the Balance: Fundraising

LEGAL COMPLICATIONS

Campaigns in the Internet age had to face a variety of legal uncertainties. It was unclear, for example, whether independent supports, those without any formal political organization ties who created a website that cost more than $250 to express their support for a candidate, would need to register with the Federal Election Commission (FEC) as a political lobbyist. A Bill Bradley supporter, Jonathan Price, was one such independent supporter who tested the legal boundaries. In a CNN story, he explained, "It's a new medium, and they're trying to apply the old rules to a new world, and these old rules do not work in this case" (*Inside Politics*, August 6, 1999). The FEC was also determining whether e-mails sent by political organizations, such as the Republican National Committee, would need to be considered publications and therefore would be required to include the types of disclaimers found on newspaper ads.

As campaigns were beginning to surface, another pressing legal issue emerged, one that served as a major impediment to harnessing the Internet for contributions. Credit card donations were ineligible for consideration as contributions for the federal matching program; only checks and money orders from supporters counted. Bill Bradley challenged the FEC, urging it to allow credit card contributions. The commission's concerns had focused on security and verifiability of credit card contributions; however, the commissioners decided in June 1999 to allow such contributions to be matched. They saw a need to be flexible and encourage political participation over the Internet, noting security concerns were less of an issue as the Internet matured.

TAPPING THE UNTAPPED RESOURCE

With a major obstacle to fundraising removed, campaigns tested the best ways to harness potential resources of cash via the Internet. Brian Jones of the Lamar Alexander campaign noted: "If someone could figure out a way to really successfully raise money (on line), that would tilt the balance. It's like TV in the presidential campaign of 1956—everybody's searching for the right formula."[12] Campaigns in 2000 saw the potential for the Internet to bring needed cash to campaigns; they just did not know how to do it effectively yet.

Money is inherently important to campaigns, but online contributions had a unique appeal. Internet consultant John Phillips of Aristotle Publishing, a private contracting firm that sells databases of voter records to campaigns, explained the advantages this way:

> When you're on the Internet and able to take contributions twenty-four hours a day, one of the big advantages is you don't have to depend on a network of fundraisers for that money or fundraising events, and you also don't have to use very expensive means such as direct mail or telephone solicitation. Any individual that wants to contribute to the campaign can get to your site; they can make a contribution on the spot. The campaign does not have to rely upon an envelope that has been mailed to the potential contributor to be in his or her mailbox on the very day at the very moment they decide to make a contribution.[13]

The efficiency of contributing online, especially the speed of it for a candidate, might be the difference between staying in the game or having to quit. It is noteworthy that Phillips was not thinking of the importance of social networks of people online helping campaigns raise money—something political professionals still conceptualizing campaigning in the paradigm of mass-mediated communication would miss.

The first successful test of Internet fundraising came during the Republican primaries. John McCain, out of sheer necessity, found a way to make Internet contributions fuel his insurgency campaign. To understand his success, one first needs to appreciate what he was up against.

Texas governor George W. Bush, during the surfacing phase of the campaign, amassed an astounding amount of money compared with his Republican rivals. His success enabled him to forgo federal matching contributions and established him as a frontrunner. The Bush campaign fundraising prowess came through a practice called "bundling," in which supporters collected contributions from friends, coworkers, employees, and family members typically offline, and in return received publicity and favor with the candidate and the campaign. "Pioneers" included major lobby firms in Washington, DC, as well as a brother and a sister of Bush's. His top bundlers each brought in over $100,000 through traditional offline fundraising techniques. Thus, in the first quarter of 1999, Bush had nearly $8 million, compared with just under $2 million for McCain, $2 million for Quayle, and a modest $700,000 for Elizabeth Dole. That financial imbalance continued through 1999 with the exception of billionaire publisher Steve Forbes, whose self-funded campaign kept him insulated from the quest for contributions.

Arizona senator McCain faced a daunting challenge in trying to beat the early favorite. His campaign put its meager resources into the New Hampshire primary, spending twice as many days campaigning in the state as Bush, traveling on the "Straight Talk Express," McCain's campaign bus. By December 1999, polls confirmed that McCain's strategy was working: he was leading in public opinion polls in New Hampshire. When the Iowa caucuses happened a few weeks prior, Bush finished first, followed by Steve Forbes, and Alan Keyes. McCain garnered only 5% of the votes. Thus, when he won New Hampshire with a margin of eighteen percentage points over Bush, a substantially greater margin than expected, it generated renewed excitement and attention for his candidacy.

The McCain campaign, from the start, had experimented with ways to generate contributions online. Although Dan Schnur, his communications director, confessed that when the website was set up, "we didn't anticipate raising very much money off of the site at all,"[14] by December they had managed to raise $1 million, or 6% of his campaign money, that way.[15] When McCain won the New Hampshire primary, the campaign saw an opportunity. Michael Cornfield, a scholar of politics and the Internet, mused to a *Washington Post* reporter: "The Net doesn't necessarily convert buzz into votes. [McCain] can't create the wave. He can only be ready with his surfboard."[16] McCain's surfboard came in the form of a pop-up window when visitors came to the website, either through a search engine or from campaign literature with the URL on it. The pop-up window invited visitors to contribute or volunteer. In the twenty-four hours following McCain's New Hampshire win, the campaign brought in half a million dollars online—an unprecedented sum.

The campaign further capitalized on the win by broadly announcing an online fundraiser ten days later. It was live video streamed using an on-demand audio/video service from the company Intervu.[17] Supporters could give $100 to watch the video stream and to pose questions to the candidate through a chat messaging program. Campaign aids picked the questions and McCain answered them on the live video feed.

The fundraising stunt garnered him substantial earned media. It was touted by journalists and pundits as the first of its kind, intimating that it was slightly risky but also worthwhile and in keeping with the persona of the maverick senator with the insurgent campaign. McCain capitalized on that free media when giving interviews, reporting the URL for his website to further drive traffic to the site. He proudly declared on CNN's *Inside Politics*, "We had almost no money when we were using the corporate jets. I could not get around from one place to another and meet my campaign schedule without it. Now we have a lot of money, thanks to the Internet and our successes, and we're able to charter a jet" (February 7, 2000). The campaign reported that over one-third of contributors were younger than forty, and that 40% of the donations were from first-time givers. The average contribution amount was $115.[18]

The cash infusion not only kept the campaign afloat, but it also served to provide a contrast to Bush and his contributors. A commentator on ABC's evening news described the contributions coming to McCain from the Internet as "clean": "It is the cleanest money that we're seeing in the system now" (February 11, 2000), as compared with contributions to Bush, which were coming heavily from lawyers, the oil and gas industry, and bankers. One newspaper reporter wrote, "McCain advisers regularly tout the influx of Internet donations as evidence of campaign momentum and McCain's appeal to 'new voters,' many of whom are giving to a candidate for the first time in small amounts that will be matched by the federal government."[19] One campaign staff member noted that the senator "may not win because of the Internet, but he would not be able to win without it."[20]

Although less impressive given Bradley's inability to win any primaries, his campaign also strategized ways to bring in needed cash through the Internet. An underdog, the former basketball star and senator from New Jersey raised over $500,000 through contributions made online by September 1999, three months out from the first election in Iowa. By comparison, the Gore campaign had only raised about $90,000 online by then.[21] Because Bradley was a challenger of an incumbent vice president, explained Lynn Reed, Bradley's Internet director, the campaign had to use every opportunity available to achieve success at the polls, and that included the Internet.[22]

Constructing Image in a New Millennium

Campaign image construction through the design of websites evolved considerably from 1996. The campaigns were using advances in HTML, including the use of cascading style sheets to better design sites. The enhanced use of visuals, from pictures to videos to carefully chosen font types, and more carefully laid-out pages suggested that campaigns recognized the importance of a well-crafted website to the image construction of the candidate.[23] Content, however, did not change drastically from the 1996 campaigns. Still present across the candidates' sites were biographical information, issue positions, press releases, and speeches. Much more prominent than in 1996 was the link to a "contribute" page. Most websites also featured a campaign store, where supporters could stock up on baseball hats and campaign buttons. One new feature was a Spanish-language version of the website, which the two front-runners, Bush and Gore, had as part of their sites.

Campaign staff in 2000 were still unsure who was likely to visit their website, and they worked to appeal to multiple audiences. In two separate studies, interviews were conducted with staff of presidential and state-level campaigns, and researchers found that they primarily targeted supporters,[24] providing information that would reinforce their opinions of the candidate while trying to move those supporters to get more active in the campaign.[25] Bimber and Davis noted that campaigns also had content that would speak to undecided voters, whom they expected would more likely visit the site as Election Day neared.[26]

Bimber and Davis, as well as Ku, Kaid, and Pfau, identified a third audience of campaign websites: journalists.[27] To that end, content on the sites included press releases, detailed policy positions, and texts of speeches. Ku, Kaid, and Pfau found that both Bush's and Gore's websites had an agenda-setting effect on the news, with Bush's site being even more effective at creating content that drove news coverage. The rest of this section describes the digital efforts of several candidates at constructing their image for these audiences.

STEVE FORBES: "HE WANTS YOU TO WIN"

Steve Forbes beats Howard Dean as the first candidate to loudly and prominently beat the drum of the potential of the Internet in campaigning. Forbes launched his campaign online, touted the fundraising and support he was receiving through his website, and took every opportunity to herald the mobilizing properties of the Internet on the stump and during televised interviews. On CNN's *Crossfire* on June 2, 1999, for example, he declared: "The American people, when they're aroused, when they mobilize—as we're starting to mobilize people through the Internet and other means—change, real change, fantastic exciting change can happen." The campaign even declared that "The Internet for Steve Forbes in 2000 will do what TV did for JFK in 1960."[28]

Forbes more than any other candidate in 2000 produced emancipatory rhetoric, highlighting the potential for ordinary citizens to become directly involved in the campaign via the Internet. He was asked on CBS *This Morning* why he would announce through the Internet that he would run for president (March 16, 1999). He answered:

> Well, as we speak, each year, tens of millions of more [sic] people do come online, and I think it's a wonderful combination of cutting-edge technology, but also a tool of bringing individuals back into the American political process, trying to end the discord and the disconnect between Washington and the American people. We're going to have online chats. We're going to involve people as individuals. It's going be a wonderful way to get our message across.

In the interviews he conducted in the early days of his campaign, his strategy with journalists was to start by noting he had launched his campaign online, mentioning the URL, and touting how many hits his website had received, how many people had signed up as donors. On Fox News Network's *Hannity & Colmes* show on April 13, 1999, he even bragged that he had received his first $1,000 contribution online, in addition to his 9,000 volunteer sign-ups and 30 million hits in four weeks. As CNN analyst Bruce Morton astutely noted on *Inside Politics*, Forbes's work to herald the Internet "was a way of getting attention. He wants to be seen as modern, as cutting edge, as high-tech, and if the picture's a little fuzzy, so what, it's new."

His campaign website, however, became increasingly hard to use. Indeed, for all of the touting of the power of the Internet to energize Forbes's campaign, the website was cluttered and visually uneven, featuring over sixty-four buttons to navigate into the site (See Figure 3.1). The main menu items were on the right of the page rather than the customary left, and each seemed to be a different font or size, competing with the images and content in the center of the page. On the left side of the site were "Your Personal Control Panel," which listed the "Steve Forbes Flat Tax That's a Tax Cut," "The Steve Forbes Personal Retirement Security System," "The Steve Forbes Power to Parents Plan," and "The Steve

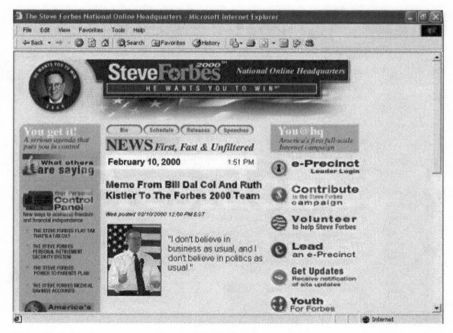

Figure 3.1 The home page of Steve Forbes's website

Forbes Medical Savings Accounts." The branded plans competed with the slogan of "He Wants You to Win," suggesting that "He Wants You" to feel you might win by electing him.

JOHN MCCAIN: STRAIGHT TALK ONLINE

The John McCain digital media brand worked in concert with the rest of the messaging for the campaign. In 2000 McCain rode a campaign bus called the Straight Talk Express. He made himself significantly more available to journalists than is typical of candidates, and used the Straight Talk Express as both a symbolic and an actual vehicle of his message to plainly and openly talk with the American people about his policies and leadership traits. Similarly, his digital media were clear and easy to use, and opened him up to the public in interactive ways.

His campaign's website design was simple and clean, featuring a banner along the top with a two-dimensional American flag icon and block lettering of McCain 2000 in white and red (See Figure 3.2). The menu was on the left side of the page in the customary location, and it provided links to expected content: contact

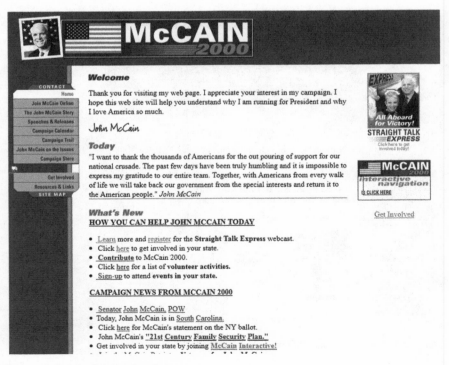

Figure 3.2 John McCain's website

the campaign, speeches, a biography, the campaign's event calendar, McCain's position on the issues, as well as links to contribute, get involved, and purchase from the store.

McCain used the website and the contributions he received from it as a counterpoint to Bush's traditional big-donor contributors. During a CNN debate on March 2, 2000, for example, Judy Woodruff asked the candidates if they used the Internet. Bush explained how his campaign was doing so, and highlighted that he listed his contributors on the website, using the opportunity to tout his philosophy of full disclosure. When McCain was asked the same question, he compared Bush receiving $7 million from "the interests in Washington" to his receipt of $7 million from "people just coming in on the Internet and contributing to our campaign because they want reform." McCain implied through this message that his support via the online contributions was coming from ordinary folks, whom he was better representing than Bush's elite and special interests.

BILL BRADLEY: AN INFORMATION BUREAU

Bradley's website, similar to John McCain's, fit with the image the campaign constructed. Bradley ran as the more liberal and principled insurgent to Gore's more centrist incumbency. Bradley's website had a clean design of a blue left column and a white center body that contained the featured content (See Figure 3.3). The graphics and layout sported cutting-edge design principles with rounded corners of menu buttons and the banner along the top. In the top left corner, anchoring the menu, was an image of the candidate that looked much like a campaign button. The menu of options provided links to a four-part biography of the candidate including excerpts from his books, campaign news, activities, and ways to get involved "In Your State," a press center, and a store. His issue positions were detailed and lengthy, and situated him to the left of Gore on issues such as gun control, tax reform, and universal health care. On Iowa caucus night, Bradley had a special website for Iowa voters with a look-up to tell them where their caucus site was.

Bradley's campaign created a negative website called www.moreaboutgore.com during the early primary season.[29] The campaign ran a TV ad in Washington state, where Bradley decided to put all of his focus rather than the Super Tuesday states after his losses in Iowa and New Hampshire. The ad directed viewers to the attack site, which made accusations about Gore's position on gun control, and provided images of newspaper and magazine articles to support the claims. The Gore campaign responded by creating a "Bradley Information Bureau" on the main Gore campaign site (www.algore2000.com). The section provided rebuttals to several of Bradley's claims against Gore.

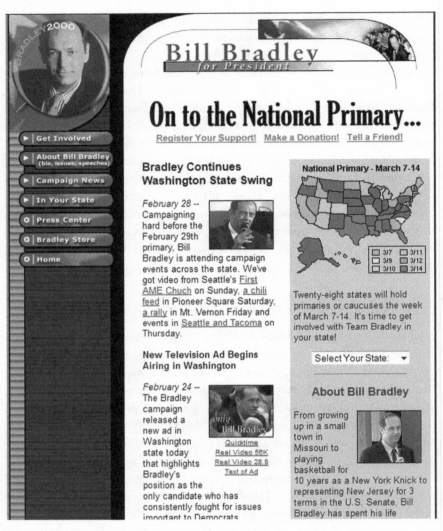

Figure 3.3 Bill Bradley's website

AL GORE INVENTED THE INTERNET AND OTHER IMAGE TROUBLES

Of the four major competitors in the primaries—Bush, McCain, Bradley, and Gore—Gore had the most substantial image troubles. Rhetorical analysis of Gore's speeches and press interviews highlighted that although he was in effect the incumbent in the election, given his role as sitting vice president, he ran as a challenger.[30] His verbal communication was more likely to attack Bush's record, call for change, and highlight how he would govern differently than Bush. In contrast, Bush's communication had the markers of an incumbent, highlighting his executive successes as governor and refraining from significant direct attacks on Gore by remaining "above the trenches." Yet Gore's digital communication strategies were those of an incumbent who played it safe, innovating where there was less risk to do so.

This relative caution when it came to his digital presence was especially noteworthy given Gore's persona. His first book on climate change, *Earth in the Balance*, published in 1992, established him as a forward-thinking, technology-focused, science-oriented politician. Coming into the 2000 presidential election, technology watchers had high expectations that Gore would run a savvy digital campaign, but then Gore made a noteworthy gaffe that reverberated through the rest of the campaign. Al Gore in a CNN *Late Edition* interview on March 9, 1999 uttered a statement that would haunt him. He was asked by Wolf Blitzer why Democrats should vote for him and not Senator Bill Bradley. Al Gore answered:

> Well, I will be—I will be offering my vision when the campaign begins, and it'll be comprehensive and sweeping, and I hope that it'll be compelling enough to draw people toward it. I feel that it will be. But it will emerge from my dialogue with the American people. I've traveled to every part of the country during the last six years. During my service in the United States Congress, I took the initiative in creating the Internet. I took the initiative in moving forward a whole range of initiatives that have proven to be important to our country's economic growth and environmental protection, improvements to our education system. During a quarter century of public service, including most of it long before I came into my current job, I have worked to try to improve the quality of life in our country and in our world. And what I've seen during that experience is an emerging future that's very exciting about which I'm very optimistic and toward which I'm—I want to lead.

The somewhat convoluted statement of Gore's qualifications and motivation for running for president had embedded in the statement "I took the initiative in creating the Internet." It quickly was twisted by Republican commentators and politicians as "Al Gore invented the Internet," which seemed ridiculous for any one person to declare his or her own invention.

To highlight the absurdity, Republicans took to the airwaves to declare what they had invented. Representative Dick Armey, then House Majority leader, joked that he had invented the highway system, Representative Trent Lott offered that he had invented paper clips, and former vice president Dan Quayle joked that he had invented spell checking, playing off his infamy as a bad speller.

Trying to quell the jokes and attacks, ten days after the CNN interview in which he clarified what he meant, Al Gore delivered a speech explaining in detail the role he had played in promoting the DARPA-NSF funded Internet into what it became by the year 2000. The corrective speech came too late. To make matters worse, the *New York Times* ran an article the same day as the speech that reported on an interview with President Bill Clinton and his efforts to highlight all the good he had done as president while acknowledging his one mistake of lying to the American people. The article ended by highlighting Gore's exaggerations on the campaign trail. This unsavory characteristic had become a stock frame journalists would use thereafter when covering candidate Gore.[31]

This construction of Gore, with the ridicule he received for the misstatement, set up expectations of Gore relative to his digital media strategy. By most accounts, though, the website was ordinary in its design and affordances. The site was rated by *PR Week* magazine as having a clean design but interactive features that did not work as well as they should have.[32]

He launched his website on April 8, 1999, later than his rivals. It featured the predictable position statements, press releases, and speeches. It also had photographs from the campaign trail, some of them taken by his wife, Tipper Gore. There was a children's section with a quiz and information about the vice president once Connecticut senator Joe Lieberman had been tapped as his running mate. It provided ways for people to sign up to volunteer, join an e-mail list, and provide names of friends to the campaign. Gore also streamed his campaign TV advertisements on his site.

Although the campaign's slogan changed during the campaign, one message that was consistent was Gore's declaration that he would open a two-way dialogue with the American people. To that end, the campaign offered some noteworthy innovations in digital strategy. In the summer of 1999, for example, he held a synchronous town hall in which about 5,000 people participated, and over 1,000 questions were posed, though only eleven were answered by Gore.[33] The campaign also embedded a note in the HTML source code of the site inviting programmers to contribute their web skills to the campaign (See Figure 3.4). Green explained that they did that to directly invite programmers into the campaign. He noted that it was met with a mixed reaction. Although new supporters were engaged by the invitation and contributed to the campaign, others declared it a gimmick and derided it.[34]

Another innovation, a precursor to social media of today, was the Gore instant messaging network. Supporters with an instant messaging program—AOL's Instant Messaging program, Yahoo! IM, or ICQ—could sign up (See Figure 3.5). They were also prompted to provide their geographic location and issues of interest to the campaign. When people logged into the network, they could see others in their geographic area who also were online at the same time

```
6    <script type="text/javascript" src="/static/js/jwplayer/jwplayer.js" ></script>
7    <script type="text/javascript" src="/static/js/video-embed-rewriter.js"></script>
8    <script type="text/javascript">
9    function initYTVideo(id)
10   {
11       _wmVideos_.init("/web/", id);
12   }
13   </script>
14   <!-- End Wayback Rewrite JS Include -->
15   <META NAME="keywords" CONTENT="al gore, gore, algore, gore2000, al gore campaign, gore 2000, tipper gore, president, presidential
         candidate, democrat, campaign, election, 2000, vote, MP3 files, family, education, health care, social security, medicare, environment
         liveable communities, crime, technology, science">
16   <META name="target" content="al gore, gore">
17   <META name="description" content="algore2000.com is the Official Gore 2000 campaign web site">
18   <HTML LANG="EN">
19   <HEAD>
20   <TITLE>Welcome to algore2000.com, Al Gore's official Presidential campaign web site</TITLE>
21   <SCRIPT language="JavaScript">
22   <!--
23   NewWindow = window.open
         ("/contrib_popup_new.html",'child','toolbar=no,location=no,directories=no,status=no,menubar=no,scrollbars=no,resizeable=yes,width=300,
         ight=350');
24   // -->
25   </script>
26   <!-------------------------------------------------------------------
27
28   Thanks for checking out our source code!  I plan to use this space to post
29   special messages to those who are helping to improve our web site -- by making
30   our site the best it can be.  The fact that you are peeking behind the
31   scenes at our site means you can make an important difference to this Internet
32   effort.  I'm grateful for your help and support in this campaign.  Now let's
33   keep working to build the 21st Century of our dreams!
34
35   Al Gore
36
37
38
39        ---------------------------------------------------------------->
40
41   <script language="JavaScript">
42
43   //     Select a random number.
44          today=new Date();
45          jran=today.getTime();
46              var number = 7;
47              var random_number="";
48              var image="";
49              var text_color="";
50              ia=9301;
51              ic=49297;
```

Figure 3.4   The Gore campaign site embedded note to programmers in the source code

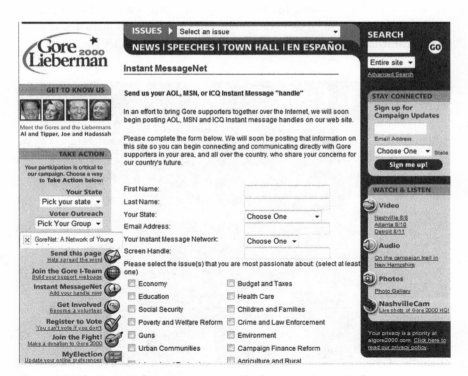

Figure 3.5   The Gore-Lieberman page to join the "Instant MessageNet"

and could chat with them. Green estimated that around 5,000 people signed up for the network. Green himself would log in and disseminate talking points, and around critical events, such as the debates, would give people in the network debate spin and encourage supporters to go to online message boards and forums to "amplify the message of the campaign."[35]

The Gore campaign collected other types of information from supporters. The website had a pop-up window for new visitors that asked them to sign up for the campaign by giving their name, e-mail address, and zip code, a trend-setting addition to the campaign website genre. Those who did this experienced a tailored Gore website with an image of the person's state flag and campaign events happening in their state or area. "We immediately give them something visual that provides a connection to where they live," explained Green.[36] He also provided a town hall section, which claimed to hold online discussions with citizens. In effect, however, people posted questions, and the campaign featured a selected question from the submissions and posted Gore's answer, in some ways a rudimentary blog.

The Gore campaign produced additional websites to attack George Bush during the general election, as well as to counter any momentum that Ralph Nader's Green Party candidacy might have to siphon voters from Gore's campaign. It released a website www.bushinsecurity.com to attack Bush's plans on Social Security (See Figure 3.6). Gore campaign staff secured the domain name: www.realplansforrealpeople.com, which was the title of Bush's policy book, and then

Figure 3.6 The Gore campaign's attack site

used it to critique Bush policy proposals. Green explained that they created separate attack sites not to move attacks off of the main campaign website, but to capitalize on the slogan so that their attack message was further driven home through the URL.[37] Indeed, research about news releases online found that the majority of them were attacks of opponents, suggesting campaigns were not shy to attack their opponent on their main website.[38]

The Gore campaign recognized by October that Ralph Nader could be a threat to his campaign by capturing 3% or 4% of potential Gore voters, which in the tightly contested election could be the difference between Gore winning or losing. The web strategists allied themselves with a third-party website, www.nadersraidersforgore.com, that spoke to Nader supporters and justified why they should instead vote for Gore.

NADER TRADERS

Consumer advocate Ralph Nader's insurgent campaign began in the late spring of 2000 as a challenge to the two major parties. Running on the Green Party ticket, Nader set out to raise a large part of his campaign's $5 million budget online. Within three days of announcing the website, www.votenader.com had 4,000 visitors.[39] When Gore and Bush remained essentially tied in public opinion surveys in September and October 2000, websites cropped up encouraging people to engage in vote swapping, meaning that Nader supporters in swing states would pledge to vote for Gore in exchange for Gore supporters in safe states voting for Nader. The justification for this vote swapping was to help secure 5% of the popular vote for Nader and the Green Party, which would in turn help the party secure federal and state campaign matching funds in future elections for their candidates while presumably not hurting Gore's chance of winning the presidential election. Nadertrader.org and Voteexchange.org were two such sites set up to facilitate the exchange. They faced legal challenges in California for attempting to interfere or subvert voting. Moreover, Pat Keaney, a Nader spokesperson, derided the online vote swap sites:

> It leaves out the grassroots level because there are people working hard in these battleground states for the Green Party that need those votes to gain ballot access in those states, to reassure their new supporters that they are going to be a viable option. So for people to turn tail and go to Gore this close to the election, as the result of some swap that they have done over the Internet, doesn't sit well with us.[40]

It was unclear in the end how many people potentially swapped their votes based on their pledge. More clear was that the Nader campaign distrusted and had concerns about the self-organizing that Gore and Nader supporters were attempting online to try and help both candidates.

BUSH'S EVOLVING DIGITAL IMAGE

Bush's digital presentation evolved considerably over the election. The initial website, his exploratory committee website, was relatively simple, providing a biography, information about his wife, Laura Bush, a list of his accomplishments, including his time as governor of Texas, speeches, poll results, and opportunities for supporters to volunteer and contribute. The site also featured a Spanish-language version.

Two additional redesigns followed. In the fall of 1999, the site's design included a more patriotic-themed banner with a background image of a waving American flag, and Bush's image appeared in the top left corner. Additional menu options included W.tv, a page that streamed TV ads and videos from the campaign, a list of contributors to the campaign in PDF format, an e-mail sign-up page to receive campaign announcements and updates, and a newsroom that listed press releases. Just a few months later, another graphical redesign was created, removing Bush's image from the top right corner, and replacing the banner image with a simple gradient blue with white lettering of georgewbush.com, and a bread-crumb trail to "My Campaign" for those who had customized the page to their interests. *PR Week* rated Bush's site before the primaries as dull, and commented that it seemed the campaign had put little effort into it.[41]

A final major visual redesign occurred in the summer of 2000. The traditional patriotic red and blue was replaced with black and an accent of yellow. Contribute, get involved, download, and register to vote options appeared along the top of the site, and GwB.TV was prominently featured on the right side of the home page (See Figure 3.7). This site invited customization for visitors by allowing them to personalize it according to issues and interests. The personalization required people to create an account with their name, login, and password, and an optional e-mail address.

The Bush campaign spent only $57,000 on the website during the surfacing stage, and the campaign did not push online fundraising. By the end of 1999, the campaign had only raised $180,000, or less 0.5% of his campaign funds online.[42] In the words of Phil Noble, CEO of Politics Online, "If I were George Bush, I wouldn't pay a hell of a lot of attention to the Internet either. Why would he want to? I mean, he's got a gazillion dollars. He's got every Republican in the country who's a sort of a party leader of [sic] official. He doesn't need it as much as somebody who is coming from behind."[43]

Figure 3.7 The home page of the general election website for Bush and Cheney

When the Bush campaign received attention for its substantial contributions, especially coming from wealthy and influential "bundlers," the campaign responded by providing the financial information as images from the 800-page report filed with the FEC. Scott McClellan, Bush's campaign spokesman, reported that at least 100,000 people had viewed the listing of Bush contributors on the campaign website.[44] The move garnered Bush earned media coverage, and it gave Bush ammunition to argue that he was running a transparent campaign by making available the names of contributors. Yet, because the database was not searchable, it was difficult to use. The Bush campaign defended the approach, saying it was the fastest way to make funder information available to the public.

Once Bush had secured the nomination, the campaign began emphasizing online fundraising in its press briefings. After an e-mail and online campaign in April, they brought in $1.5 million. Greg Sedberry, Bush's Internet campaign director, explained that the goal of the site was to "create an atmosphere in which the user feels they are part of the campaign," including sharing audio and video from the campaign trail.[45] Sedberry also highlighted how the campaign used the Internet for organization and mobilization efforts: "When 'John Smith' from Iowa signed up for the campaign we got his general profile here and the state office the profile for what he signed up to do. That's very powerful when you consider that at some points during the primary we were getting seven to eight thousand volunteers signing up a day."[46]

URLS AND DOMAIN NAMES

One special aspect of image construction for the candidates emerged through their domain names. In 1999 and 2000 they were a source of intrigue for journalists and citizens and a source of consternation for candidates. Domain name practices were starting to become clearer, with most campaigns including the candidate's name in the URL and using the .com domain extension, but the purchases sometimes fueled unwanted speculation by the press and forced campaigns to deal with a pervasive challenge: the cybersquatter.

In January 1999, before any candidate had even established a formal candidacy, speculators were buying up domains that included names of possible candidates. Some campaigns, in turn, in a preventative move purchased domain names to preempt ownership of the candidate's moniker. Journalists reported on the purchases, fueling speculation about campaign strategy and potential vice presidential picks.

The two biggest domain name purchasers were the George W. Bush and Steve Forbes campaigns. In addition to the two main domain names, Bush2000.org and GeorgeWBush.com (the latter of which became the official URL for the campaign), Karl Rove, Bush's campaign strategist, registered the domain names of anti-Bush sites (e.g. www.bushsucks.com) and pro-Bush sites, and redirected them back to the Bush campaign official website. He also purchased domain names around potential running mates, including New Jersey governor Christine Todd Whitman, Pennsylvania governor Tom Ridge, and New York governor George Pataki (e.g., www.BushPataki.com).

Steve Forbes's campaign registered two dozen domain names that indicated a possible partnership with Jeb Bush, governor of Florida and brother of candidate George Bush, as Forbes' vice president. Domain names included www.steveandjeb.com, www.steveforbes-jebbush.org, www.forbes-jebbush2000.com, and www.forbesandgovernorjeb.com. The Bush campaign response was that Forbes must be playing a joke on journalists and political watchers. The Forbes campaign responded by hinting that it had registered the names simply to irritate George Bush.

The purchases generated press coverage. Political pundits used them as a reading-the-tea-leaves approach to determining Bush's strategy in selecting a vice president. Spokesman Greg Mueller, for Steve Forbes, in an effort to spin the purchases to Forbes's political advantage with conservative primary voters, said, "This is an early indication by the Bush campaign that they intend to campaign to the more liberal wing of the party, which will raise a lot of red flags with rank-and-file Republicans and conservatives."[47] Mindy Tucker, Bush's spokeswoman, irritated with all of the speculation about the purchases, was quoted in a news story saying: "An enterprising young staffer [Karl Rove]" was to only buy negative and positive domain names but went a bit too far in purchasing domain names of possible vice presidents.[48]

Yet, for all of the effort to control domain names, the Bush campaign was unable to secure every domain that might be used against them. Some of them ended up in the hands of people who were hoping to make money from the campaign, known in the pejorative as "cybersquatters." Others purchased the domains to make a political statement against Bush. One independent voter, Brian Rodgers, had registered GeorgeBush2000.com because he simply did not want Bush to be president.[49] Another cybersquatter filled a Bush domain with links to anti-Republican websites and to pornography. The Bush campaign responded with disdain to a *Washington Post* journalist: "The person who registered the domain name approached the campaign and offered to sell it to us for tens of thousands of dollars, and we declined. Clearly, now he's decided to use the site to peddle falsehoods and pornography."[50] In the same article, a Republican National Committee spokesman said that it is "a rather nasty, dirty trick by somebody who's obviously supporting Al Gore." The response was to minimize the content creator by suggesting the motive was personal profit, and to associate the dirty tricks indirectly with Gore.

One site in particular especially irritated Bush. The site was a political parody created by Zack Exley, then a computer programmer from Boston and more recently a staff member of the liberal political group MoveOn.org. It was professionally designed and appealing with a theme similar to the official George W. Bush campaign website. The content, however, attacked Bush for an alleged history of cocaine and other drug use.

The Bush campaign, fed up with this site, threatened a lawsuit against Exley and appealed to the FEC. The campaign argued that Exley was operating as a political action committee and should be shut down. During a press meeting, Bush was asked about the site and described Exley as "just a garbage man." Exley responded by creating on his website a link: 'Click HERE for an earlier Bush 'garbage' initiative," which led to accusations of questionable financial dealings by the Bush family. The Bush campaign then sent a cease-and-desist letter to Exley: "In your wholesale misappropriation of the georgewbush.com website, you violate a host of copyright and trademark laws."[51] Exley posted the letter to the site along with his response (See Figure 3.8). Bush did not get the justice he sought, however. In April 2000, the FEC dismissed Bush's complaint against Exley, stating that the site did not intend to violate election law and was not serious enough to be reviewed by the commission.

The purchase of domain names that implicated the Bush name and the legal and political tug of war with Exley illustrate how seriously campaigns took URLs as extensions of their campaign, and also as indicative of their efforts to control their online image. A mischievous citizen or a person with an axe to grind could

Georgewbush.com vs. Gwbush.com

Despite all its great work, GWBUSH.COM has recently been
hounded by a pesky, upstart web site called
GEORGEWBUSH.COM. That web site, a dead ringer for the one
you're now visiting, first attacked GWBUSH.COM claiming that
we were using some of GEORGEWBUSH.COM's copywritten
material. The nerve!

But it gets worse! Unsatisfied with our response, the unusually
litigious site then filed a complaint with the FEC.
GEORGEWBUSH.COM claimed that GWBUSH.COM stood a
chance to affect the outcome of a presidential election or some
such thing!

Check out the legalistic ravings of GEORGEWBUSH.COM's
lawyers:

Cease & Desist Letter

Complaint to the FEC

And our fearless response:

GWBUSH.COM answers GEORGEWBUSH.COM's FEC
complaint

Figure 3.8 Zack Exley's gwbush.com political parody site

purchase a domain name, set up an attack website, and from the campaign's perspective, potentially do political harm to the candidate's image. At times the web
for campaigns looked like a risky endeavor, one over which they had much less
control than the much safer world of broadcast television where the rules of the
game were better understood.

Inventing Ways to Involve Citizens Just Enough

The theme of 2000 for challenger campaigns was *invention*. Candidates and citizens alike were trying to figure out how to make this technology work for them.
As is historically true of campaigns, they look to the past to see what worked. In
1999 what seemed to work was the approach of Minnesota Reform Party candidate and former World Wrestling Federation wrestler Jesse Ventura. His campaign started well behind in the polls and had a shoestring budget. The Ventura
campaign developed an elaborate website in bold, nontraditional colors of green
and white that laid out the candidate's background, his reasons for running for
governor, and his issue positions. It also sported an online bulletin board, one
of the firsts for political campaigning, and one of only a few sites in the 1998
election cycle to do so. The campaign used the bulletin board and an e-mail list

of supporters to announce campaign stops around Minnesota. The campaign could not afford an advance team or expensive venues, so the bulletin board and e-mail list became the way for supporters to find Ventura on the campaign trail and to build support and momentum for his campaign. Thus, in 2000 the campaigns looked back and saw potential to experiment in new ways with the interactive affordances of DCTs in an effort to get ahead of the competition.

NECESSITY IS THE MOTHER OF INVENTION: CHALLENGER INNOVATIONS

Both Bradley's and McCain's digital operations, in line with Ventura's campaign, experimented with ways to bring in new supporters, raise more cash, and garner free publicity through digital strategies. Bradley's site, for example, was successful in converting people into supporters by having them fill out a form on the website to get more involved in the campaign. The campaign had a community involvement kit that provided a list of fifteen activities people could do in their community to support the Bradley campaign (e.g., hosting a dinner, registering voters). Forbes similarly kept track of supporters' locations and what activities they would like to do for the campaign.

McCain's site emphasized his Straight Talk Express tour. Supporters could click on a map and see if and when McCain's bus would be coming through their town during the primaries and caucuses. Supporters of the campaign got special designations, "insurgent" or "rough rider," for example, as they became more involved in terms of contributions, online action, or volunteering.[52] McCain touted in an interview with Dan Rather that he had 50,000 people sign up on his website to volunteer.[53] The campaign also invited people to make phone calls for McCain in primary states. If they signed up, staff would e-mail a list of names and telephone numbers to the supporter, though the campaign had no infrastructure in place to track whether calls were made. In Virginia, the campaign created a flier and asked people to print it and make copies to distribute to friends and neighbors.

The Bradley staff made their website an integral component of their strategy. They heavily advertised the website, displaying it on podiums, lecterns, and advertising online, especially news websites. The efforts worked. Bradley's campaign manager reported that on an average day they were getting 5,000 visitors to their website and were receiving about $7,000 a day in contributions online.[54] Lynn Reed, Bradley's Internet strategist, sent out an e-mail request to 5,000 supporters in the Northeast to invite them to New Hampshire to canvas. Reed explained, "We were able to get 300 folks, free. If you had to make phone calls for the same return, it might not be worth it [financially]."[55]

The community involvement kit, another Reed invention, provided a list of actions supporters could take for Bradley. As supporters carried out those activities, they were included as part of a "Team Bradley" photo gallery.[56] Bradley's campaign engaged in ad watching of Gore's primary ads, sending an e-mail after a Gore ad on health care, critiquing it for stealing Bradley's words about the plight of the uninsured.[57] The ad watch itself was not noteworthy, but the channel through it operated was—an unprecedented move to use e-mail to directly contact a large number of reporters and try to steer the news.

Forbes's website invited supporters to sign up to become a leader of an "e-precinct" where they were urged to organize their friends on behalf of the Forbes campaign in a form of multilevel marketing. The originator was rewarded with special access to website content and a chance to meet the candidate in person. This strategy generated over 5,000 "e-precincts," some with thousands of members. The Forbes campaign developed a detailed e-mail list with location information of supporters.[58] He also innovated with streaming videos of speeches, including a live stream with schoolchildren from eighty-five different schools.

RECOGNIZING THE POWER OF THE PERSONAL

Both the McCain and Gore campaigns recognized the power of two-step flow in digital media to help people to feel connected to the campaign and to enable them to organize their own network of friends and supporters. The McCain campaign developed the most extensive voter e-mail database of any of the primary campaigns.[59] Fose explained in an interview with a journalist that the purpose of e-mail was to help supporters organize for the campaign.[60] In a highly prescient observation, he also noted the following: that in the past the neighborhood was where most organizing happened; if a campaign mobilized a few people in a neighborhood, then those people would get their neighbors involved or at least in support of the candidate on Election Day. The neighborhood is no longer the strong community it once was. Instead, people have a community that spans across the country, connected through the Internet. Mobilizing supporters and activating them to work with their nationally distributed social network was the key to success, Fose thought. As became evident in subsequent election cycles, Fose was right.

Campaign staff recognized the potential power of activating supporters to become super-advocates who could work on behalf of the campaign. The Gore campaign, for example, established several different venues meant to help supporters mobilize and engage their friends and family members. In addition to the Instant Messaging network, they heavily used e-mail to communicate with supporters. A *New York Times* article a day before the election highlighted the role of e-mail in the campaign as a cost-effective, efficient way to mobilize supporters.[61] The article described the Gore campaign e-mail strategy to implore recipients to forward the message to their friends and to bring ten friends to the polls on Election Day. Campaigns were beginning to recognize that people contacting and organizing their friends was likely more effective and more efficient than the campaign trying to mobilize those same friends.

Out of that support from ordinary citizen activists, however, emerged a tension for the campaigns about how to control the message and ensure no damage was done by rogue supporters. For example when George Bush was exploring his vice presidential pick during the summer of 2000, a group of supporters of a Republican representative from Ohio, John Kasich, created a website, www. BplusK.com, to promote Kasich as Bush's vice president. A spokesperson for Congressman Kasich interviewed by a reporter said, "We're aware of it. That's all I can say" about the citizen-generated website.[62] His tone suggested that the campaign was not happy about the site. One journalist captured the concerns political campaigns and parties had:

> On one hand, grass-roots websites represent a wellspring of new activists for candidates and parties to tap, especially when so many political observers have lamented a decline in voter participation. But this new medium also created a series of what-ifs for the parties: What if a well-meaning website contains information the candidate or party believes misrepresents it? What if confusion arises between official party and candidate websites and grass-roots ones? What if some of these websites contain links to groups on the far right or far left that a candidate would rather not be associated with? And, even more basic, what if these websites begin to shift political power away from candidates and parties and to individuals with a large electronic presence?[63]

The challenge for campaigns was in determining which risks with digital campaigning were worth the reward.

DATA ANALYTICS: REPUBLICANS LEAD THE PACK

The Bush campaign used e-mail and the website to engage citizens with the campaign, and used the two in concert to advance the campaign's work to build a database of voters to target with Bush's message. Bush hired Aristotle Publishing to help with this objective. Aristotle devised one clever way to collect information about voters, running interactive banner ads on popular websites inviting people to learn their tax savings under Bush's economic plan.[64] If they were intrigued, they could interact with the banner ad directly by providing income information. When they got back the result of their tax savings, they were invited to give their e-mail address to stay in touch with the Bush campaign.

Aristotle in 2000 was already starting to combine voter behavior online with state voter rolls offline. Jay McAniff, a spokesperson for Aristotle explained,

> direct marketing people are like insurance salesmen—people don't like them much. However, there's a need for political candidates to start targeting people on the Internet. We came in and we said, "How can we reach voters without pissing people off?" Candidates are legally allowed to use voter rolls, so we take that and add it to a list of people who say we can use their e-mail addresses to receive messages.[65]

Aristotle's voter database allowed campaigns to begin to more carefully target voters.[66]

The e-mail address is, metaphorically speaking, the key to the city, the primary means data aggregators have to connect various bits of information about potential voters into a database, which they can then analyze to better target messages. According to Michael Turk, who worked on Bush's campaign in 2000, the Republicans were more effective at building big donor lists with e-mail addresses than the Democrats.[67] Indeed, the Republican National Committee's strategy in 2000 was to build as massive an e-mail supporter list as possible, using whatever gadgets and gimmicks might get a supporter to provide an e-mail address. By the start of the general election, the RNC had a database of 250,000 people, and the RNC chairman's motto was "Digital or die."[68] About 150,000 received daily e-mail updates during the Republican National Convention. The RNC also invested significantly in terms of resources and staff, budgeting nearly $5 million and dedicating fifteen staff to digital campaigning. Part of the RNC's motivation for going digital was to more effectively and directly communicate with supporters and the electorate. In the words of Larry Purporo, a deputy director at the RNC, "The Web gives us the power of direct, one-on-one communication. It allows us to totally leapfrog the Fourth Estate [the media]."[69] He also hoped to be able to convert supporters into activists: "You can turn soccer moms with laptops into a labor force."[70] Haley Barbour, former RNC chairman, declared that Web users in 2000 were more likely to lean Republican, and so a strong digital presence was to the party's advantage.

Not only is an e-mail address the key to connecting information about a potential voter or supporter, e-mail is also the "hammer of an e-campaign," as Mike Shannon, a digital strategist for the Bush campaign, explained insightfully in a postelection memo to Karl Rove, Matthew Dowd, Ken Mehlman, and Jack Oliver, senior staff of Bush's campaign. Because e-mail is a push medium, meaning that people get a message in their inbox without having to go out and find it, the campaign can get information more easily in front of supporters. If, as Shannon urged, campaigns kept the messaging short and memorable, helping it to break through the clutter often found in people's inboxes, and a message was effectively targeted to the people who were most receptive to it, then e-mail was potentially the most potent messaging weapon a campaign had.

Conclusion

The presidential campaigns in the primaries and the general election experimented with a variety of digital campaign practices. Digital campaign staff were better integrated into the strategic planning of the campaign, enabling richer opportunities to try untested tactics in the hopes of big payoffs. It is evident that by 2000 insurgent campaigns, and those with less to lose but much to gain, were at the leading edge of experimentation. They had staff and candidates who recognized the potential of the Internet to aid their success. For Bradley and especially McCain those speculations seemed to pay off. Bradley was able to run an efficient campaign on the backs of volunteers, some of whom found their way to the campaign and to New Hampshire through a digital path after learning about the campaign through more traditional campaign messaging channels. McCain was able to effectively use his website and digital campaign to ride the wave of his win in New Hampshire, thereby enriching the campaign far more quickly and effectively than he would have otherwise. All the campaigns were beginning to recognize that there was a potentially new paradigm of campaigning by mobilizing the strongest supporters to work on behalf of the campaign through the two-step flow process of talking with their own social networks. In doing so, those supporters would likely be effective at convincing those contacts in the social network to get involved in ways that the campaign could not.

Much of the experimentation was focused on two objectives: (1) driving money to the campaigns; and (2) building databases of e-mail addresses and voter information to send messages to particular voter segments who met a particular profile or expressed a particular interest that the campaign wanted to target. Relatedly, inventions, such as Lynn Reed's online organizing kit for Bradley supporters, provided super-advocates with organizing tools to help them coordinate their offline social network on behalf of the campaign. Some staff even began to create point systems and leader boards of sorts to gamify campaign activities, as Max Fose did for the McCain campaign, and induced motivation among supporters to do more for the campaign.

For all the experimentation, what campaigns were cautious about was genuinely opening up for direct citizen engagement and interaction with campaign staff. Although campaigns invited feedback and stories from supporters, such as on Gore's website, unused were message boards or chat rooms to allow supporters to begin to meet each other online, discuss the campaign, or coordinate online to act offline. The rudimentary social media system created by Ben Green through instant messaging programs was an experiment in crafting a community online and arming members with talking points to spread through other digital media channels. Yet campaigns were still generally distrustful of what might happen if they threw open the doors and let their supporters drive the campaign. As hierarchical organizations with professional and highly paid senior staff who in their gut and through their experience *knew* how to campaign, the idea of opening up campaigns for more citizen-driven efforts in the way that Ventura did in 1998 was unthinkable.

4

2004: The Paradigm Shift

Digital campaigning in 2004 can be understood by looking back to 1960. In that election year something revolutionary happened in the world of political campaigns: television. Although television had been in America's living rooms for a decade and political campaigns aired TV advertisements in the 1952 and 1956 campaigns, TV was at the cusp of coming into its own as a key component of presidential campaigns by 1960. The fabled Nixon/Kennedy televised debate, in which TV viewers purportedly preferred Kennedy over Nixon because of Nixon's sweaty, unshaven, and rumpled appearance, compared to the clean-cut and handsome Kennedy, has been heralded since as evidence that a paradigm shift had occurred in American politics.

In 2004 the paradigm shifted again, though this time it was brought about by campaigns' use of digital communication technologies (DCTs). The mass diffusion of Internet access in the US population meant that by 2004 American political actors began to feel that change was upon them. Although dramatic change effectively ended with Democratic primary candidate Howard Dean's mighty "Yeeaahhh!" when he lost the Iowa caucuses, his campaign's inventive uses of DCTs to genuinely open up and be responsive to the energy and ideas of supporters helped advance an underdog candidate to front-runner status and demonstrated the power of digital campaigning.

Although many today recognize the influence the Dean campaign has had on the practices of digital campaigning since, fewer give credit to the Draft Wesley Clark campaign, a truly grassroots, or perhaps *netroots*, affair[1]—that is, until it collided with the rigid and hierarchical practices of the formal Wesley Clark campaign, in which the know-how of professional political consultants collided against the creative and loosely organized energy of the netroots. The clash that occurred, looked at from the lens of actor network theory, helps reveal underlying power dynamics and relationships between political actors.[2]

This chapter examines the nature of the practices that suggested a paradigm shift from campaigning based on the impersonal dissemination of mass messaging in the broadcast era to recognition of the value of interactivity by supporters *with* the campaign. This transition to a networked era of campaigning manifested in this election cycle, as campaigns began harnessing supporters to drive them to self-organize, to tap their existing social networks with the aim of disseminating the campaign message to undecided and less-involved voters via two-step flow, and to give up their data so campaigns could more effectively microtarget.

This chapter provides the contextual background that shaped the efforts of the campaigns, examines efforts by several to fundraise and to craft their image through DCTs, and looks at how campaigns lost and worked to gain control of interactivity with and among supporters. Finally, this chapter highlights how the organizational structures of campaigns changed this election cycles, and the reasons those changes mattered.

Background and Strategic Environment

POLITICAL BACKGROUND

In early 2003, during the surfacing stage of the 2004 presidential campaign, the nation was in a remarkably different situation than it had been in the lead-up to the 2000 election. Instead of peace and prosperity, the nation was now at war in two countries, Afghanistan and Iraq, and the economy was sluggish at best.

The nation was fighting what President Bush described as a war on terrorism following the attacks on September 11, 2001, in which members of the group Al-Qaeda hijacked four US airplanes; two were flown into the World Trade Center towers in New York City; one flew into the Pentagon in Washington, DC; the other crashed in a field in central Pennsylvania when passengers attacked their hijackers. Over 3,000 people were killed that day, and President Bush rhetorically declared war against Al-Qaeda, putting troops into Afghanistan a month later because its Taliban-run government gave safe harbor to the militant group. Then, after months of public messaging about the dangers of President Saddam Hussein of Iraq holding what the Bush administration characterized as weapons of mass destruction, the United States launched an air and ground assault in Iraq in March 2003, just as Democratic candidates began to officially launch their campaigns against the incumbent president.

The US economy was sluggish, although climbing out of a recession that occurred briefly after the terrorist attacks of 9/11 in conjunction with the dot-com bubble bursting. President Bush pushed for a broad set of economic measures to help stimulate the economy including tax cuts for most Americans, lowering the rate of capital gains tax on investment income, increasing the size of deductions households could take, and gradually eliminating the estate tax.

Bush was unchallenged in the Republican primaries, but several candidates surfaced to compete for the Democratic nomination to contest Bush in the general election. Public opinion polls suggested that the nation was strongly divided, with Democrats being more likely to oppose the war and much more likely to feel negative toward the president. Democratic presidential hopefuls saw an opportunity to unseat the incumbent. Those hopefuls included Senator John Kerry, Senator Joe Lieberman, Governor Howard Dean, Representative Dick Gephardt, Senator Carol Mosley-Braun, Representative Dennis Kucinich, and eventually General Wesley Clark. Ultimately, none of them were successful in their quest, with Bush narrowly defeating Kerry in the general election.

The Democratic surfacing stage was remarkably unpredictable in terms of accurately identifying the probable nominee. Political pundits in early 2003 predicted John Kerry, John Edwards, and Dick Gephardt as likely front runners. By the end of 2003, however, those prognostications had changed.[3] At the top of the pack was now General Wesley Clark, who had entered the race in the early fall, after a prolonged and visible Draft Wesley Clark campaign by the netroots. Former governor Howard Dean also was at the top of the pack, demonstrating that his people-power fundraising and insurgent digital media tactics had the power to garner him significant media attention, money, and poll numbers.

THE INTERNET

The Internet by 2004 had matured substantially from 2000 in terms of its diffusion as well as the activities occurring through its many channels. By 2004, just over 60% of American adults were using the Internet. Of those with Internet access, almost 60% reported looking for news and information about presidential campaigns online, which was more than double the number of 2000, according to surveys from the Pew Internet & American Life Project.[4] As well, 40% of Internet users were sending instant messages, nearly 70% were buying products online, and just under half were conducting online banking. Web video compression technologies combined with greater diffusion of broadband Internet meant that over half of Internet users were now consuming audio or videos online.

One important digital communication channel that grew in popularity in 2004 was the weblog, or blog. Primarily these were used for personal journaling by ordinary people, updated chronologically with newer posts presented at the top of the page, and typically with a *blogroll*, a list of links to other blogs.[5] In 2002 they also began to be used by political commentators on both the left and the right of the political spectrum.[6] Kerbel characterizes blogs as capturing "the decentralized, bottom-up nature of the Web" because they can be easily produced by anyone with Internet access.[7] Through their technological openness of original posts, commentary on those posts, and links to other blogs and sources of information they enable a free flow of conversation and information exchange on political and social issues. The communication technology of blogging, as described further below, was used first by the Dean campaign, and later by other candidates, to provide a place for interaction to occur directly between campaign staff and supporters. The blog, more than any other communication channel on the Internet at the time, was the driving technological innovation that helped decentralize the campaign hierarchy and enabled greater voice and visibility of supporters to the campaign, to the media, and to each other.

Another important actor in the 2004 election cycle was the left-leaning political group, MoveOn.org. It started as an online petition in 1998 to urge Congress to censure President Bill Clinton rather than impeach him and then "move on" to tackling more pressing issues the nation faced. By 2003, MoveOn had grown into a notably large activist group for progressive causes. It played a vital role in the 2004 campaign by drawing attention to the primary candidates vying for the Democratic ticket and sending resources to those identified by its membership as worthy of support. For example, MoveOn launched the first ever online Democratic primary. It became a noteworthy political organization that helped channel the netroots and organized them to promote Democratic candidates.[8]

Finally, a nonpolitical organizing tool, MeetUp.org, was used first by ordinary people who were politically interested and subsequently by political campaigns to help supporters organize themselves for the campaign. A minority of people in 2002 was skeptical of the run-up to war in Iraq being pushed by the Bush administration, and they began to find channels online to express their frustrations and find others who shared their concern on such sites as Andrew Sullivan's blog, the Daily Dish. Sullivan, a proponent of candidate Howard Dean because of his antiwar stance, helped turn a group of antiwar progressives into Dean supporters. These Dean supporters in turn began to find each other offline using MeetUp. org to "meet up" at coffee shops or bars where like-minded antiwar or pro-Dean supporters could commiserate about the state of politics. These MeetUps (for Dean, for Clark, etc.), like blogs, helped supporters find each other and begin to plan together ways to change not only the national conversation about the war but also something to help nominate and elect an antiwar candidate.

Political uses of DCTs increased in 2004 as well. The Pew Internet & American Life Project issued a report on the use of the Internet in the election.[9] Half of adult Internet users reported getting news and information about the election online. E-mail was used by over one-third to discuss politics and especially to share jokes about the candidates. The demographic profile of those who were getting political news online widened. For example, only 34% of female Internet users in 1996 consumed political news, compared with 66% of men. By 2004, the gender gap was closing, with just under half of female and just over half of male Internet users consuming political news online. Of note, the study found that Kerry supporters were more active online, with a greater percentage participating in online polls (31% of Kerry supporters vs. 18% of Bush supporters), getting information online on where to vote (25% of Kerry supporters vs. 17% of Bush supporters), and contributing money online (9% of Kerry supporters vs. 2% for Bush supporters). The Internet and the channels of communication through it were becoming mainstream socially and politically.

EXPANDING FUNDRAISING EFFORTS ONLINE

McCain and Bradley demonstrated in 2000 that with the right strategies a campaign could capitalize on the affordances of DCTs to raise needed cash. The key strategy in 2000 was to use a catalyzing event, such as winning a primary in McCain's case, or manufacturing fundraising goals with a message that resonated with supporters, such as in Bradley's campaign. Being an insurgency campaign also helped energize those who felt disillusioned about the front runners but also motivated enough to mobilize around an alternative. The clever campaign that recognized or manufactured a fundraising opportunity also had to have the right infrastructure to draw people from the home page to the contribution page, such as the pop-up window—an important innovation in 2000. Some of the 2004 campaigns understood the lesson and worked to hone the practice of online fundraising. Those stories are described next.

PEOPLE-POWERED GIVING

The Howard Dean campaign's use of DCTs facilitated a lasting shift in an essential component of the campaign, fundraising, by generating small contributions from a large number of supporters, often repeatedly. Some journalists and pundits used the metaphor "sea change" to characterize the shift.[10] Yet at the start Governor Dean was hardly a blip on the radar in terms of early estimates of potential contributions as compared to the front runners. After a surprising groundswell of support at MeetUp events across the country in early March 2003, Dean campaign staff began to craft careful pitches for small contributions to the network of supporters, many of whom were people without large cash reserves to contribute $2,000 to a candidate. On the eve of the first quarter of 2003, when campaigns must report their past three months of contributors and amounts to the Federal Election Commission, Howard Dean wrote a short e-mail message urging his supporters to contribute to the campaign to help establish his viability and by extension his supporters' vision. The message worked, and the Dean campaign was able to report $2.6 million, over $700,000 of which was generated through online contributions. Although the total amount was well behind other candidates, it positioned Dean as a contender in the eyes of the news media, and his surprising fundraising abilities meant that he garnered a healthy dose of positive earned media coverage. Joe Trippi, Dean's campaign manager, emphasized in interviews that the contributions over the Internet were typically less than $100. This signaled to pundits and campaign watchers that Dean, though raising a smaller amount of money than others, was nevertheless garnering a great deal of enthusiasm. Any member of the electorate who puts "skin in the game" in the form of a campaign contribution, even if it is a small contribution, is a serious supporter. This is part of the reason that the news media focus so heavily on campaign fundraising numbers in the surfacing stage of a campaign; it is a heuristic of the viability of the candidate.

The political campaigns experimented with ways to drive small-donor contributions, with the Dean campaign at the leading edge. Trippi experimented with personal appeals via e-mail and on the blog as the campaign neared the quarterly reporting deadlines to urge new rounds of giving.[11] In addition, he had his web staff create an art logo of a red baseball bat that was featured prominently on the website. Dean supporters were urged to "hit a grand slam for Dean."[12] His personal and emphatic appeal paid off, sharing with the world the campaign's internal fundraising goals, though it was viewed as risky by some in the campaign because it was not information campaigns share typically.[13] The red bat and fundraising goal spurred more than $700,000, giving the campaign slightly more than $7 million for the second quarter.[14]

Dean's experimentation was profoundly successfully. By the campaign's end, he had raised $51 million in contributions, 61% from donors giving $200 or less.[15] The campaign's success led strategists to do something that is typically unthinkable for a campaign that relies on the largesse of others: to eschew federal matching money—the first Democratic primary candidate to do so since 1976.[16]

Other campaigns followed suit, establishing fundraising goals, promoting them publicly, and even creating their own visuals. John Edwards's campaign sent an e-mail to supporters telling them about Edwards's love of jogging. Noting that the race for the White House was his most challenging terrain yet, the e-mail invited supporters to contribute $44 and get four friends to contribute $44 and receive "a really cool fuzzy 'Jog with John' headband as a token of our gratitude."[17] Clark tried to motivate giving by challenging online donors to pick a World Series winner, the Clark04 Baseball Challenge, putting a contribution toward the team they were betting on to win the Series. Lieberman was able to generate nearly $1 million from an e-mail fundraising request, demonstrating that Dean was not the only candidate who could activate his supporters in a time of need.

The campaigns had discovered that an advantage of small donors is that they keep giving. Most campaigns' small-donor givers had not reached the $2,000 campaign limit by the end of the 2003, suggesting a resource the campaign could continue to tap through the primaries.[18] The new fundraising goals and sometimes corny gimmicks were meant to go back to the well of small donor givers and bring forth a new outpouring of money.

Kerry's fundraising strategy evolved over the life of his campaign. Although he ran the traditional large-donor fundraising strategy of the typical front-runner candidate during the surfacing and primary stages, his staff experimented with generating cash infusions online, especially at the end of the financial reporting quarters. They further tuned their online fundraising strategy when they hired Josh Ross in the late fall of 2003, who originated in the digital start-up world of Silicon Valley. Ross was able to convince senior staff to include a mention of the campaign website in Kerry's speech when he won the Iowa caucus, which, as Ross promised, drove traffic and vital money to the campaign. Ross focused on e-mail, shifting the writing in messages from the more direct mail style of lengthy argumentations that the campaign had been using, to one that had a shorter, more conversational feel. Ross also pushed the website design on the contribution page to facilitate a quicker and easier donation experience for users. Ross explained, "I came from Silicon Valley. I took an e-commerce approach to the process and simplified it."[19] After it became clear on Super Tuesday that Kerry was likely the presumptive nominee, the campaign brought in $2.6 million within a twenty-four-hour period, which at the time was the most money raised online ever in such a short period.

As Kerry turned his attention from winning the nomination to beginning a general election campaign, in May 2004 the campaign launched a $10 million in ten days online fundraising drive. Howard Dean, who backed Kerry after quitting the campaign, posted a red bat on his newly created Democracy for America website and urged his supporters to help the Kerry campaign fill it. He sent an e-mail to his substantial e-mail list, driving $500,000 in contributions to Kerry in one day.[20] The campaign also established fundraising goals and drummed up energy and excitement for those goals through e-mail, on the blog, and on the website. The campaign also implemented a splash page, the first page a visitor saw, that typically invited the visitor to get involved, give an e-mail address, or contribute.[21] By June 2004, almost three-quarters of Kerry's fundraising was coming through Internet channels.[22] Of particular note, the Kerry campaign did A/B testing, a way of testing the effects of different messaging or images, of its e-mail messaging to see what messages were more likely to drive visitors and donors to the site.[23] The campaign also tested the best locations for the "Donate" button and other design elements, according to Peter Daou, a Kerry online media strategist.[24]

THE STANDARD: LARGE-DONOR GIVING

Historically, presidential campaigns relied primarily on the wealth of large donors and *bundlers*—those who have substantial wealth of their own to give maximum contribution amounts to campaigns through traditional means (e.g., attending fundraising dinners) as well as those who have substantial networks of contacts they can massage into giving contributions. Front-runner John Kerry had established a network of potential large-donor contributors that he had been cultivating since the 2000 election, as did John Edwards. Dick Gephardt focused on capturing union endorsements and support that he could convert into financial contributions. Each front runner was expected to raise more than $4 million in the first four months of 2003 that way.

The Bush campaign continued its strategy from 2000 to encourage core supporters to become bundlers for the campaign. His Pioneers in 2000 had raised millions, so in 2004 a new class of Rangers was created with a target goal for each to raise $200,000 in the primaries, twice what each Pioneer had been tasked with raising the campaign before.[25] In the second quarter of 2003 Bush raised $30 million, substantially more than any of the Democratic primary challengers.[26] By comparison, his campaign had only generated about $700,000 online throughout the second quarter. By December 2003, Bush had over $100 million in the bank, nearly all of it raised through traditional offline means.[27]

Through the general election the Bush campaign continued with its traditional fundraising strategy. It also continued to build a deep list of supporters, gathering e-mail addresses, demographic information, and prior voting history, and combining that data with consumer purchases and web-browsing activities to develop carefully targeted e-mail messaging to raise contributions. Contributions from online giving, approximately $14 million of the overall $270 million, was never a substantial focus of the Bush fundraising effort.[28]

IMAGE CONSTRUCTION IN A TIME OF WAR

What was most noteworthy about image construction in DCTs in 2004 was the increasing reliance on streaming video to convey a unified message across media channels: online and on TV. The Bush and Kerry campaigns heavily used streaming videos, with the Bush campaign even featuring a W.tv link on the website to a bank of ads the campaign had created. The web videos campaigns created often were more hard hitting and controversial than broadcast ads because they were not regulated in the same way. Dean and the Draft Wesley Clark campaign relied less on streaming video and more on their campaign blogs to construct the story of the campaign and candidate, highlighting the important role that supporters played in making their campaigns into a movement. This section describes in detail the major contenders' efforts at image construction through digital means.

THE DEMOCRATIC WING OF THE DEMOCRATIC PARTY

By the spring of 2003, Dean constructed himself as the anti-Iraq war candidate who also was a revolutionary user of DCTs, striking a chord that resonated with a segment of the electorate. Before then, Dean had campaigned in Iowa and New Hampshire, but had gained little interest among voters. When he opposed the vote that most of his Democratic rivals made to authorize funding for the war in Iraq in October 2002, he found his message. He began to attract local news coverage and more people turned up at his events.

Seeing the resonance of his image as an outsider running against opponents such as Kerry and Lieberman, who had voted for the resolution, Dean shifted tactics. He hired Joe Trippi, who had helped with the campaign of insurgent candidate Jerry Brown in 1992 and had helped Dean with his TV ads when he ran for governor. Trippi, who had become disenchanted with politics but enamored of the interactive capabilities of DCTs, assembled a campaign with a strong focus on them. As Trippi explained in his book, *The Revolution Will Not Be Televised*, the campaign lacked much by way of an organization or a strategy when he joined it in early 2003. He turned to DCTs to help build an inexpensive insurgency campaign.

Dean embraced a rhetoric of empowerment for his supporters, evidenced especially on the campaign's weblog, establishing them as important and agentic. Dean declared in speeches, on his website, and in e-mail messages that his supporters "have the power to take back the Democratic party." Trippi contributed to the messaging that Dean was the right candidate at the right time, stepping into what he called in a blog post in the summer a "perfect storm of democracy," explaining, "It's the confluence of the right candidate, the growth of the Internet and our willingness to give up control and allow people to organize themselves.... It's a bottom-up approach—the way this country was built."[29] Dean's website in September 2003 told visitors: "Time will tell whether the special interests and the Bush administration have underestimated me. But I know in my heart that they have underestimated you." The red fundraising bat on the website became a symbol of that power. One supporter wrote on the blog that the bat has "become a metaphor for a big club we can swing at the political status quo (or George W. Bush—however you want to look at it) with our combined muscle. Howard Dean will go down in history as having given this club to a huge bunch of political nomads.... I love you all, and I love this movement."[30] The campaign blog referred frequently to the campaign being "your campaign," investing ownership of it, including its successes and failures, in supporters.

When interviewed by journalists and in speeches, Dean and his spokespeople routinely highlighted their Internet-driven campaign, the vital role his support- ers were playing in his success, while attacking other Democrats for abandoning their principles, characterizing Dean as representing the "Democratic wing of the Democratic party." The image the campaign had constructed resonated with potential primary voters. By December 2003, Dean was the front runner, polling ahead of Kerry, Gephardt, Edwards, and Lieberman.

The campaign website design further underscored this message. The site, which went through a few major overhauls during the surfacing stage, with Trippi complaining that he had trouble getting the web designers to get the link to MeetUps at the top of the page, eventually landed on a slightly uncon- ventional color scheme, with the menu along the left side and the top having a black background and white lettering.[31] Eventually, Trippi got his wish, and the right column of the website was devoted to the key ways that supporters could work for the campaign, including a "Join the Dean Campaign" where visi- tors could provide their e-mail address and zip code, and above that the "My name is" MeetUp badge design with a note of how many MeetUps had occurred (See Figure 4.1). The menu options along the top featured the "official blog," "get local," "Deanlink," and "Contribute." The red bat showed fundraising goals achieved and the invitation to "click here to contribute." The center of the page was a featured article or picture.

Yet the apparent insurgent and liberal image that had emerged early in 2003 conflicted with many of Dean's policy positions and the endorsements he received, creating a confusing image of the candidate. Pundits declared that Dean was another George McGovern, a reference to the 1972 presidential campaign, in which antiwar and liberal South Dakota senator George McGovern took on Republican president Richard Nixon and lost badly. This comparison reinforced ideas among supporters that Dean was a strong liberal. Dean's policy speeches and positions on a variety of issues, however, showed a moderate streak. Though he was against the Iraq war, he was hawkish on war generally. Although his state of Vermont had legalized gay marriage, which Dean supported, he was moderate on most social issues. Moreover, he was fiscally conservative. In December 2003 he was endorsed by Al Gore, a politician viewed as a consummate Washington insider by many. Some political watchers, including participants on Dean's blog, attributed Dean's demise to Gore's endorsement. The core issue was that Dean's image was complex and many of his policy positions were at odds with much of his base of supporters.

Dean had another image problem, one that had circulated primarily among the press corps, but cropped up in news coverage of the candidate especially in December 2003, when he received heavy scrutiny by the press, which was further aggravated by misstatements Dean made while on the campaign trail.

Figure 4.1 Howard Dean's campaign website

The trouble was that he was perceived as being intemperate and a hothead. The culmination of these brewing troubles occurred when he lost Iowa. Dean's third-place finish came as a surprise to him and to observers who were unaware of the poor organization the Dean campaign had in the state. He had not prepared a concession speech that night, and so when he took the stage to address his disappointed followers, he spoke extemporaneously and from the heart. Failing to recognizing that his audience was not the disappointed "perfect storm" of volunteers standing in front of him, but voters in primary states to come who had tuned in on television to watch his concession speech, Dean launched into a full-throated declaration of the states that they were heading to next, leading to taking back the White House, followed by a cowboy's charge of "Yeeaahhh." That guttural cry reverberated on cable news for the next forty-eight hours, further fueled by late night talk shows and viral videos on the Internet, some of which were created by staff from rival campaigns. The press began declaring the end of the meteoric rise of the Democratic wing of the Democratic Party, his emotional expression a violation of permissible public speech.[32]

CLARK AND HIS ARMY

General Wesley Clark, a retired army general, hired by CNN as a commentator on the war in Iraq, flirted with the idea of running for president through the summer of 2003. As Kathleen Hall Jamieson, professor of political communication, commented to the Associated Press: "If you wanted to raise your visibility, cost free, at a time when visibility on a major network should translate into viability in the polls, you should be a respected general who is a commentator on a widely viewed network."[33]

Through the surfacing stage of the campaign it was disgruntled Democrats, unenthused by the other candidates, who crafted Clark's image. Prominent left-leaning bloggers Markos Moulitsas Zuniga and Andrew Sullivan drafted a petition site and eventually merged forces with John Hlinko, who had launched his own effort, and who eventually managed public relations for the Draft Wesley Clark movement. The movement heavily using the World Wide Web, a blog, an e-mail list, and organized MeetUps to promote the candidate, increase name recognition, and build a base of supporters. The website urged visitors to write a letter to the general and pledge to contribute (See Figure 4.2).

Hlinko generated publicity for the candidate by holding visibility events and encouraging others supporters to do so. These included handing out Clark bars, a chocolate candy bar, to people on the street in an effort to simultaneously forestall their rejection and hear the pitch and to give them something that would boost Clark's name recognition.[34] Hlinko argued on the Draft Wesley Clark blog that he was the right candidate to beat George Bush. Clark's record as a Vietnam veteran and a general who commanded the allied forces in the war in Kosovo served as a contrast to Bush, who was drafted but deferred service in Vietnam, and who had launched a war in Iraq that had fallen under criticism for poor execution. Thus, "Clark's Army" constructed an image of a seasoned war veteran who was boosted by a groundswell of support from an authentic grass roots and netroots.

When Clark finally announced he was running in late September, he was substantially behind his opponents, offering vague statements on foreign and

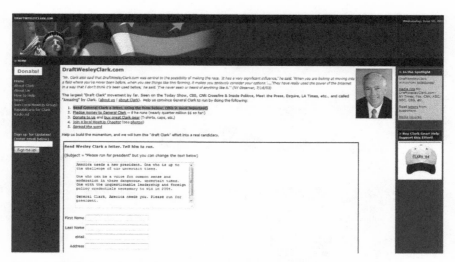

Figure 4.2 The home page of the Draft Wesley Clark movement

domestic policy, and declaring he would be boning up on the issues and offering his positions in the weeks to come. He was faced with a campaign infrastructure, in the form of draft Clark supporters, that he had not cultivated and did not control. His campaign website exhibited the efforts to frame the netroots as a movement, yet Clark's welcome statement conveyed to visitors that they take a moment to learn about his background and proposals. Typically, a movement already knows where it is heading and what motivated it, but the message construction suggested that Clark was still trying to catch up to his movement. His patriotic themed website, underscored by the slogan "new American patriotism," looked and read more like a traditional presidential campaign, not the kind of insurgency the netroots supporters had cultivated (See Figure 4.3).

Although he jumped to the top of public opinion polls after his announcement, he quickly received negative press about the disorganization of his campaign and the turmoil within the netroots over apparent resistance by his old-school campaign staff to fully engage them. The links to MeetUp and a blog, "Generally Speaking," came online in early October, but were not nurtured in the same way as they were on Howard Dean's site, underscoring the challenge for a campaign when the two paradigms—the mass mediated and the networked—collide.

VETERAN KERRY

John Kerry was in many ways the perfect candidate to carry an antiwar message to contrast himself with the Bush administration's policies. Kerry had served as an officer-in-charge of a swift boat in Vietnam, and upon his return to the states

Figure 4.3 The official Wesley Clark campaign website.

became a vocal activist against the war. During the slow, hard work in the surfacing stage of the campaign, Kerry kept up a steady pace of meetings, events, and fundraisers, constructing a straightforward image of a Vietnam vet who knew firsthand the price of war and would serve honorably as commander in chief. His website showed images of Kerry in his military uniform as a young man, highlighting his own and his father's military service in his biography, and emphasizing his positions to strengthen the military (See Figure 4.4). Kerry received a boost when one of his fellow swift boat veterans called him up and asked to join him at a campaign event in Iowa. Kerry agreed, and Jim Rasmussen, a Republican but a loyal friend to Kerry, joined him onstage at a rally in what media reports described as an emotional reuniting.

Figure 4.4 John Kerry's website in early June 2004

The Kerry campaign, like others of Dean's rivals, attempted to play catch-up with digital communication. Campaign staff launched an Internet petition related to a Bush administration policy change to tighten overtime pay rules. The campaign also paid $2,500 a month to MeetUp to facilitate meetings, including receiving e-mail addresses of Kerry MeetUp fans in the summer of 2003.[35] While Dean's numbers were increasing, though, Kerry's MeetUp groups were canceled at a greater rate each month through the summer and fall of 2003, contributing to an image that his campaign was losing the Internet organizing battle with Dean.

Kerry had another problem, one that rendered him unpalatable to the antiwar faction of the Democratic Party, and that contributed to the solidifying theme that Kerry would be a potentially weak leader. Kerry had voted for the appropriations bill to pay for the combat mission in Iraq, making his position as an antiwar candidate impossible. In order for Kerry to secure his position with the base of the party and those Dean and Clark supporters who were against the war, Kerry had to explain his vote. His explanation came in the context of a Bush attack ad that ran in March 2004 when Kerry became the presumptive Democratic nominee. The Bush attack ad declared that Kerry was not supporting Iraq's troops because he voted against a military funding bill. In a public forum he was asked about his votes on Iraq and Kerry explained:

> Ladies and gentleman, the president made the decision as to when to send our troops to war, no one else—he decided the date. And on the date they went into Iraq, they didn't have the armament on the Humvees, the armored doors…and they didn't have the state-of-the-art body armor at that moment when they went in. Secondly, this is very important, I actually did vote for the $87 billion—before I voted against it.[36]

Bush's strategists pounced on it, editing the existing attack ad with the new snippet and deriding Kerry in interviews with journalists for his apparent flip-flopping. Indeed, flip-flops became the iconic image at the Republican Convention, where attendees were given pairs of the sandals as noise makers and props to underscore the theme of Kerry as indecisive.

Kerry also faced a barrage of attacks from the Bush campaign and outside groups that questioned his heroism and the facts surrounding his war injuries. These criticisms also began soon after Kerry became the presumptive nominee. Kerry released his military records on his website in an effort to quell the attacks, but without success. Indeed, Kerry's image as war hero slowly eroded as the Bush campaign and an independent action group, Swift Boat Veterans for Truth, attacked him. The latter operated in the newly created category under the Bipartisan Campaign Reform Act of 2002 of influence or interest groups, known colloquially as "527s," the label applied to groups under section 527 of the tax code. The Swift Boat Veterans for Truth issued an open letter to Kerry in March 2003 criticizing his actions of protest against Vietnam when he returned from his tour of duty. A set of advertisements followed, initially posted on a website, SwiftVets.com, and then aired on TV as an issue ad campaign. The ad campaign featured veterans who served on swift boats during Vietnam, disputing Kerry's stories of valor, heroism, and injuries, although most did not serve at the same time or place as Kerry and did not witness the actions in question. The campaign was funded primarily by two prominent Texans who were supporters of Bush and the Republican Party.[37] The damage the ad campaign online and on TV had on Kerry's image was substantial.

The Kerry campaign's lack of attention to DCTs, especially during the primaries, was ultimately damaging to his candidacy. Digital media scholar Michael Cornfield points out that when Kerry announced his run for the presidency on the Sunday morning political show *Meet the Press*, he did not mention his website.[38] If he had, he likely would have generated traffic and cultivated supporters that the campaign could have harnessed. If the campaign staff had been monitoring the political blogosphere, they would have observed that soon after that *Meet the Press* announcement, a story was already beginning to form that Kerry was a politician of expedience who "flip-flopped" on issues when it was convenient to do so. The campaign initially ignored the attack by the Swift Boat Veterans for Truth because TV ads were airing only in a few smaller media outlets; staff dismissed the fact that the ads were on the Swift Boat Veterans website and were being heavily discussed on the blogosphere. When they finally began to respond on television and on their website, it was too late. The campaign's lack of attention to DCTs proved costly at reading sentiment and understanding the likely attacks that would be lodged against Kerry.

COMMANDER IN CHIEF

Coming into his re-election campaign, George W. Bush was fighting wars on two fronts, Afghanistan and Iraq. He constructed himself as a tough, decisive commander in chief. Back on March 17 of 2003 he told Saddam Hussein, president of Iraq, in a televised speech that if he and his sons did not leave their country the United States and a coalition of other countries would have no choice but to come into Iraq to free its people from lawless men and secure the world from some of the most lethal weapons ever devised. When the United States attacked Iraq two days later, Bush's approval rating was 70%.

His image as a successful war president eroded in the coming months. He promised a swift, inexpensive war, with a minimum number of US casualties. On May 1, he gave a speech on the aircraft carrier *USS Abraham Lincoln*, which had returned from the Persian Gulf. Bush gave his speech under a banner declaring "Mission Accomplished." The publicity stunt was met with derision, especially among war bloggers. It became clear by the fall of 2003 that the war was not over, as a guerrilla campaign grew against US and coalition forces. By December 2003 over 450 US service personnel had died. By March 2004, as Kerry became the Democratic Party's presumptive nominee, 125 additional military fatalities had occurred and Bush's public opinion numbers had dropped to 50%. Thus, coming into the Republican National Convention and the general election contest, it was evident that his re-election was not guaranteed.

Bush's official campaign website constructed the image of a successful incumbent president with many reminders that he was president and commander in chief: the color theme, messages from "President Bush," and photos of the

Figure 4.5 The Bush-Cheney website

president engaging in diplomacy, deplaning Air Force One, walking on a stage with the American seal (See Figure 4.5). Campaign slogans were prominently displayed in the banner along the top: "Steady Leadership in Times of Change" and "Building a Safer World and a More Hopeful America."

The campaign also used the website as the home for a substantial volume of online advertising. Because of the change in campaign advertising laws with the Bipartisan Campaign Reform Act, ads aired on television had to include a recorded statement from the sponsor that he or she approved the message; those rules did not hold for online advertising. Scholars speculated that the striking increase in online ads in 2004 was due to this change in election law.[39] Starting in February 2003, the Bush campaign began creating web videos, starting with an advocacy ad that was a montage of statements from the candidate, paired with inspirational music, and an image of a little girl running. As it became evident that Kerry was to be the presumptive nominee in late February, the campaign crafted attack ads against him. He was painted as a hypocrite for taking money from special interests while declaring he was not beholden to them, and the ad was posted to YouTube and on the campaign website. Staff also sent e-mail messages to supporters and the press directing them to view the ad when it was released. The goal was to begin to undercut Kerry's message and short-circuit his rise in the polls following his wins in the Democratic primaries. Mark McKinnon, Bush's media strategist, explained to a *New York Times* reporter the goals: "Senator Kerry was getting a free ride from a lot of the Democrats, and we felt it was important to point out what he was saying was inconsistent with his record, but we were not prepared to engage that fully yet. The Web offered a modulated way of engaging."[40] Kerry's campaign countered quickly with its own web-based attack video, highlighting Bush's relationship with special interests, including Enron, a disgraced energy company. This counter did not have the intended effect. Instead, journalists began reporting that Kerry seemed rattled by the Bush attack.[41]

Citizen Involvement in the Service of Winning

It seems easy to declare that the 2004 election was the first in which the full interactive potential of digital media was harnessed by presidential campaigns. Howard Dean, Draft Wesley Clark, and eventually most of the other campaigns deployed MeetUps and blogs to render citizen-supporters more visible to the campaign, to the media, and to other citizens. Yet I have argued elsewhere that although there were genuine efforts to throw open the campaigns to supporters in ways historically unseen, ultimately there remained something of a simulacrum, a facade, of openness and interactivity as supporters engaged with the campaign.[42] This was especially true of Dean's and Clark's web campaigns as supporters realized that while the curtains opened for a time to reveal the inner workings and strategies of the campaign, and included them in that vital work, eventually those curtains closed and they were excluded. In the case of the Clark campaign, the networked, interactive campaign that emerged when it was in the hands of the netroots collided with the hired campaign professionals who knew the mass-media paradigm, and did not understand the emerging paradigm that the netroots was creating. This section details the digital technologies and techniques that the innovators and front runners deployed in the service of winning.

MEETUP AND MOVEON

Two digital media-based organizations were used by presidential campaigns to identify and then draw in supporters. Howard Dean's case is the most noteworthy. Early in 2003 Trippi had devoted some staff time to coparticipating in local MeetUps, noting that there seemed to be a groundswell of them for Dean. He was right. In early March 2003, Dean attended a fundraiser in Manhattan and found more than twice as many people as expected, over 500, in attendance. Trippi exclaimed to a *New York Times* reporter about the event: "I've never seen anything like that, with no advance people, totally self-organized by a bunch of citizens. It was a really great moment."[43] Seeing the organizing power of DCTs, Trippi put significant resources into developing tools to help these self-motivated supporters convert their friends and the less politically active to support Dean.[44]

The marriage of the Dean campaign and MeetUp was a strong one. The campaign sent staff and volunteers to MeetUp events to help coordinate supporters. A paid staff member at the campaign headquarters was tasked to support MeetUps full time, and the Dean campaign paid MeetUp for organizing technology, and gained access to most of the e-mail addresses of MeetUp users who had signed up for Dean events. By the summer of 2003, Dean was paying MeetUp $2,500 a month to use its infrastructure to help supporters coordinate for Dean's candidacy. Dean explained in a speech that "The MeetUp people have made it possible for me to no longer just be an insurgent candidate because they've given us an organization that we otherwise would have had to pay for."[45] Trippi proudly boasted to a *Washington Post* reporter, "We have the largest grass-roots organization in America right now, and we are going to try to utilize it. If television took the grass-roots out of politics, the Internet will put it back in."[46] The synergy was remarkable: over 185,000 people signed up via MeetUp to support Dean.[47]

None of the other presidential candidates had nearly the volume of supporters organizing through MeetUps in the early surfacing months. By August, however, the Kerry campaign was also paying $2,500 a month to do coordinated organizing for the campaign via MeetUp. As well, the Draft Wesley Clark movement relied heavily on MeetUps in the summer months to further build name recognition and momentum for Clark to join the race.

MoveOn had a different role that it played in the Democratic primaries. In June 2003, MoveOn announced via e-mail to its 1.4 million "members," people who gave MoveOn their e-mail address or a contribution, to vote in the first ever online primary. The top vote recipient would receive support in the form of endorsements from MoveOn, encouraging members to send financial contributions to the winner. All nine primary candidates encouraged their supporters to register with MoveOn and vote. Howard Dean, John Kerry, and Dennis Kucinich were the top three contenders. The voting received great interest. On the first day of voting, so many visited the MoveOn website that it crashed and the news media faithfully covered this novel primary and its outcome.

There was some concern and frustration expressed by the candidates that the MoveOn primary seemed rigged for Dean, given his close ties to MoveOn and to the constituency of their members. Nevertheless, John Kerry's spokesman Robert Gibbs explained that although "we've never believed that we would win this...we saw it as a chance to increase the number of people interested in the senator's campaign, a way to increase the number of donors in the campaign and a way to bolster our long-term online communications capabilities."[48] Dean finished first, but without the 50% needed to secure the kind of endorsement that MoveOn had promised. All the campaigns benefited from the primary in the form of lists of e-mail addresses of MoveOn voters who agreed to allow it to share their e-mail address with their chosen candidate.

CONSTRUCTING PARASOCIAL INTERACTION

Perhaps the most novel and important change in presidential campaigning came with the adoption of the campaign blog. The weblog, technologically speaking, was better able to facilitate a sense of connection, of parasocial interaction, for visitors with the campaign than other components of the campaign website. Parasocial interaction, a term first applied to television by scholars Horton and Wohl, describes an "illusion of [a] face-to-face relationship."[49] Television watchers, they observed, feel a sense of connection, as if they know the actors and television personalities whom they watch in their living rooms. The weblog, when used effectively by a campaign, promotes the same illusion. As a campaign diary with photos of campaign staff, the candidate, and supporters, first-person accounts by staff and the candidate from the campaign trail, and direct, first-person address to supporters letting them in on the strategies and plans of the campaign, it facilitates a psychological perception by visitors of involvement with the campaign. The blog also invites a kind of intimacy with the major actors of the campaign: the digital media staff who serve as the link between the campaign and the citizen-supporters who spend time on the blog.

Dean's campaign was the first to figure out the power of parasocial interaction for campaigning, and the other campaigns followed. The campaign blog was launched after Trippi observed the noteworthy organizing work being done on former journalist Andrew Sullivan's blog, the Daily Dish. The Draft Wesley Clark's website also had a blog, and eventually the official campaign site. Clark's Internet strategist explained to a *Washington Post* reporter that the value of the blog was in its sticky nature: "The idea that people know that any time they come back there's going to be new content is great, because it's a new way to draw them back to the site."[50] Bob Graham, a senator from Florida, who was also running a long-shot campaign, sported one, and his campaign even had a chat room. The Kerry campaign had a blog by the summer of 2003. George Bush's campaign site featured a blog, though it did not allow commenting.

By far the most active blog was Howard Dean's. In the early months of the primary campaign, the blog, called Dean Call for Action Blog, was a place for a running commentary by campaign staff; it did not allow comments. In June, the campaign shifted blogging platforms to MoveableType and opened the blog to comments. It very quickly became the most visited element of the campaign website. The blog featured supporters and innovative ways they were helping, urged them to help fill the red bat to meet fundraising goals, kept readers abreast of activities and events as well as missives of life on the road with candidate Dean, provided news coverage summaries and sometimes called supporters to action to respond to the news media, and revealed to supporters and readers the campaign's strategy for getting Dean elected. Supporters used the blog to commune with other supporters, to encourage each other to fill the bat, to tell stories of successes on behalf of the campaign, and to brainstorm and coordinate actions that they thought would help get Dean elected, like painting the sides of barns with Dean's name.

Although the Dean campaign heavily used the blog and talked about it with journalists, there is little evidence that staff were actively interacting with visitors who were commenting on the blog.[51] Four campaign staff posted the bulk of new blog posts. In December, when the campaign was at its height, those staff wrote 411 blog posts, averaging 13 new posts a day. The last day of the fundraising quarter, December 31st, they produced 21 posts. Those 21 posts generated 4,236 comments in a twenty-four hour period, averaging 200 comments per blog post. The energy, excitement, and camaraderie of supporters were palpable in the comments section. Campaign staff reported to the press that they routinely read comments posted by visitors to the blog. Rarely, though, did they comment or interact with commenters. After Dean's loss in Iowa, a flood of armchair strategizing was unleashed by Dean's supporters. Mathew Gross, one of the campaign's blog writers, said that he was reading the comments and suggestions, but when pressed could not say whether any of the suggestions had been adopted by the campaign.[52] The comments themselves suggest a profound frustration among many who had built the community of Deaniacs who believed the campaign was not listening to them. Some even suggested that they should just take over the campaign from the professional staff and run it themselves.[53]

By contrast, the Bush campaign's blog functioned as a daily diary of the campaign, crafting a careful story of the campaign, highlighting Bush's policy vision and successes, and focusing the story on the ways for supporters to get involved, but it did not allow comments. Michael Turk, who was a digital strategist for the campaign, explained that the campaign did not allow comments for two reasons. The first concern was logistical: senior staff did not have the person-hours needed to monitor the blog. Turk explained, "The level of vitriol aimed at President Bush, together with the anonymous trolls that are the hallmark of the Internet, combined to create a concern that we would be unable to keep up, and it would detract from staff efforts in other areas."[54] The second concern was that commentary on the blog was generally unproductive for the ultimate objective of the campaign: getting Bush reelected. Turk and other senior staff felt that the idle "chatter" on the blog was unlikely to help get the candidate elected. "We would prefer that our supporters be out talking to voters, rather than gathered around our blog talking to each other. So we spurned blog comments in favor of more action-focused online activities," explained Turk.[55] The Bush campaign, while not actively promoting a blogger-commenter community on the official website, worked to cultivate relationships with prominent conservative political bloggers, even linking from the campaign website to a blog roll of "Bloggers for Bush."

DRAFTING CLARK

The Clark campaign serves as a novel case of digital campaigning because motivated and involved citizens used digital media to grow a movement around a candidate who had not indicated he would run. The Draft Wesley Clark netroots movement was groomed by John Hlinko, a Democratic activist who in 2002 contemplated the 2004 election and wanted to see a strong Democratic candidate unseat the incumbent president. He happened across a listing of the top 100 potential contenders for the Democratic nomination, and he noticed one candidate with "General" in front of his name. As he began to research General Clark, he found a compelling biography, especially his prior military experiences, that Hlinko thought might be the type of resume a candidate could use to beat Bush. Yet Clark's name recognition was only at about 10% in 2002, suggesting substantial work was needed to grow Clark's name recognition.[56]

Over the early months of 2003, Hlinko established a website, www.extreme-campaigns.com/draftwesleyclark. The URL was of a domain he had registered for a business he hoped to launch. The simple web page he created invited visitors to leave a message about why they wanted to draft Clark. Relatively quickly the site had more than 50,000 of those statements, and plenty of traffic from people visiting the site to read the statements. Hlinko also began cultivating an e-mail list of potential Clark supporters. Those messages were sent from a listserv he had created for a dating website for Democrats, so messages were sent from draftclark@actsforlove.com. By March, Hlinko had the resources from his dating website to pay for a domain with the URL of DraftWesleyClark.com. Using Microsoft FrontPage to create the HTML, he invited people to sign up to receive e-mail updates, and he began encouraging draft supporters to e-mail their friends with information about Clark and to generate visibility for Clark by visiting blogs and online forums where politics was discussed to spread the idea of a Clark candidacy.[57]

By Labor Day, the Draft Wesley Clark movement was a coalition of liberal bloggers and antiwar activists that was frequently turning up in news articles about the presidential campaign, and journalists and pundits speculated about whether Clark would announce a run. For his part, Hlinko was growing concerned that Clark was not seizing the opportunity and announcing his bid. He and three of his friends and fellow movement leaders flew to Los Angeles for a meeting with Clark. Hlinko made his pitch that running would continue Clark's long line of service for his country. Hlinko explained that the Draft Wesley Clark movement had developed a network of supporters and volunteers, and that hundreds of people had pledged to contribute to the campaign, giving Clark an almost guaranteed $1 million at the start of the campaign's launch.[58] Clark was polite and friendly, and seemed genuinely intrigued by the idea of running, but was non-committal. When he did announce his bid on September 15, he failed to include Hlinko and the other leaders of the Draft Wesley Clark movement in that announcement; Clark had not even notified them when he decided to run.

Clark's candidacy quickly faltered. His campaign had only three months to establish enough of an organization, with all that such entailed (e.g., fundraising, supporters, field organizations), to be a credible contender in the first voting states. Although the seeds had been planted for that organization by the draft Clark online efforts, including the substantial $1 million in pledges, it was not enough to overcome the realities of a presidential campaign and the need for a rigorous ground game.

To continue to engage the grassroots organizers in the Draft Clark movement, the official campaign engaged in a couple of visibility stunts. Clark held weekly synchronous "wire-side" chats with supporters. More than 6,000 people logged on to participate, which helped the campaign collect e-mail addresses to add to its database of supporters. Hlinko, who was brought into the campaign as director of Internet strategy, likened what they were doing with FDR's fireside chats when he was president. The other publicity event was what one journalist compared to a reality show,[59] in which two teams traveled across country in recreational vehicles; on their journey the teams uploaded reports, videos, and photos of their road trip, and supporters were enticed to vote on the website for the team they liked better. It served as a way to reconnect and draw in supporters and gather e-mail addresses, but was quite devoid of a political message or an explicit organizing component to advance the Clark candidacy.

UNLEASHING INTERACTIVITY AND MANAGING THE CHAOS

Of the presidential campaigns, Dean's and Clark's struggled with managing eager supporters, attempting to direct their energies in productive ways for the campaign, but not always with success.

Trippi's philosophy as campaign manager for Dean was to run an insurgency, taking risks by experimenting with potential but untested means for messaging, organizing, and fundraising. Trippi vowed to "let the momentum and the decision making come from the people—stop trying to control the river... just open the flood gates and see where the current took us."[60] The campaign seemed to especially energize younger voters. A site called GenerationDean.com aimed to register young voters, for example, and help them organize on college campuses. One young journalist told a *New York Times* reporter that she quit her job to volunteer full time for the campaign: "It's just, like, so inspiring. These people get it. The campaign is transparent—or it at least appears that way. You feel like you're involved. You feel like you matter."[61]

Campaign staff experimented with ways to open up the floodgates of supporters and channel the flood in ways beneficial to the campaign. They did this in a number of ways. Staff attended MeetUps in order to explain to volunteers how they could best help. The strategists established concrete fundraising goals to fill the red bat and meet quarterly objectives. They held the Sleepless Summer tour, in which Dean traveled to a dozen cities, holding rallies, meeting with many of the netroots who were energized by his campaign and signing up an additional 450,000 supporters. They orchestrated a letter-writing campaign online, in which supporters were to "adopt an Iowan" and write a letter to an undecided Iowa voter explaining why they supported Howard Dean, an idea that reportedly came from a Dean supporter. Staff developed "Get Local" tools, which provided a rudimentary infrastructure to find other Dean supporters and to organize events for the candidate. Zephyr Teachout, one of the campaign's Internet strategists who went on the road to meet Dean supporters in the fall, explained to a *New York Times* reporter: "The goal of all our online activity is to move it off-line."[62] In the late summer, the campaign launched "Dean.tv," which archived web videos from the campaign that were shown at MeetUps to help keep supporters on message and motivated to work for the campaign. They created unique pages for active volunteers to keep track of events and fundraising successes. The people-powered campaign even invited supporters to vote on whether Dean should opt out of federal financing of the campaign. When people voted, they were asked to supply their e-mail address, which helped the campaign continue to build the e-mail list. The vote also gave Dean rhetorical cover when he announced he would opt out, pointing to the views of his supporters as the rationale for bucking a system of campaign finance that Democrats had supported since the 1970s.

The Dean and Clark campaigns embraced computer programmers and software engineers to help as volunteers and as staffers to build tools that would enable self-organizing for the campaign. The Dean campaign openly called for programmers to volunteer to help build applications. These programmers typically adopted open-source infrastructures, existing applications and tools whose source code is made publicly available for other programmers to tweak, build on, or modify as they desire. Though most campaigns typically buy off-the-shelf products to help manage their information, these two campaigns decided to craft their own products based on existing open-source software. For example, the Dean campaign built DeanSpace (initially called Hack4Dean), which created lists of potential voters' addresses or phone numbers for volunteers to write letters or make phone calls. Clark's campaign built several tools, including eBlock, which helped volunteers to contact undecided New Hampshire citizens to remind them to vote on primary day, and EventFinder, which let supporters search for nearby campaign events. Both campaigns also used Really Simple Syndication (RSS) to automatically feed announcements, fundraising appeals, and photos to independently maintained websites whose creators had signed up to receive the RSS feeds.

The advantage of building campaign tools, rather than using third-party vendors, includes tailoring the application to the unique requirements and data needs of campaigns, and also being able to access all of the information users might supply to use the application. In the early surfacing stage for Dean MeetUps, for example, the Dean campaign did not have access to the names and e-mail addresses of those who were meeting up. Eventually, MeetUp agreed to share that information, but at a cost to the campaign. The campaign also required MeetUp.com to change its user agreement to specify that e-mail and other contact information would be shared with third parties.

Even with those efforts to provide focused activities for supporters and to keep their messaging with their social network consonant with the campaign's, there were challenges. For example, blog commenters wanted Tom Harkin, one of Iowa's influential public and political figures, to endorse Dean. A blog commenter proposed that supporters call Harkin's office to urge him to do so. Harkin's office was then flooded with calls, prompting a Harkin staffer to contact the Dean campaign to ask it to urge supporters to stop. More innocuous activities, such as such as painting haystacks in South Dakota with Dean's name, were not what the campaign needed in December when Dean's name recognition was already high.

CHANNELING SUPPORT WITHOUT INTERACTIVITY

Both the Kerry and Bush campaigns used fewer of the interactive affordances of digital communication technologies to open up their campaign to supporters. The Kerry campaign, for example, featured a blog and built many of the same get-involved applications to help supporters volunteer for the campaign as other Democratic candidates. The website also added gamification elements, such as a point system. Supporters who were advocating for the campaign could keep tallies of their activities, from raising money to holding house parties.

The Bush campaign was masterful at carefully managing supporters with limited interactivity. While Dean was letting people organize with limited direction from the campaign, the Bush campaign was carefully crafting digital technologies to focus supporters in a managed way. Some of the activities included providing an application on the campaign website in which visitors entered their zip code to send a campaign-written message in their local newspaper's letter-to-the-editor section, and encouraging visitors to call in to talk radio stations to deliver a message crafted by the campaign. A campaign spokesperson told the *New York Times* that the website reflected where the campaign stood: "It is an online reflection of what is going on out in the states" (August 19, 2003), getting people to express themselves in support of the president through their community's media outlets.

Rather than pouring energy into open discussion forums and applications to facilitate supporters to self-organize, the Bush campaign harnessed the energy of motivated campaign event attendees. Those who came to political speeches and rallies were often shepherded into directly volunteering for the campaign at the end of the event. A *Washington Post* article details, for example, that after a Bush speech at the Orange County Convention Center in Florida, attendees got on buses or moved to calling stations to register Republicans and identify potential volunteers and supporters of the campaign.[63] Rather than using digital channels to help people work for the campaign, they were using analog means of organizing.

The Bush campaign built on what it had started in 2000, a massive voter file and e-mail list. By 2004, the campaign had amassed a list of six million e-mail addresses, an order of magnitude over Dean's much-vaunted e-mail list. The Bush campaign used this e-mail list for carefully targeted messaging, as well as a mass-dissemination platform of updates from the campaign. Rather than financial appeals, which became the commonplace pitch in the Democratic candidates' e-mail messages, many of the Bush e-mails detailed events and ways to volunteer.

The campaign also continued to build upon its list, collecting new information as means to do so appeared. For example, one intriguing way the Bush campaign channeled volunteers was by giving them a list of their neighbors, often within a few blocks of where the volunteer lived. The list included contact information, a script, and a list of questions to ask, including party affiliation, attitudes toward the president, and positions on a number of issues, like abortion. In this way, the campaign continued to enrich its data file of potential voters.

Campaign Organization and Digital Media: Change and Stasis

Most of the campaigns in 2004 were organized in traditional, top-down fashion, with a campaign manager holding substantial prior political campaign experience, a set of senior staff, including communications, field organizing, and finance, and subordinates of those senior staff. There was no agreement within and among political campaigns about where digital media staff reported. Some campaigns, like Bush's, made sure that staff who were focused on Internet strategy had an equal seat at the senior staff table. Lieberman's campaign only hired a full-time Internet fundraising staffer in June 2003, after faring poorly compared to Dean and others through the second quarter of fundraising.

The eventual Democratic nominee, John Kerry, although personally understanding the importance of the Internet to his campaign strategy, did not bring on a dedicated Internet strategist until the late fall of 2003, eventually building a staff of approximately fifteen who focused on Internet strategy.[64] Indeed, his campaign launched with the traditional model of the modern mass-media presidential campaign, being led and organized by a set of consultants used to running traditional, cautious political campaigns, with a clear hierarchy of management from the top down. There were challenges as a result, for example, around messaging. The communications staff wanted to use the same message and approach on e-mail as through the news media, direct mail, and in the get-out-the-vote messaging. Josh Ross explained that some of the Internet strategists were frustrated trying to convince others in communications that e-mail should have a distinct style from other communication channels. Ross explained that the Internet strategists understood that the messaging in e-mail should more explicitly speak to interests and motivations of supporters, rather than the more muted messaging that might be produced for independents and undecided supporters because anyone who actually opened and read an e-mail message from the campaign was likely a hardcore supporter.[65] .

One challenge for Kerry's organization was how to respond to the Swift Boat Veterans attacks. Ross and others on the digital team recognized that core Democrats were "furious and terrified" that the Republicans were going to "do to us like Dukakis" with the Swift Boat Veterans for Truth attacks.[66] He also said that campaign staff were aware of the growing attack in the blogosphere about Kerry's Vietnam service. They knew it was going to be a big story, yet Ross noted that it was unclear the best way to respond to the attack.

The Kerry campaign, while facing some organizational challenges early in the campaign, ultimately built a stable and effective organization. Early on, the campaign was rife with conflict at the top between one of Kerry's key advisors, Bob Shrum, and his campaign manager, Jim Jordan, who disagreed on everything from messaging to strategy. Kerry mediated the disputes until November 2003 when he fired Jordan. Under his new campaign manager, Mary Beth Cahill, the campaign continued a steady, focused strategy in the early voting states, sending needed resources on the ground in Iowa, generating positive earned media coverage with a sensational presentation at the Jefferson-Jackson dinner, an Iowa political tradition, and running positive ads highlighting Kerry's vision as president and his leadership and sacrifice during his service in the Vietnam War.[67]

Consonant with Kerry's image and message as a veteran, he organized vets from other states and from within Iowa to canvas Iowans, sending a focused and clear reinforcing message to potential caucus-goers.

Of all of the presidential campaigns, Howard Dean's organization established the digital media team as central in the campaign, a key component to the success the candidate enjoyed.[68] Trippi was deeply involved in and worked to integrate digital media and strategy into the core of the campaign, sometimes to the detriment of other components, such as field offices in Iowa.[69] Trippi sought out political blogger Andrew Sullivan to guide and advise the campaign in its earliest days,[70] and he also hired staff members from MoveOn.org and MeetUp.org to help with strategy. Indeed, when Zack Exley took a leave from MoveOn to help the campaign in the early summer of 2003, he was able to help Dean staff develop a more coherent digital strategy that was more aggressive and strategic than what it had been, which was reactive.[71]

If the celebration for Dean's meteoric rise rested on DCTs, part of the cause of the campaign's demise was in its organization and strategy. In early January 2004 polls were predicting a Dean win in Iowa; when Dean came in third, it shocked many in the political world. The reasons for Dean's surprising upset loss in Iowa included at least three problems. The first resided with the staff. Trippi was so intently focused on Internet strategy that he paid less attention to the vital ground organizing that needed to happen in Iowa.[72] Other senior strategists realized by the early fall that the campaign was severely behind Gephardt, Kerry, and Edwards in field organization. Although a steady stream of volunteers and staffers were shepherded to the state, they were unable to make up for lost time. A related problem was the tension among senior staff. Trippi felt that Dean never really trusted him, and that Kate O'Connor, Dean's personal assistant who traveled with him everywhere, ultimately dictated what the governor heard and did not hear while he was on the campaign trail.[73] There were persistent complaints that decision-making did not happen effectively and efficiently. When Dean was under intense scrutiny in December, the campaign was ineffective at responding to the negative attacks and failed to stop the damage after Dean's Iowa concession speech. Reports by journalists suggested that state and regional organizations struggled to get decisions from campaign headquarters on strategy and messaging, and there seemed to be tension within the campaign, as staff who felt they had political know-how were ignored by Trippi, who seemed to "adopt ideas from the blather on its Web log."[74]

A second cause of trouble was TV advertising. The trouble here was twofold. First, one of the few moments of intense negative TV advertisement in the primaries happened between Dean and Dick Gephardt. Iowans historically tend to be repelled by negative ads, and 2004 seemed no exception. Second, the ad buys were expensive and the purchasing seemingly without much forethought or strategy. Inexplicably, in the fall the Dean campaign ran ads in Texas, many months before people in that state would even be paying attention to the political campaign.[75] The overall set of ad buys drained the campaign of money and seemed to have little strategic benefit.

Third, the Dean campaign, in an effort to make up for the lack of organizing, and as a way to give supporters in other states that were meeting online something to do offline, the campaign created the "Perfect Storm" campaign. Named after a blog post by Trippi, the idea of the campaign was to mobilize 5,000 Dean supporters to come to Iowa and canvas for Dean. The campaign encouraged volunteers to travel to Iowa to door-to-door canvas. In the few weeks before Iowa's caucus, around 3,000 "Deaniacs" in their campaign-issued orange stocking caps showed up to knock on doors and persuade undecided voters to caucus for Dean. One Associated Press reporter, for example, described an interaction this way: " 'Hi there, ma'am,' Scott Davis, 21, said to Mary Morlan in a thick Tupelo, Miss., accent. 'Will you be going to the caucuses?' She was standing outside her home here, stamping her feet on the icy sidewalk while her dog sniffed out a tree. Davis' accent was a bit jarring in suburban Des Moines, Iowa, but not as much as his appearance: Long hair, scruffy beard, a dirty baseball cap and jeans."[76] Some cited the cultural clash evident between the undecided Iowans and the Deaniacs who were knocking on their door as one of the flaws of the "Perfect Storm."

That was not the only problem, though. As Kreiss explained in his ethnography about the Dean campaign, the voter information that these Dean supporters were using to determine whom to contact was in disarray.[77] As a result, undecided voters were being contacted repeatedly by Dean supporters, causing them to feel harassed by out-of-towners. Trippi, seemingly unaware of any organizational trouble, told one news outlet, "If you have 3,500 people and you say 'Here's a voter list, just get three people to this caucus,' that's 10,000 people. It doesn't have to be a real complicated organizing thing. It's pretty simple."[78] Yet it turned out not to be that simple after all.

Unlike the poor field organizing in Iowa, the campaign had a complex and deep field organization in place in New Hampshire. As in Iowa, the campaign invited volunteers from across the country to come to New Hampshire to canvas, but there the campaign had a much better organized data infrastructure for managing contacts on the ground. Moreover, they had been better trained and organized for months, unlike Iowa, where the staff was scrambling to catch up in the late fall. Dean had invited Professor Marshall Ganz to come to New Hampshire and train campaign volunteers in the style of community organizing he had been involved in in the 1960s. This strategy of actively training super-supporters in organizing techniques would be honed in subsequent elections.

By the end of January, when the campaign was nearly broke, having spent $7 million on television ads produced by Trippi's consulting firm,[79] and with the back-to-back losses in Iowa and New Hampshire, Dean brought in Roy Neel, a Washington lobbyist and aide to Al Gore, to direct the campaign. Dean wanted Trippi to stay on the campaign as an Internet and media strategist, but Trippi resigned instead. Hard core Dean supporters in the netroots were distraught by the change. The blog was alight with complaints and concerns about the changes that Neel would bring. Although there were discussions and complaints about the fact that Trippi had not managed to turn money and support into victories in Iowa, and jaded skepticism about Trippi's purchase of TV ads produced by his own firm that cost a fortune, there was also genuine fear about what Neel would do with the campaign. His status as a Washington insider raised concerns that he would run a standard, mass-media campaign, which would close out their role and the work the netroots had put into it. On a more personal note, the netroots felt a connection to Trippi, whose missives from the campaign trail and revelations of strategy created that parasocial interaction that invested supporters in the campaign. A Washington University student explained to an Associated Press reporter, "I've read that the Gore influence is growing and I'm a little apprehensive that it will become another staid, kind of boring campaign, just another establishment organization. I'm still committed to it, but I think it's lost a lot of steam."[80]

The Clark campaign, when it finally got underway in September, brought onto the staff several Washington insiders who were prepared to run a traditional political campaign. After initially approaching a McCain strategist to run it who declined, a thirty-five-year-old former campaign field organizer for Al Gore's 2000 presidential election was tapped—mostly because he was already there at the nascent Arkansas headquarters when more senior political operatives arrived. Quickly a clash occurred internally as the young campaign manager, Donnie Fowler, pushed for the voices and ideas to be heard of the netroots volunteer base of self-organized "drafters" who were working hard for Clark before his official campaign. Fowler's specific concern was that the Washington insiders were not taking the netroots supporters seriously.[81]

Thus, a profound clash occurred. The netroots, which had relied on the interactive affordances of DCTs to organize themselves to make Wesley Clark a household name suddenly were confronted with campaign professionals who understood only the power of mass media and were leery of the networked netroots. The campaign professionals, instead of immediately working to further nurture the MeetUps that had sprung up around the country to support Clark, for example, turned to traditional fundraisers and strategizing, which resulted in Clark losing the MeetUp organizing contest with Dean.[82] Many of the draft

Clark activists relatedly grew disgruntled as they watched what they cultivated shrivel in the neglect of the Clark campaign consultants.

As a particularly potent illustration of the clash, Hlinko explained that he was shocked to learn on a conference call with senior staff and the candidate that they had decided not to try and build an organization to compete in Iowa. Hlinko was dismayed because he knew that the Draft Wesley Clark campaign had 3,000 Iowa volunteers who were loyal and motivated. He was certain that they could have established a competitive field organization on the backs of those volunteers in Iowa and finished in second place. When he mentioned that there were 3,000 volunteers in Iowa ready to help organize caucus-goers, he learned that the senior staff had already leaked to the *New York Times* that Clark would not contest the state.[83] There was no going back.

Organizationally, then, the netroots base that the draft Clark movement cultivated over the spring and summer months of 2003 was set aside by the senior strategists who did not know what do with the people they generally regarded as "unhinged."[84] Not only did they not tap the netroots for volunteers and organizers, they actually told them to stop their activities because some senior staff worried that creating signs and organizing for the candidate might be viewed as an in-kind donation. The Draft Wesley Clark organizers, including Hlinko, were marginalized in the campaign hierarchy. Initially, he was part of strategy meetings, but over the next months invitations no longer came to him. He did not quite know what he should do, and because he felt ignored but still committed to the movement he had cultivated, he moved to New Hampshire to organize the volunteers and netroots that had been with him since Draft Wesley Clark.[85] The activist who had started the movement and helped build the momentum to move Clark to agree to run was effectively sidelined.

Conclusion

In 2004 a shift occurred in presidential campaigning. A confluence of forces was at work that came together in this election cycle to cause turbulence, choppy waters, and eddies most visible during the run-up to and the actual voting contests of the primaries and caucuses. The interactivity of the Internet, more directly harnessed in this election cycle than those that preceded it, ran up against the campaign practices of the mass-media era; this confluence was rendered most visible in the collision of the Draft Wesley Clark movement with the formal Clark for President campaign.

The Dean campaign catalyzed the potential of DCTs to propel it, because of a campaign manager who saw the potential, combined with a candidate who was willing to run an insurgent campaign on a message that resonated and empowered a set of voters who were searching for exactly that message. Yet even the most innovative campaigns need also to ensure that core fundamentals of campaigning are followed, which in the days leading up to the election requires the hard work of knocking on doors, delivering a persuasive message, and securing pledges of support, and then on Election Day turning those supporters out to vote, something both Kerry and Bush executed well. In Iowa, the ground game for the Dean campaign was not well executed, and Dean's infamous scream sealed the demise of the campaign. Digital media helped the campaign, but it was clear that more work could be done to hone the interactive affordances of DCTs while also structuring the enthusiasm of supporters into more productive work for the campaign.

5

2008: Networked Campaigning and Controlled Interactivity

If the 2004 presidential campaigns experimented with digital communication technologies (DCTs) to alter the power dynamic between campaigns and supporters, the 2008 election shifted from experimentation to control. The 2004 campaign of Howard Dean and the netroots movement to draft Wesley Clark showed the tremendous interactive capabilities of DCTs and the energy such interactivity unleashed among networks of supporters. By opening up the campaign to greater citizen involvement with staff and with each other, the collective work of supporters propelled those insurgent campaigns to front-runner status, though not to electoral success. By contrast, the major party nominees, George W. Bush and John Kerry, ran more restrained digital media efforts, especially around interactivity. Bush used DCTs to build massive voter files for targeted messaging, and Kerry pushed farther than prior campaigns had in testing their digital message and website design.

The controlled experimentation that emerged in 2008 came as staff recognized that a central benefit of DCTs was in two-step flow: identifying and structuring the work of what might be called super-supporters,[1] those energized and engaged citizens willing to give money, put in time, and proselytize about a candidate. Thus, when looking at the relationships that emerged in the 2008 elections, using the approach of actor network theory to examine the positioning of citizens to campaigns through DCTs,[2] what becomes evident is the following: interactive affordances of DCTs when carefully deployed could be quite effective at leveraging supporters to do the vital work of the campaign. Thus, in some ways, in 2008 we saw shifting practices that further opened up the presidential campaigns to include a greater role for and visibility of citizens in the daily work of campaigning; at the same time the practices were substantially more directed by the campaign staff to ultimately advance the objectives of the campaign.

To the victor go the spoils, as they say, and so Barack Obama has received the bulk of attention from scholars,[3] pundits, and journalists as being *the* candidate who really innovated with DCTs and changed the practice of campaigning. Yet, as the prior chapters attest, the Obama campaign's work built upon not just the innovations from the 2004 campaign, but also upon the earlier experiments and practices from 2000 and 1996. Moreover, other candidates, especially Democratic primary candidate Hillary Clinton and Republican primary candidate Ron Paul, experimented with and centralized DCTs as key components of their campaigns. Finally, the financial disadvantage John McCain's campaign faced relative to Obama's in the general election cannot be overemphasized when considering why McCain lost. Accepting federal financing, from which Obama opted out, meant that McCain was effectively hamstrung. His campaign had little choice but to focus on tried-and-true mass-mediated campaigning, and could not effort to fully build out DCTs to work to his advantage.

Thus, this chapter explores the historic 2008 election, highlighting the important contextual forces that structured the tactical environment for campaigns, describing how organizations and fundraising shifted in this election, examining the ways several campaigns used digital media to construct their candidate's image, and lastly explaining how controlled interactivity with supporters took shape for maximum candidate benefit.

Background and Strategic Environment

THE POLITICAL CONTEXT

The 2008 presidential election started early. Most candidates began forming exploratory committees in late fall of 2006 and announcing formal campaigns at the start of 2007. Some, such as Senator Joe Biden, made his intentions known in March 2006. This early race meant that the campaigns had to raise substantial sums of money in order to be seen as viable over a year later when Americans finally voted.

This campaign cycle also featured no incumbent president or vice president, thereby opening up the primaries to a large number of contenders from both major parties. The social and political context suggested, however, that the political winds were against the Republicans. The Iraq war was going poorly by 2006. The sectarian violence in the country was dramatic, and the news featured nearly daily reports of bombs and deaths in the country as civil society broke apart, and attacks on American and British soldiers increased. Public opinion on the war, which in 2003 at its launch was at 70% favorability, had dropped to 35% in September 2006.[4] Indeed, it seemed that the Iraq war would be the most important foreign issue that presidential candidates would need to address in their campaigns.

A second difficulty facing Republican candidates was that the incumbent president, George W. Bush, experienced only modest support from the public. In the 2004 election, Bush's approval ratings hovered around 50%, but by October 2006, they were at 37%.[5] By January 2008, when the primary and caucus voting began, Bush's approval rating was at 32%. Low approval ratings for the leader of the party make it even more difficult for the party in power to hold onto its position.

On the domestic front, two issues dominated: health care and the economy. In February 2007 Americans believed that the second top priority of government was health care (27%), behind the Iraq war (76%),[6] and by March 2008, the economy was Americans' top domestic concern.[7] Just as the general election was in full swing, on September 15, 2008, the investment bank Lehman Brothers collapsed. This collapse signaled the start of a national and then global panic about the health of the global banking industry, and by extension the overall economy. It remained Americans' top issue as people went to the voting booth in November 2008.

The Republican field was wide open, and in the end four candidates competed aggressively for the nomination: former mayor of New York City Rudy Giuliani, former governor of Massachusetts Mitt Romney, Arizona senator John McCain, and former governor of Arkansas Mike Huckabee. By Super Tuesday, held on February 5, it became a two-man race between McCain and Huckabee. Huckabee ended his candidacy after losing the Texas primary on March 4.

The Democratic contest started with a large field of eight contestants, but quickly became a two-person contest between a black senator from Illinois,[8] Barack Obama, and former First Lady and senator from New York, Hillary Clinton. A third contender, former senator from South Carolina and vice-presidential candidate in 2004 John Edwards, dropped out after losing in the first four contests, including his home state of North Carolina. The presidential campaign in 2008 proved historic, not only for the uses to which DCTs were put, but also for the remarkably intense and hard-fought primary contests between two historic figures: the potentially first black and the potentially first woman Democratic nominee.

THE STATE OF THE INTERNET

Between 2004 and 2008 several changes occurred in DCTs. Internet adoption rates jumped another 10% in the United States., climbing from 63% of adults to 73%.[9] Cell phone access increased to 75%. The smartphone was just emerging as a new technology. The first iPhone was released in the summer of 2007, and the iPhone 3G came out a year later.

As important as Internet penetration rates, a philosophical shift had occurred in software development generally, and World Wide Web applications specifically. This philosophical shift was coined *Web 2.0* by Tim O'Reilly, founder of O'Reilly Media, which publishes guidebooks on software design. Web 2.0 as a concept highlighted the shift in software programming to consider the World Wide Web as a platform in which the applications built for it enable the user to have greater interactivity with them, configuring and remixing data and media as need dictates, and greater interactivity with other people through the platform. O'Reilly called this new way of conceptualizing software that channels communication and information over the Internet an "architecture of participation."[10]

That architecture of participation gave rise to what many label *social media*, those digital media applications that allow for connection with others for social or professional purposes. Popular examples include Facebook, Twitter, and Flickr. In 2004, the social sharing site Myspace was popular; by 2008 Myspace had shrunk in size and Facebook had grown. In February 2005, the first year the Pew Internet & American Life Project asked the question, 7% of American adults were using an "online social or professional networking site." By 2008 that number had jumped to 35%. Video-watching online also exploded, with 50% of adults reporting watching on a site like YouTube.[11] Twitter was still a nascent communication channel, with about 9% reporting using it, primarily as a texting service that was used through cellular phones. Blogging was still popular, with 36% reporting ever having read a blog, while just over 10% were actively reading blogs.

By the spring of 2008, while Clinton and Obama were intensely involved in an unprecedented primary contest, 55% of Internet users were looking for news about the campaign, according to a Pew Internet & American Life survey.[12] It also found increased participation among African Americans in searching for news and information online, 40% in 2008 as compared with just 19% in 2004. As cell phone and text messaging expanded in the United States, Pew found about 8% of those surveyed reporting sending or receiving text messages about the campaign at least once a week. Of particular note for efforts by the campaign to create two-step flow of targeting super-supporters to advocate for the candidate within their social networks, by the spring of 2008 9% of all adults reported signing up to receive e-mail from a candidate, and 14% of Internet users reported forwarding or posting political commentary or writing. By the end of the campaign in November, almost 75% of Internet users went online to get news and information about the campaign.[13] Nearly 60% of Internet users used a variety of social tools, from Twitter to e-mail, to send or receive information or talk about the election. Yet analysis of Pew's postelection survey data suggests that there remained a sociodemographic divide, with younger Americans being more likely to participate in political activities, especially involving social networking sites, than older Americans.[14] Even so, that survey analysis also suggests that the increased involvement online did not translate into voting offline. A survey of young social media users in early 2008 similarly found that they were not more likely to be politically involved.[15] Thus, the hope that political activities online would translate offline, especially for younger voters, was not borne out.

Digital Media Staff Get a Seat at the Senior Staff Table

By 2008, senior staff and advisors to the presidential candidates recognized that DCT strategy was going to be integral to the campaign. Nearly all the presidential primary candidates, on both the Republican and Democratic sides, had a digital media or Internet strategist who was part of the senior staff team involved in strategy. Katie Harbath, deputy e-campaign director for Giuliani, explained that by 2008 his campaign as well as the others were "finally starting to realize it's more than communication. It's fundraising, strategizing."[16] In the Giuliani campaign, she initially reported to the communications director, but by May 2007 the Internet team became its own department and worked with the strategy group.

Many of the candidates also understood the importance of digital media to their overall campaign strategy. Mike Huckabee, for example, was deeply involved in using DCTs to campaign. As Vincent Harris, the campaign's Iowa online director and a campaign blogger explained, Huckabee "loves the Internet. He realized early on that a lot of his support was coming from the online community."[17] With Harris's help, the Huckabee campaign reached out to conservative websites and bloggers, and began hosting telephone calls with the candidate. Huckabee enjoyed those calls and saw value in connecting with the conservative netroots. Hillary Clinton also was fully cognizant of the importance of the Internet. Peter Daou, Clinton's Internet strategist, explained that when he was hired, they talked about the importance of progressive online organizations in increasing energy and support for her campaign.[18]

Some of the primary candidates hired digital media directors who had little by way of prior presidential or even political campaign experience, but who did have passion, interests, and experience with digital media. Ron Paul's e-campaign director, Justine Lam, had no prior experience working on a political campaign.[19] Her prior job was as a project manager of a nonprofit. She had a connection with the Paul campaign chairman through a fellowship program she directed. When she sent in her resume to volunteer for the campaign, she was instead offered a paid position to direct the digital campaign and became the second paid staffer. She and others hired after her largely had to learn *how* to run a campaign *while* they were running it.

Others, such as Katie Harbath, Giuliani's digital director, and Tim Tagaris, Chris Dodd's Internet director, had prior political campaign experience. Harbath had worked at the Republican National Committee doing digital strategy during the 2004 campaign. Tagaris had worked as Ned Lamont's digital director when Lamont ran successfully against Joe Lieberman for the Democratic Senate nomination in Connecticut. The Clinton campaign hired Daou, a prominent blogger who wrote on Salon.com, to serve as Internet director.

Unlike Paul or Huckabee, who had brought on relative novices to help with e-campaign strategy, the Obama and McCain campaigns hired digital media firms. Obama hired Blue State Digital (BSD) to build the technology and help establish digital strategy. BSD was formed by four former Howard Dean e-campaign staff. One of them, Joe Rospars, dedicated himself full time to the Obama campaign as its e-campaign director. BSD was hired just a week before Obama's presidential campaign announcement, and in that short period of time built the website and the related organizing, fundraising, and social networking technologies that would become a major source of revenue and field organizing.[20] McCain hired Campaign Solutions, one of the prominent Republican digital media companies in the United States. Headed by Rebecca Donatelli, who had worked for McCain's campaign in 2000 and Bush's in 2004, the firm had a depth of experience with presidential campaigns generally and digital media specifically. Deputy e-campaign manager Mark SooHoo worked full time on the campaign and had been at the firm for ten years.[21]

The question in 2008 was whether senior campaign staff recognized the importance of DCTs to the ultimate success of the campaigns. Andrew Rasiej, a Democratic strategist, summed up nicely the issue to a *Washington Post* reporter: "Every campaign will tell you that they get the Web, that they understand its power, but you have to look at where the power lies. How much influence do their online people have?"[22] He concluded that the presidential campaigns, at least by May 2007, did not fully recognize that DCTs would be a key element.

In many ways, he was right. Mark Penn, a senior advisor to Hillary Clinton, declared in November 2007 that Obama's supporters looked like Facebook, which was perceived by some in the pundit class as an insult. David Plouffe, Obama's campaign manager, was quoted by the press saying, "Don't get me wrong, the Internet is a powerful organizing and fundraising tool, and it's getting more and more important every day, but it's still not the persuasion and message tool that TV is."[23] Both comments highlight that attitudes at the very top of the presidential campaign hierarchy still did not appreciate the organizing and communication advantages of DCTs.

This lack of insight also was observed organizationally in some campaigns. Harbath, Giuliani's e-campaign director, explained that she and the e-campaign director were relegated to a subunit under communications, reporting to the communications director. Eventually, the e-campaign became its own department.[24]

Other senior staff generally appreciated the potential of DCTs and situated them equally with other functions of the campaign. For Tagaris and his small Internet team on the Dodd campaign, they were a separate department but worked closely with the communications staff. He noted that it was recognized that the campaign could be "successful if it [DCTs] served as a compliment and not subservient to the other areas."[25] Rospars, Plouffe's views aside, reported directly to the campaign manager. Daou reported to Howard Wolfson, who served under Clinton's campaign manager, Patti Solis Doyle.[26]

If we look back at the digital media teams and the tools and practices they created, it is almost a truism to say that the Obama campaign understood the importance of digital and put resources and staff there at a rate the other campaigns ultimately did not. Yet that is not fully the case. The Clinton campaign also put significant resources and attention organizationally into digital media. Daou explained that the campaign from the start recognized the importance of digital media as a communication, fundraising, and organizing platform.[27] As evidence for this, the campaign launched with a prominently featured web video of her announcement and a listening tour, in which Clinton invited the public to participate in three live web chats with her.

Yet the spending priorities of the campaigns reveal that the Obama campaign was banking on digital media ultimately in ways that Clinton's was not. Obama's top paid employee was Joe Rospars, his e-campaign strategist; for the Clinton campaign it was the finance director and fundraiser.[28] The difference is that Rospars was fully involved in fundraising, organizing, *and* messaging strategy for the campaign, the new paradigm of organizational structure in networked campaigning, while Clinton's top staff were more compartmentalized into distinct activities, the more common organizational structure in the paradigm of mass-media campaigning.

Shifting Tactics to Fundraise

If Howard Dean in 2004 and John McCain in 2000 had shown the potential of fundraising through digital means, then the 2008 election solidified effective practices to raise unprecedented amounts of money, often in small, repeated increments from many people.

THE FINANCIAL FIGHT: EARLY MONEY

During the surfacing phase, one of the most critical elements that determine a candidate's viability is fundraising prowess. Candidates who lag behind in fundraising tend to receive less media coverage and therefore do not do as well in public opinion polls. Hillary Clinton was expected to raise significant amounts of money after she announced her candidacy given her well-recognized name and political and social connections. Barack Obama, however, was a relatively unknown senator from Illinois. Nevertheless, his campaign was able to raise nearly as much money as Clinton in the first fiscal quarter of 2007. He raised $25 million to her $26 million.[29] Half of Obama's contributors gave online, for a total of $6.9 million compared with Clinton's $4.2 million.[30] This initial sign of strength on Obama's part helped fuel speculation that he would be a major contender against Clinton.

Such speculation continued for the remainder of 2007. In the second quarter Obama raised $32.5 million to Clinton's $27 million. Although the bulk of that money actually came from large-donor contributors,[31] the campaign touted that it had signed up 154,000 new donors in the second quarter.[32] In the third quarter, Clinton out-fundraised Obama, but by only $4 million. In dealings with the press, the Obama campaign continued to herald the large number of small and first-time contributors.[33]

In February 2008, as primary voting was underway, Clinton replaced campaign manager Patti Solis Doyle with Maggie Williams, a longtime aide. Doyle had promised to build but failed to deliver the kind of small, online repeat donor base that the Obama campaign effectively built.[34] In March, Clinton's staff more aggressively promoted the campaign's website. Clinton referred to its URL in speeches after her victories in Ohio and Texas, and staff sent out more e-mail messages to followers and placed more advertisements online.[35] These efforts succeeded, with an increase in small-donor contributions to her campaign. After the primary win in Pennsylvania, her campaign brought in $10 million in approximately twwenty-four hours through the Internet.[36] By May, as her delegate count fell behind Obama's, the online contributions waned.[37]

In early 2007, McCain had weak fundraising numbers that fell far behind those of Romney and Giuliani.[38] One way that staff tried to drive online traffic and contributions was through Google search advertising, bidding on keywords, such as "earmarks" or "Abu Ghraib," that people might search and then showing a link to the campaign website in the paid advertisement section of the Google search window.[39] SooHoo noted that the campaign was highly cost effective in targeted ad campaigns online to drive money to the campaign.[40]

CAMPAIGN FINANCE REFORM'S DEMISE: THE MOUSE VERSUS THE LION

During the general election McCain's hands were effectively tied when he decided to accept federal matching money. Back in 2002, he was one of two key advocates for legislation, the Bipartisan Campaign Reform Act (know typically as the McCain-Feingold Act), that restricted contributions to political parties and required new labeling and disclaimers on television advertising. Given his highly visible role in advocating campaign finance reform and his persona as an opponent of lobbyists' influence on politics, he had no choice but to take public financing as a sign of his commitment to his reform efforts of prior years.

This commitment put him at a substantial disadvantage because his general election opponent, Barack Obama, eschewed federal dollars. Obama raised a jaw-dropping $150 million, for example, in the month of September alone.[41] By way of comparison, McCain received only $75 million in public financing money that needed to last through October and early November. Moreover, by accepting federal financing, his expenditures were capped at $84 million.[42] The financial fight between McCain and Obama was about as uneven as a mouse fighting a lion.

MONEY BOMBS

One of the most effective campaigns at raising substantial sums of money online was that of Ron Paul. Similar in some ways to the Dean campaign of 2004, supporters largely led the campaign. One vital benefit was the remarkable flow of money that supporters raised on two separate occasions during the surfacing stage. Called "money bombs," supporters selected two days of symbolic significance to flood the campaign with online contributions: November 5, 2007, which coincides with Guy Fawkes Day, commemorating the Catholic revolutionary who aimed to blow up the House of Lords in London in 1605 to kill Protestant rulemakers; and, December 16, 2007, the anniversary of the Boston Tea Party in 1773.[43] The latter garnered the largest single-day cash infusion of over $6 million during the surfacing stage for any candidate. In the fourth quarter of 2007, Paul raised as much money online as Clinton and Obama, almost $20 million.[44]

Supporters found other creative ways to bring awareness and money to the Paul campaign. The supporter behind the money bomb idea created a business, Liberty Political Advertising, through which it sold shares of a blimp that advertised the Paul campaign across the Eastern Seaboard.[45] Other supporters teamed up to develop and then fundraise for a full-page advertisement in Iowa's influential newspaper, the Des Moines Register. It was a montage of faces of supporters that combined to create an image of Paul with a message that urged people to vote for him. These citizen-generated money bombs capitalized on the event-driven nature of fundraising, not only to raise needed cash for the campaign, but also to generate earned media from the shock value of the "bomb" of money.

Constructing Image through DCTs

The 2004 election demonstrated that a campaign's use or failure to use DCTs factored into how the candidate was perceived in the media and by the public. Dean developed an image, via earned media coverage of his remarkable online fundraising success, as the first Internet candidate (although Steven Forbes would dispute that, declaring he had been the first in 2000). By 2008, all of the campaigns integrated DCTs as a key component of their overall media, fundraising, and outreach strategy.

The prevalence of social network sites, such as Myspace, solved a problem that Bimber and Davis highlighted in their research on the 2000 presidential campaign, that of finding ways to draw attention to the website and to the campaign online.[46] If a candidate could generate name recognition and excitement and eventually get people connecting to the campaign on Myspace or YouTube, then a set of people could be contacted and urged to share what they were learning about the campaign with their network of friends. Some, such as Obama and Paul, were more successful at it than others. Although DCTs were only one small part of the hypermedia environment that is still largely dominated by television,[47] this section examines several primary and the general election candidates' uses of DCTs to shape their image.

GOOGLE RON PAUL

The mainstream news media mostly dismissed Ron Paul's candidacy. Paul, a libertarian-oriented Republican member of the House of Representatives and a physician, had served in Texas for over two decades before this run for the presidency. Lacking media coverage, he still gained a substantial following, especially with young, male voters. They found appealing his strong opposition to the Iraq war and his libertarian stance that citizens and government return to what he described as the original principles the founders of the Constitution established, liberty and self-government. Paul decried intrusions by the federal government into issues that should be left to the states, including gay marriage, abortion restrictions and legalizing drugs. This stance resonated with a group of politically interested but disillusioned voters who found Paul genuine and authentic. They saw him as not just another politician but someone who expressed his views because he thought they were right, even when they went against Republican orthodoxy. One supporter, Cheryl Scott, told a *USA Today* reporter that Paul was "really one of us" and that "he doesn't seem like a politician."[48]

Supporters were frustrated by the lack of mainstream news coverage about the candidate, who was raising substantial money online and had a cadre of supporters. Born out of this frustration was the Google Ron Paul campaign. The idea was to circumvent the news media by getting people to learn about Paul for themselves via articles they would find through the Google search engine. Supporters placed signs around in their neighborhoods, on major roadways, and other visible, highly trafficked areas. The signs, mostly handmade, simply said "Google Ron Paul." The implied message of the campaign was that Paul's ideas were powerful and scary to mainstream politicians and press, which is why they did not get covered. People who looked for the information about Paul could discover for themselves the wisdom of his vision of governance for the US. The simple message also underscored and was made possible by the changing information landscape, where people no longer needed to rely on traditional news to learn about politicians; they could do their own research on a candidate quickly and easily through the Internet.

Paul's self-organized supporters, who primarily met online through Paul-supporter-sponsored blogs, Myspace, or Facebook, or who met offline via MeetUps, further fueled the notion that Paul was a cutting-edge candidate with a savvy Internet presence. One GOP strategist told a *USA Today* reporter, "Ron Paul is no laughing matter. He's tapping into a side of the Republican Party that's never had its issues addressed. And he's doing it by running a truly Web 2.0 campaign."[49] The problem for Paul was that his supporters were organizing primarily out of the field of vision of the campaign. The official campaign website provided only the typical information about the candidate and requests to contribute or check a box to volunteer. There was no platform to help supporters interact with each other and effectively self-organize there until December 2007.

Paul's supporters also caused trouble for his image. News media described Paul supporters as young, unkempt, and slightly confused about their political views.[50] Jesse Benton, Paul's campaign spokesman described "Paulites" as being driven and inspired by the candidate. Yet their inspiration often led to their engaging in activities that other campaigns and organizations found irritating. For example, CNN partnered with YouTube to hold the first presidential primary debates in which the candidates were asked questions from the public submitted as videos via YouTube. Anderson Cooper justified CNN's decision to not let the videos be chosen through popular vote because of the concern that Paul's digital-savvy supporters would game the vote system and rig the questions for Paul.[51] Indeed, the blog Redstate.com banned Paulites. "People would post on the blog that they were going to the bathroom, and a Ron Paul supporter would say, 'While you're there, don't forget to vote for Ron Paul,'" said Erick Erickson, RedState's editor.[52] For many, the Paulites' unbridled enthusiasm was too much, furthering marginalizing Paul from the rest of the Republican contenders in the eyes of pundits and journalists.

FAITH. FAMILY. FREEDOM: HUCKABEE SPEAKS THROUGH THE BLOGOSPHERE

The surprise upstart on the Republican side was former governor of Arkansas Mike Huckabee. A former Baptist minister, with a clear antiabortion position and a belief in intelligent design, he should have appealed to the Evangelical Christians of the Republican Party. Although he did well in the Iowa straw poll and the Values Voters Summit vote in 2007, religious conservatives were slow to embrace him, in part because former mayor of New York Rudy Giuliani had been billed early as the front runner. Conventional thinking was that Huckabee could not compete well against him or against Romney and his partially self-funded campaign. Huckabee's poll numbers and fundraising remained low until a month before the Iowa caucuses.

Huckabee was an unlikely candidate to finish first in Iowa, but that is what he did. Credit for that came largely from his appeal to evangelical Christians in the state and a disarming, country-boy demeanor that resonated with Iowa's secular voters. His website heavily focused on Iowa, prominently featuring ways on the front page for supporters to help there, from contributing, to volunteering, to learning more about his positions.

A third factor, political blogging, also played a vital role. Harris credited the heavy courting of conservative political bloggers for his success. From the start, the campaign reached out to the right-leaning blogosphere, holding conference calls, sending e-mail, and "booking" Huckabee to appear as a commentator or to participate in a question-and-answer session for a political blog. Huckabee himself blogged frequently on the campaign website (See Figure 5.1). He encouraged supporters to start their own blogs in support, generating what came to be known as "Huck's Army." Harris explained that even someone with a small blog with five followers was allowed in on the conference calls and e-mail messages because the campaign knew that was five more people whom they could reach. Harris estimated that they had nearly 2,200 bloggers who linked to the Huckabee site, which drove a steady volume of traffic there.[53] In a unique move, the campaign held a "Blogger Bash" in Iowa before the caucus and invited political bloggers in the state to come and meet the governor and Chuck Norris, the martial arts expert turned actor, who supported Huckabee.

It was part of the Huckabee strategy from the start to court political bloggers as an important constituency that would help the campaign fundraise, publicize, and support the little-known candidate. After Iowa, his campaign relied on volunteer church organizers and Huck's Army to spread the word and generate support for the candidate. This underfunded and loosely organized campaign, though, could not effectively compete against McCain once voting occurred in the crush of Super Tuesday states.

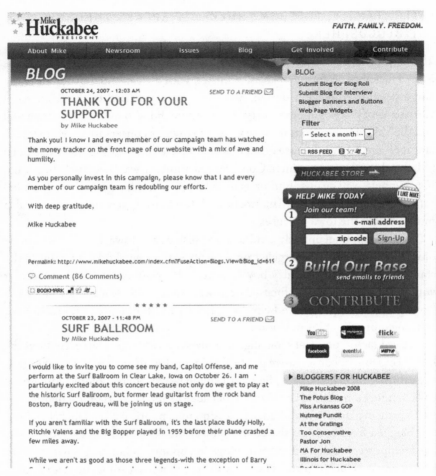

Figure 5.1 Mike Huckabee's campaign blog

COUNTRY FIRST: THE MAVERICK RISES AGAIN

Unlike McCain's run in 2000, when his image construction was clearly and strongly that of a maverick within his party, in 2007, when he surfaced as a candidate, he controlled and limiting access by the press and more carefully watched his words. One notable exception to his caution was his selection of Alaska governor Sarah Palin as vice-presidential candidate. This selection, announced the day after Obama's Democratic National Convention acceptance speech, came as a surprise. It also stepped on the expected news stories about Obama's speech. The addition of Palin to the ticket, a woman with a libertarian political streak, was read as a bold, unconventional move. Through the general election campaign, though, the choice backfired. Palin's poor performance in news interviews

and noteworthy gaffes, including her claim that she had foreign policy experience because Alaska's "next door neighbors are foreign countries,"[54] reverberated
through DCTs, mainstream media, and late-night comedy and raised questions
of her suitability to lead.

In shedding McCain's maverick image, he was remade as a statesman and
presidential. This was achieved by highlighting his foreign policy expertise,
grounding it in his firsthand experience as a veteran of the Vietnam War, and
suggesting he would be an ideal commander in chief, especially in the context of
the ongoing Iraq war. He aligned himself with President Bush's policy in 2007 to
increase American troop presence in Iraq, branded "The Surge."

McCain's alignment with Bush and efforts to highlight his foreign policy
expertise were reinforced online. The website design through the primaries
echoed design features of the Bush campaign from 2000, including a black banner
with gold lettering. The campaign highlighted McCain's foreign policy positions
and war experience on his website and in web ads. For example, they released a
web video right before the Iowa caucus attacking former governor Mitt Romney
as lacking foreign policy knowledge. The ad included graphic images of a bomb
blast in what appears to be Iraq, with a dead man dragged from the wreckage, and
images of apparent terrorists showing off their weapons.[55] The graphic nature of
the ad was inappropriate for television, but seemed perfectly designed for the
Web. It had its intended effect of capturing news media attention. In ways similar
to the dramatic 1964 "Daisy" ad, in which President Johnson implied that his
rival, Barry Goldwater, would be reckless in the use of nuclear force, McCain's ad
was channeled in a limited way, but was meant to generate big news.

McCain had image problems, however. First, he was seventy when he launched
this campaign. Questions about his health surfaced, which were of some concern
given his battle with skin cancer. Doubts also were raised about his temperament
and stability; he had a reputation of being a hothead. He also was unapologetic,
in the age of the Internet, about being technologically illiterate. In an interview
with the *New York Times*, he explained that he had never sent an e-mail because
he felt no need to do so. He explained that aides helped him get online to read
newspapers and blogs, although he preferred to get his news and opinions from
print newspapers and television.[56] An article a month later in the *Times* further
examined McCain's lack of technological savvy, suggesting that it was a sign that
he was out of touch with what most Americans now experienced as part of their
daily lives.[57] The article compared his lack of computer and technological savvy to
George H. W. Bush's astonishment at checkout scanners at a grocery store when
he was president. That apparent lack of interest in the digital world swamped his
media image online. Critical news stories suggested that McCain's fundraising
numbers were not as strong as expected given his frontrunner status because he
was not innovating with online fundraising like he had in 2000.

McCain had another image problem: he seemed initially tone deaf about the economy and then erratic in his approach to dealing with it when he finally acknowledged there was a problem. At a speech given the same day as the announcement that Lehman Brothers collapsed, he declared that "the fundamentals of our economy are strong."[58] The Obama campaign jumped on that message, arguing that McCain was out of touch. When McCain suspended his campaign in late September to return to Washington to help craft a rescue for the economy, both Obama and political pundits described McCain as "erratic," playing into questions about his temperament and ability to lead.

McCain rebounded in the last weeks of the campaign on the economy with a concerted media push to highlight the negative implications of Obama's tax policies. McCain was helped by Joe Wurzelbacher, who at an Obama event asked for clarification on how his tax policy would affect those making more than $250,000. Obama's answer included the statement that it is good for everyone when the wealth is spread around, and conservatives and McCain pounced on the answer. Wurzelbacher was rebranded by the campaign as "Joe the Plumber," and McCain took to television and the website to highlight how Obama's tax policies would hurt ordinary people like Joe, even inviting supporters to film their own "I am Joe the Plumber" videos, some of which were featured on the website (See Figure 5.2).

Through the general election, the McCain campaign worked to construct a negative image of Obama as a shallow celebrity. The message was underscored in a coordinated messaging campaign that included a web and TV ad, combined with an e-mail announcement and a blog entry, all aimed at creating a powerful viral messaging campaign. In July, after Obama's overseas trip that ended with a speech in Germany, the McCain campaign released a video linking Obama to celebrities Paris Hilton and Britney Spears.[59] The ad, according to SooHoo, was highly successful on the Internet, with several million views of the campaign's website. It had the intended effect of pushing the news media to cover the attack and discuss questions of his qualifications to be president. Yet the most watched videos on YouTube of McCain were gaffes and controversial statements he made, such as his "Bomb, bomb, bomb, bomb, bomb, Iran" to the tune of "Barbara Ann" by the Beach Boys or his statement that America should stay in Iraq for one hundred years.[60]

THE FRONT RUNNER: HILLARY FOR PRESIDENT

Hillary Clinton had been a visible, national public figure since the 1990s. Her husband, former president Bill Clinton, served two terms. As First Lady she was a strong advocate for health care reform, chairing the task force created by her husband to develop policy. The legislation and her role crafting it were

Figure 5.2 The McCain-Palin website

controversial, and she became a polarizing figure, generating "Hillary Haters."[61] In the late 1990s, she endured her husband's sexual scandal, which led to his impeachment when he lied under oath about an affair with a White House intern. In 1999 she ran for a seat in the Senate from New York and won, and became the first First Lady to win political office.

In 2008, the field was wide open on the Democratic side, but the campaign worked hard early to establish Clinton's dominance in fundraising, polling, and organizing.[62] The Clinton brand lent an air of confidence and inevitability.[63] Clinton was so confident she would win in the early caucus and primary states that the main strategists did not plan nor organize in later states. When it came clear that she would lose Iowa, the campaign scrambled to put in place field offices in later-voting states.

The Clinton campaign started with great promise to heavily engage DCTs in pursuit of the nomination, adding a cutting-edge entrepreneurial spirit to her already established policy-wonk image. The campaign constructed this image from the start of her campaign through her formal announcement via her website, www.hillaryclinton.com. She announced in a web video that she wanted to start a conversation with the American people and would do so immediately in the form of three conversations on consecutive nights in January 2007, when she would take questions from people who had signed up and answer them via live video stream. A spokesperson for the campaign explained to the *New York Times* that the objective was to speak directly to voters rather than having to talk with them filtered through the mainstream media.[64] In the conversations, Clinton sat on a sofa in a living room setting. She appeared relaxed, friendly, and personable, an effort to use this medium to construct a different image of her than Americans had of her in the past: cold, dominating, and tough.[65] Daou reported to the news media that she received 25,000 questions and over 50,000 sign-ups to watch the webcasts.[66]

Clinton had a complicated image with regard to her gender. News coverage highlighted it while simultaneously speculating that Clinton's run and likely nomination meant that the nation was now "post-feminist."[67] The implication of that conception was that sexism no longer was an issue in the United States, unlike race. Clinton, for her part, struggled with how to be postfeminist while also capitalizing on the appeal her candidacy had to women, especially to older women who made up the core of her support base, what Alexander describes as "walking the boundaries."[68] Her public persona had always been one of a no-nonsense, serious, thoughtful, well-organized policy wonk, and she often downplayed her gender. Indeed, she worked hard to establish herself, especially as compared with Obama, as a tough leader who would make the hard decisions on domestic and foreign affairs. On the other hand, especially when the contest became tight in the primaries, she highlighted the symbolic importance of being the first potential female president, declaring that she was running "to break the highest and hardest glass ceiling,"[69] and pushed back at the news media and her opponents for ganging up on her because she was a woman.

The somewhat schizophrenic relationship Clinton had with gender in debates and with the press was less evident online. Through DCTs, the campaign worked hard to target her most ardent supporters, older women, and expand her base to younger women using rhetoric on her website, for example, that highlighted the need for contributions to help her "level the playing field" (See Figure 5.3). During Women's History Month in March 2007, the campaign launched the Women's Leadership Network, a group of female supporters that the campaign harnessed to promote Clinton's candidacy among women. This included a web page where specifically mothers and daughters could share stories of "I can be president." The campaign launched a website in early October 2007 that corresponded with a speech Clinton delivered to her alma mater, Wellesley College. The website, called hillblazers.com, aimed to help mobilize women on and off college campuses to organize for Clinton.

Figure 5.3   Hillary Clinton's website after losing Nevada

The campaign used DCTs to round out Clinton's cold, wonkish image with warmth and playfulness. In early summer, her campaign released a video in which Clinton says earnestly, "I want to know what you're thinking on one of the most important questions of this campaign" and then directs the viewer to visit the campaign website to vote on the unserious topic of the campaign's theme song. The clip ends with Clinton singing the national anthem out of tune, which had been a YouTube sensation in prior months and had been used by her detractors to ridicule her. By including the clip of her out-of-tune singing, combined with her ironic delivery urging people to vote on the serious issue of a campaign song, she owned the stereotype of herself as being serious while also showing that she could laugh at herself. Daou reported that the response was so positive and strong it was "insane."[70] The video was viewed nearly a million times, and over 100,000 votes were cast for song nomination.[71] Although it generated recommendations from detractors, including Rush Limbaugh's suggestion, "Baby Got Back," and *Rolling Stone* readers who proposed "Cold as Ice," the positive earned media coverage combined with the heavy traffic to the website helped reshape Clinton's image.

Daou and her digital media staff continued to find ways to use DCTs to shape a more positive image of Clinton. The campaign's greatest digital media sensation in terms of fundraising and traffic to the website was a video that played off the popular TV show *The Sopranos*. It ended in June 2007, and the campaign's "Sopranos Video" was released just weeks later and reproduced the last, provocative scene of the show: Hillary Clinton sat at a booth looking at a menu and flipping through songs on the table-side jukebox; Bill Clinton walks to her table, sits down, and they chat; an actor from *The Sopranos* walks by and glares at Hillary, and then the screen goes black. As a faithful mock-up of the original, the video was wildly popular online and generated a fresh round of earned media highlighting her playfulness.

After Clinton lost Iowa, she and her campaign shifted tactics, capitalizing on the new opportunities her loss created. Daou explained that the Iowa defeat by Obama allowed Clinton to shift from being the front runner to an insurgent, which brought new enthusiasm and energy, especially online.[72] As she campaigned in New Hampshire, she stopped delivering her standard stump speech and just talked with the audience, answering questions until the audience was satiated. On the day before the New Hampshire primary, at a cafe with a meeting of female supporters, television cameras caught her growing emotional after she was asked how she managed to get up and campaign every day. Clinton said that it was not easy, then paused as she quelled emotion. She then explained that she could not meet the grueling schedule if she was not so passionately concerned about the future of America. Some pundits and press speculated that this was her Ed Muskie moment and predicted she would lose (in 1972, he apparently shed tears defending his wife, and then lost badly in New Hampshire).[73] Instead, voters streamed to the polls and cast a majority of votes for her.

Clinton's campaign was the first on the Democratic side to introduce a website responding to smears and rumors flowing on and off the Internet. The website, called The Fact Hub, launched with a rebuttal to a rumor that she and her traveling staff had failed to tip a waitress at a diner.[74] Phil Singer, press secretary for Hillary Clinton's campaign, noted that one of the challenges for presidential campaigns is how to deal with rumors and attacks: "Do you address something head on and risk making it into a mainstream phenomenon? Or ignore it and risk allowing it to take on a life of its own?"[75] This perennial question proved no easier to answer in the Internet age, but at least campaigns had at their disposal websites and fact checkers to disseminate counterinformation to fight rumors and misstatements.

CHANGE YOU CAN BELIEVE IN

Barack Obama, the junior senator from Illinois, surprised many political watchers with his campaign prowess. Dismissed by some for his lack of political experience, Obama turned that into an asset and a comparison with Clinton, using slogans that focused on change. In the context of two terms of the Bush administration, a war that was not going well, and an economy that was sluggish, the notion of *change* resonated with the core of the Democratic Party. The Obama campaign worked to make subtle and sometimes explicit arguments that electing Hillary Clinton would be a return to an older, institutionalized Democratic politics that would not move the country forward.

The Obama campaign cultivated an ethos in the surfacing stage that was similar in many ways to that of Howard Dean. Obama's team crafted an image of the candidate as cutting edge and next generation—both in age and in philosophy. One example of the construction of this ethos came from a viral video that did not officially come from the campaign, but nevertheless conveyed a distinct message about Obama relative to Clinton. The video, titled "Vote Different," was a mash-up of an Apple ad from 1984 for the Macintosh computer. The original ad, an Orwellian portrayal of contemporary life under rival computer company, IBM, featured a young woman in orange shorts, running toward a giant television screen in a theater full of brainwashed people wearing dingy gray clothing watching Big Brother (See Figure 5.4). The young woman destroys the television, freeing the people. In the mash-up version, the young woman's T-shirt is adorned with the Obama campaign logo, and Hillary Clinton is Big Brother delivering her announcement speech. At the end of the ad, text tells viewers, "On January 14th, the Democratic Primary will begin. And you'll see why 2008 won't be like '1984.'" The ad garnered heavy media coverage and generated 2 million views within a week of its release on YouTube. The message of the video was twofold: the Obama campaign was on the cutting edge of digital culture by creating a savvy mash-up video that had the message and the design to go viral; and the prospect of a Clinton presidency would be a step back for the Democratic Party and the country.

The ad also brought controversy to the Obama campaign. Great mystery surrounded the creator of the video. Speculation grew that someone in the Obama campaign had created it, but the official message from the campaign denied any involvement. Eventually, it was discovered that a high-level staff member at Blue State Digital, the firm contracted to do Obama's digital media, had created it. He claimed the Obama campaign had no knowledge of his creation, and he resigned from the firm.[76]

Another way the campaign constructed Obama's tech-savvy and cutting-edge image was through heavy visibility on online social networking sites. Obama was

Figure 5.4 A still image from the mash-up YouTube video "Vote Different"

first on Facebook, and the candidate himself purportedly filled in the information on his page.[77] The campaign also established an online presence on dozens of other niche social networking sites, such as BlackPlanet, a social networking site for blacks. The campaign hired one of the founders of Facebook, Chris Hughes, who joined the campaign in early 2007, just as it was launching. His title, "online organizing guru," essentially meant that his job was to bring his knowledge of online social media to the campaign. He also oversaw the campaign's internal social networking site, known as MyBo. In an interview with the *New York Times* Hughes explained that his vision for MyBo was to mirror the success of Facebook by helping people connect within their own local communities.[78]

The perception was accurate that Obama ran a highly successful digital media strategy from the launch of his campaign. The *New York Times* reported that Obama received twice as many visitors to his campaign website as Clinton for the first two months of 2007.[79] One small part of that success was the careful experimentation that campaign staff like Dan Siroker did, who was hired to do data analytics for the campaign. He experimented with page layout, button labels, and images to determine what was most effective at moving visitors to action.[80] During the general election, the Obama campaign even placed advertisements in Xbox video games of those who played online,[81] something rarely considered by political campaigns.[82] The ads were placed primarily in sports video games on banner or billboards placed in the environments that reminded players to vote. The ads were targeted at households in critical swing states, especially those that allowed early voting.

Obama, similar to Howard Dean in 2004, constructed his supporters as agentic. His message was that ordinary people had the ability and the responsibility to self-govern.[83] On his website that included emphasizing ways for people to "get involved," "build the momentum," and "make a difference" (See Figure 5.5). The campaign also enacted that vision by creating tools for supporters to self-organize. Unlike Clinton, who heavily used DCTs to soften her image, Obama used DCTs to empower his advocates by organizing online and by extension in their social networks offline.

Obama also had image challenges. As mentioned earlier, he garnered the reputation of a celebrity. Early in the campaign, a viral video posted on a website called BarelyPolitical.com and recirculated on YouTube featured a campy but

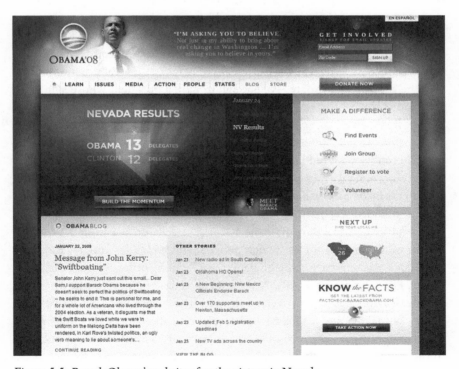

Figure 5.5 Barack Obama's website after the victory in Nevada

professionally produced R&B style music video of a woman, who came to be known as Obama Girl, singing "I got a crush on Obama." When Obama lost to Clinton in the New Hampshire primary, rap singer will.i.am of the Black Eyed Peas created a music video setting Obama's New Hampshire concession speech to music. The video featured a dozen celebrities saying and singing parts of Obama's speech, juxtaposed with that of Obama delivering the speech. The song featured the refrain "Yes, We Can," which was the slogan of the Obama campaign during the early primaries. The video generated over two million hits within five days. These user-generated viral videos, combined with the record-setting numbers of people who were turning out to Obama campaign events not just in the United States but also in countries like Germany (when Obama briefly traveled Europe), led his opponents, especially Clinton and McCain, to attack him for offering hope and beautiful oratory that moved people to embrace him as a celebrity, but not necessarily real solutions to the nation's challenges.

In the candidacy of Barack Obama, the identity politics around race came to the fore. In some of the ways that Clinton reflected and refracted US cultural perspectives of gender, Obama did the same around race. Obama, whose mother was white and an American citizen and whose father was Kenyan, complicated notions of blackness. Early in the campaign there were questions of whether he was "black enough" given that he did not share the heritage story of African Americans, with its legacy of slavery and Jim Crow laws, nor was he "purely" black, given that his mother came from working-class, white roots in Kansas. For others, especially young people in the United States, he seemed to represent the potential that the United States had advanced in race relations by demonstrating that the country was progressive enough to have a president whose skin color was read as black.

As Clinton avoided explicit discussion of gender early in the campaign, so too did Obama of race. When the candidate became the focus of scrutiny when he and Clinton were locked in a tight race during the primaries, he had to directly address race and race relations in the United States. The controversy started with comments made by Obama's pastor, Reverend Jeremiah Wright, and posted on YouTube. Initially reported by *ABC News*,[84] the videos featured statements from Reverend Wright five days after the terrorist attacks on September 11, 2001, condemning America for its foreign policies, and telling his congregation that "America's chickens have come home to roost," among other controversial statements. Five days after the *ABC News* story, a feeding frenzy grew in which the broadcast and cable news coverage showed new videos and also drove more videos onto YouTube.[85] Obama had to respond directly to the controversy. A week later he gave a speech in Philadelphia, a city with strong symbolic links to the movement to abolish slavery as well as to the founding of the nation. In his "More Perfect Union" speech he narrated the lessons from Martin Luther

King Jr.'s 1963 "I Have a Dream" speech. Obama confronted race relations in the United States while moving to transcend them by arguing that injustice should be confronted in all quarters so that everyone can achieve the American dream.[86]

Judged as an eloquent and important speech on race relations, it furthered the perception of Obama as a gifted orator, and it effectively quelled the controversy over Jeremiah Wright. The speech, which was immediately placed on YouTube, received a remarkable 1.6 million views in just two days.[87] The video and transcript were surprisingly popular items on Facebook, given their subject matter.[88]

Although the Obama campaign benefited from the complex messaging environment available through DCTs, by amplifying his message beyond initial audiences and supporters, he also was harmed by it. In April 2008, just weeks before Pennsylvanians would hold their primary and potentially break the stalemate between Clinton and Obama, a journalist recorded a controversial statement he made that raised questions about Obama's elitism. The journalist was working with OfftheBus.net, an experiment in citizen journalism by New York University professor Jay Rosen and posted on the website Huffington Post. She attended an Obama fundraiser in California, in which he described his experiences traveling through Pennsylvania's small towns. He observed that prior administrations had failed in promoting job creation in the state. He concluded by saying: "So, it's not surprising that they get bitter, they cling to guns or religion or antipathy to people who aren't like them or anti-immigrant sentiment or anti-trade sentiment as a way to explain their frustrations."[89] The journalist's report and accompanying audio posted to the Huffington Post created a firestorm of news media coverage. The controversy also extended to the journalist's role. A self-described Obama supporter, she got into the fundraising event, which the campaign viewed as off-limits to reporters. Her story raised questions about the role of citizen journalists and bloggers in the political campaign, and whether they should also be viewed as journalists.[90] For Obama, he had to answer for the quote and explain his views. The DCTs his campaign had been using so effectively had also been used against him.

The Obama campaign also had to grapple with rumors that he was Muslim. An unsourced claim in a news story in the spring of 2007 declared he converted to Islam while living in Indonesia as a boy and was educated in a madrasa, which in American culture connotes a school that teaches a fundamentalist interpretation of Islam to children. E-mail rumors circulated that declared that Obama was sworn into office on a Koran, and that he turns his back to the flag during the Pledge of Allegiance. In late 2007 an e-mail message sent by a Clinton campaign staff member in Iowa declared Obama's Muslim faith.[91]

The campaign responded to these rumors and unfounded accusations by creating a website, FighttheSmears.com, launched in June 2008 to debunk claims that Obama was Muslim, not a citizen, and that his wife had made derogatory statements about whites. The campaign also dealt with e-mail rumors by urging supporters who received such notes to forward them to local organizers who would write a rebuttal and then send the rebuttal back to all the recipients of the original message.[92]

Although it had become common wisdom that candidates had greater message control online than through traditional media, where journalists can frame or reframe a candidate's message, in the Web 2.0 era message control became more of a challenge. The complex, hybrid media system of broadcast and cable television, print newspapers and magazines, YouTube, social media, websites, and online distributions of traditional broadcast and print had matured, combined with the rise in citizen journalism and elite bloggers.[93] Such a system meant that the carefully constructed, direct messaging by candidates to citizens without the mediation of the news media was less likely. Research around the Reverend Wright controversy suggested that cable news and YouTube fed off each other, amplifying the discussion and spreading it wider to the public than might otherwise have happened.[94] Yet Obama's speech also reverberated beyond journalists' retellings, with a remarkable volume of traffic to the video of the speech posted on YouTube suggesting that people wanted to hear Obama's words unframed by journalists. Thus, rather than offering a simpler, more direct way for candidates to shape their image with the public, the hybrid media environment made the challenge of image construction even greater for candidates.

Comparative Case Studies of Citizen Involvement

By 2008, although many campaign staff who worked on digital media had not worked on prior presidential campaigns themselves, with the exception of top Obama staff,[95] most had witnessed the 2004 election and the successes and failures of those campaigns. The lore of the Dean campaign meant that staff were more willing to try new tactics. Yet the Dean campaign also served as a note of caution, given how hard Dean fell when voting actually started; the digital media staff in 2008 did not want to experience the same fate. Thus, their experimentation found effective ways to focus and control supporters. Staff recognized the power of digital media to help bring super-supporters into the campaign and unleash their enthusiasm strategically to their social networks, in the spirit of two-step flow as described by Katz and Lazarsfeld over six decades ago.[96] The trick was managing that support, not only for fundraising as described earlier, but also for identifying and enacting practices that would get supporters mobilizing their network of contacts. This section focuses on and contrasts the campaigns of Paul, Clinton, McCain, and Obama to highlight the different approaches presidential campaigns took with regard to activating their networks of supporters.

RON PAUL'S REVOLUTION: A STUDY IN NO CONTROL

Ron Paul's campaign, from the start, struggled with controlling supporters' efforts for the purpose of gaining delegates for the Republican nomination. The staff, especially at the senior level, did not effectively develop tools and ways to use DCTs to focus supporters' energy. As one example, Lam explained that the campaign chairman did not have official signs created until June 2007 because he did not think they would be useful or relevant until a month or two before voting began.[97] Supporters, though, wanted signs, in part to promote the Paul campaign and in part to express their own identity and affiliation with Paul. Rather than waiting for the campaign, they created their own. Another example was the campaign blog. Although the Paul website featured a blog that chronicled his activities and events, it did not allow supporters to post comments for several months because of concerns about what supporters might say. As a result, supporters went elsewhere, creating their own forums to communicate and organize outside of the observation or the direction of the official campaign. As well, supporters created their own MeetUp groups, but Paul staff did little to coordinate or direct their efforts. Eventually, staff held a conference call with groups, but only once, because they found it too time consuming. After that, they created a video and put it out for MeetUp groups to watch and hopefully to follow.

As a result of the lack of direction for supporters, they developed a reputation of being spammers—not only for invading online public opinion polls and taking over discussion forums of other candidates, but for literally sending spam heralding Paul's performance in a debate and detailing his policy positions through an illegal "botnet," which masks e-mail origins.[98] Thus, the enthusiasm, though well intentioned, created negative publicity for Paul, and further fueled the sense that Paul was a marginal candidate. Moreover, the energy and enthusiasm of Paul supporters was not translated by the campaign through DCTs into the hard work of grassroots organizing, such as door knocking and phone campaigning, that is essential for performing well on Election Day.

There was recognition by campaign staff that supporters needed tools and goals to focus their efforts that would be productive for Paul, yet little action was taken in that direction. Eventually, they developed a tool but it did not launch until December 2007, too late to be effective in coordinating action on the ground. The tool, which Lam called a "precinct leader tool," was designed to help people coordinate campaign activities in caucus and primary states at the precinct level. Its development was slowed because of a lack of resources and staff. No single staff member was responsible for making the tool a reality. When it was built, it had to be approved through several channels, which slowed its launch. Lam also felt that it was not easy to use, and there was not much information for supporters on how to use it to their advantage or what a "precinct leader" even meant. Nevertheless, by the end of the campaign, it had 28,000 such leaders identified. The energy and enthusiasm was there, but the campaign lacked vision, resources, and a model to help channel that enthusiastic support into electoral success for Paul.

MCCAIN AND CLINTON: A STUDY IN TOO MUCH CONTROL

Both McCain and Clinton struggled to develop a set of practices with DCTs that would harness the support they were receiving while giving enough leeway for those energized supporters to creatively work on behalf of the campaign.

Clinton had the resources and the staff to push campaign practices with DCTs in new directions. Her campaign at the start constructed a message of openness that was quickly countered by the actual practices of the campaign. When she launched her campaign with the promise of starting a conversation with the public, backed up with live web chats, this seemed an auspicious start to a front-runner campaign. In these early days, when she was already declared the likely Democratic nominee, she was suggesting a historic shift in presidential campaigning in which the front runner, not just the insurgent, genuinely opened up to greater interactivity with the public.

As the web chats unfolded, though, it became evident that the Clinton campaign's digital media strategy was not going to shift the ground of power from the campaign to its supporters and the broader public. Political observers described her announcement video as "an old fashioned broadcast message for a new digital era," not something new, and the conversations "stale."[99] The event drew scorn from political observers Andrew Rasiej and Micah Sifry, who wrote: "But what kind of conversation involves random questions followed by longish and meandering answers when the person talking never says, 'Well, what do you think?'"[100] Clinton's digital media team were using DCTs to grab attention and positive media and to drive interested people to the campaign to deposit e-mail addresses and contact information, but those supporters' voices were from the start relegated to secondary status.

Indeed, Clinton as well as McCain used DCTs to craft pseudo-interactive events to create a perception of involvement and agency by supporters and the public, but did little to genuinely engage supporters. Clinton's voting contest to select the campaign theme song or the mock *Sopranos* video were meant to help construct a playful image of Clinton and drive new donors and supporters to the website, but were not themselves designed to help supporters self-organize to work on behalf of the campaign. For McCain's part, the "I'm Joe the Plumber" videos, which were meant to coincide with the campaign's efforts to highlight the plight of middle-class Americans in the United States, generated many submissions, but beyond posting the video, there was nothing else for supporters directly to do for the campaign.

As for social media, although Clinton and McCain established presences on such sites, they never had the volume of followers that the Obama campaign did. The McCain campaign created an online social networking tool on its website called McCain space, but it was not heavily used by campaign supporters.[101]

A specific challenge for Clinton was one of demographics when it came to organizing and mobilizing via DCTs. Daou explained that the enthusiastic supporters for Clinton's candidacy were older women who were less involved in Facebook and other social networking platforms.[102] Indeed, the quote from Mark Penn earlier that "Obama's supporters look like Facebook" was meant not as a caustic comment but as a statement of the reality the Clinton campaign faced: it had to speak to their supporters where they were, and they were not online to the same degree as Obama's supporters. Thus, the website and other digital communication were meant to generate enthusiasm and draw potential supporters to the website to contribute and to sign up to volunteer. This entailed developing messaging that would draw in supporters, such as the *Sopranos* spoof or the contest to pick the campaign theme song, by appealing to their tastes and interests, and then teaching them how to use digital tools to organize, which took time and effort. Josh Ross, senior digital strategist on Clinton's campaign, felt that her digital infrastructure was more advanced than Obama's,[103] but it could not compete with the reality that Obama's supporters tended to be those that "look like Facebook."[104]

Although both Clinton's and McCain's campaigns established some of the vital DCTs that can facilitate genuine interactivity and bottom-up agency by supporters, they had neither the same traction nor quite the same vision for these features as did the Obama campaign. The McCain and the Clinton campaigns had blogs where people could comment, for example. SooHoo explained that staff read comments on McCain's blog. He even noted that they surveyed core supporters about design elements and features of the website and made changes based on that input.[105] Much effort by SooHoo and others, though, focused on web videos and games that they hoped would go viral and spread a message or generate awareness of McCain in new quarters. In describing the role of the Internet in campaigning, SooHoo explained that his company, Campaign Solutions, worked to impart to clients that the Internet should be a part of every aspect of a campaign: fundraising, advertising, message, communication, even administration. The website was a way for people to submit comments, register for events, and print tickets for those events, and he noted that campaigns could better track voter contacts and develop metrics to measure effective and ineffective tactics and messaging. At no point did he argue that campaigns should think about digital media in the ways that, for example, Joe Trippi had in 2004 when he highlighted the importance of DCTs to open the campaign to the ideas and strategies that supporters might invent.

It is important to note that when the shift occurred within the Clinton campaign—when she lost Iowa and South Carolina and thus became an insurgent—a new energy infused her campaign. Both her core supporters and new ones grew energized to do more to ensure her win. The campaign capitalized on that shift to facilitate greater self-organizing by super-supporters. For example, when the campaign began preparing for California's primary, they encouraged "BYOP" (Bring Your Own Phone) house parties to make calls for Clinton. The campaign also structured the calling parties so that volunteers entered the information they learned during the phone calls into a form on the campaign website, giving them instant information about likely and unlikely voters. On the day of California's primary, Clinton was able to mobilize enough supporters to call one million California voters.[106] Indeed, the Clinton campaign argued that as voting proceeded, they matched Obama in terms of field organizing and digital media efforts. Yet the Clinton campaign did not open up to supporters in the same way that the Obama campaign did; the data sharing and self-organizing of volunteers was not as advanced.

Resources proved a major challenge for innovating with DCTs in the McCain campaign. Because of the lean financial situation McCain faced once he accepted federal matching money, staff could not build the digital infrastructure that the Obama team did. For example, Rebecca Donatelli, a media consultant for the campaign, had mocked up an iPhone application that would help supporters mobilize friends and report data of voting propensity back to the campaign. She never had the money to commission the application.[107]

Looking back at the 2000 McCain campaign, much of the time it also ran on a shoestring budget, but staff found ways to innovate. By 2008, in the thick of the general election, McCain focused more on traditional, mass-media campaigning, spending precious resources on television ads. Although digital media staff had dreams of cool applications that they wanted to try, they did not contemplate effective but inexpensive ways to innovate with DCTs to mount a super-supporter-driven campaign.

MYBARACKOBAMA: A STUDY IN CONTROLLED OPENNESS

Although the Obama campaign was not immune from the impulse to control the message and the means of organizing in DCTs, relative to the other campaigns it found the magic formula of providing enough openness to foster genuine engagement while directing that engagement in ways ultimately beneficial for the campaign. Obama's candidacy, a challenger candidacy from the start, worked synergistically with DCTs to lead to electoral victory.

Obama announced on February 10, 2007, that he was planning to run for president. From the start the campaign website was oriented to getting supporters involved in the campaign. Obama's much heralded my.BarackObama.com, known by his campaign staff, consultants, and supporters as MyBo (pronounced "My Boh") was a social networking site created internally to help supporters network with each other, advocate for Obama, and organize offline. Rospars was the progenitor of MyBo, taking the lessons he learned on the Dean campaign and channeling the energy and motivation of supporters into concrete activities that advance the candidacy, and in ways that the campaign could monitor.[108]

The difference between MyBo and other organizing tools created by campaigns was the high level of individual customization that supporters had who downloaded the tool. It gave noteworthy control to individuals to organize in ways that suited their interests and levels of commitment. That control extended to the sharing of data, specifically voter rolls, that organizers could access and share with their network of volunteers. In Texas, for example, precinct captains were provided unprecedented access to lists of voters to target and the freedom to decide how to contact them. "The scale of this is not anything anybody's tried before, giving this many people this much control over the campaign" explained Rospars to a reporter for *The National Review*.[109] Ultimately, the platform was used to organize over 35,000 volunteer groups.[110]

The Obama campaign from the start stressed both rhetorically and practically the need to build a community to help launch a movement to elect Obama. His prior experience as a community organizer served as the inspiration to harness DCTs for organizing, according to Rospars.[111] The emphasis on community, captured by the slogan that emerged in 2008, "Yes we can," was supported by the networking tools like MyBo that were established as critical components of the campaign.

The blog was a vital place where community was built. As with the Dean campaign in 2004, the Obama campaign blog became an important place for information updates from the campaign and communing with supporters. Sam Graham-Feisten, a blogger for the campaign who eventually became director of blogging and blog outreach, explained that the campaign saw the blog as a central reason that people came back to the website. As such, it became an important messaging channel to facilitate community and also move people to action. He explained that the campaign was "intensely, obsessively focused on return on investment, on making sure that everything we did had a definitive purpose and was going to absolutely impact the campaign in a positive way. We were not interested in any activities for the sake of 'oh look at this cool, shiny, fun activity.' Everything was about how to make us win."[112]

How to make the campaign win rested on storytelling: about the candidate, about the mission of the campaign, and especially about the supporters. Graham-Feisten explained that their goal was to create a movement, and the prime mover for that was stories. When people told stories of what inspired them to get involved, these would be infectious and bring others into the campaign.[113] He also noted, "We would raise money on the concept of telling stories." He explained:

> People weren't just going to get engaged for no reason. They were getting engaged because they liked Obama. They wanted to be engaged over the long haul. The average donor gave more than twice. We wanted people to have a reason to keep going, and you can't keep going unless inspired. The most inspiring thing is being part of a movement: reading others' stories as a way of inspiring them to tell their own stories.[114]

Thus, the campaign built parasocial interaction,[115] a feeling of connection with the Obama campaign, and fostered community in an effort to inspire supporters to keep giving. That is, the goal of the authentic and inspired stories was to motivate people to open up their wallets (again) and move from casual supporter to activist on behalf of the candidate.

E-mail was another way that staff worked to build that parasocial relationship. Kreiss explained that Rospar's goal was to wrest control of e-mail from the hands of multiple staff and control it entirely, cultivating a carefully constructed image and story that was meted out in e-mail messages with the express purpose of developing a relationship with potential donors and activists for the campaign.[116] He, like other e-mail writers for the presidential campaigns, experimented with more informal, chatty subject lines, such as "hey" and "let's do lunch" from celebrities or from the candidate or Michelle Obama—ways to draw people in and make them feel part of the campaign. Jon Henke, the Internet strategist for Fred Thompson's Republican presidential primary campaign, observed that the practice also was evident on the website: "Other candidates' websites immediately ask you for money. Obama's website builds a relationship with a user before asking for money."[117] Another way the campaign did this was by finding supporters willing to match the contribution of another. Those who agreed were paired up, and why they were donating shared with each other to foster the sense that they were part of a larger movement.

The campaign used social media, like the then small but growing Facebook, to activate two-step flow: targeting supporters and getting them to like Obama's Facebook page, which in turn allowed the campaign to post status updates to the supporter's news feed rendered visible to others in that person's social network. The campaign set up pages on a wide variety of social networking sites, from

AsianAve to LinkedIn. Scott Goodstein, who updated Obama's profiles on those sites, explained, "Some people only go to Myspace. It's where they're on all day. Some only go to LinkedIn. Our goal is to make sure that each supporter online, regardless of where they are, has a connection with Obama."[118]

Like all campaigns, Obama's identified particular demographic groups that were more likely persuadable. They identified women and African Americans as key groups and encouraged super-supporters in those demographic groups to use DCTs to mobilize others. For example, they helped female super-supporters to connect and interact through the blog, to post and cross-post on blogs elsewhere in cyberspace with women readers, and encouraged offline gatherings, such as reading groups and cocktail parties.[119]

Key to their digital success with Democratic voters as compared with Clinton's campaign was that Obama drew younger supporters to his campaign. Obama's image construction of being young and progressive combined with his policy messages about student loan debt and quality education spoke to younger voters. Thus, Obama had an advantage in the digital media space because that is where young voters live. Content analysis of the Facebook pages of Obama and McCain, for example, found substantially more activity by young people on Obama's page.[120] In terms of sheer numbers of "friends," Obama had nearly four times as many as McCain. Thus, young people were accessible to Obama on social media, and in turn the campaign made itself accessible to them. Indeed, to the surprise of the Clinton campaign, Obama turned out 50% more younger voters to caucus for him than the Clinton campaign expected.[121] Obama's Facebook page reached the million marker when Hillary Clinton dropped out of the race in June 2008. MyBo saw a million members in June 2008 as well.[122]

Obama's digital media staff took a long view to organizing super-supporters through digital media. The campaign organized "Camp Obama" in Chicago, a volunteer training camp. Hans Riemer, the national youth vote director, explained to National Public Radio: "We are training them, teaching them how to be effective, showing them what their role is in our strategy to win the election.... We're taking people from raw enthusiasm to capable organizers."[123] The idea was so successful that the Obama campaign took the camps on the road to swing states, recruiting professors, union activists, and religious leaders to host training seminars. These trained volunteers began organizing using the MyBo tools weeks and sometimes months before the official campaign set up shop in the state. This organizing led to the remarkable success the Obama campaign had in caucus states, such as Idaho and Nevada. The strategy of focusing on caucus and small-delegate states while not conceding the big states, meant that although Obama lost the overall popularity contests in some large states, his delegate count remained substantial and eventually beat out Clinton.

Monitoring and tracking of supporters was key to building relationships and then further crafting targeted messaging. One challenge the Dean campaign had in 2004 was tracking potentially interested people because many were organizing on third-party sites, such as MeetUp. As Rospars and the team from BSD began ramping up their DCTs, they recognized the importance of that careful tracking. The campaign engineered events and opportunities for potential supporters to give information about themselves and their friends. The campaign's iPhone application, for example, rearranged the user's contacts by the states that were the highest priority for the campaign. If called, the application had a reporting feature where the supporter could report back information about the call.

Although the Clinton campaign adopted text messaging into strategizing in May 2007, it was the Obama campaign that pushed experimentation with the platform. Establishing a Short Message Service (SMS) a month later, the campaign invited people by e-mail to text-message the campaign with their e-mail address to receive an Obama campaign bumper sticker and also to get updates from the campaign on their cell phone. They could also download campaign ring tones and add wallpaper to their phone in ways that were reminiscent of the experimenting Dole's campaign did in 1996 for computer desktops.

More intriguing than just the media-interactivity of downloading ring tones was the invitation to text questions. Staff promised that questions would be answered by volunteers as soon as possible through SMS. One news report provided an example: if someone sent a text about Iraq, the sender would get a response back that provided the candidate's position ("Barack has been strongly against the war since 2002") and the URL for the website, where specific information was available.[124]

Campaign staff found other ways to collect information from supporters to facilitate further contact. In the week before the start of the Democratic National Convention, the Obama campaign announced that it would text-message the vice-presidential choice to supporters. The goal was to collect additional cell phone numbers that could be used during the general election to mobilize supporters. These efforts had positive benefits. The announcement produced a fair amount of positive earned media for the campaign.[125] Moreover, a study at the University of Michigan found that people who received a text message reminder were 4% more likely to go to the polls.[126] Scott Goodstein, a staff member on the Obama campaign, oversaw text messaging. In an interview with the *New York Times*, he noted that he experimented with text-messaging etiquette, aiming to not be too annoying to recipients of the messages. He also wanted there to be dialogue, so if someone replied to an Obama text message, an automated response came, or a reply from a staff member or volunteer. The messages also encouraged recipients to pass the message on to others.

The Obama campaign also stumbled at times in its efforts to unify and control messaging in social media. In 2007 Myspace was the hot social networking site. Obama had a page created by a volunteer supporter for the campaign, Joe Anthony. The page, which was pointed to by Myspace's own "impact channel," had over 150,000 friends by late spring of 2007. Rospars and Anthony had a good working relationship until the Obama campaign decided it should have complete control over messaging on the page. Anthony in turn requested a consulting fee for his work, and Rospars refused to pay the requested $39,000. Rospars ultimately appealed to Myspace to create an official Obama page. The move triggered a barrage of mostly negative commentary on the blogosphere and in the news about the incident. Rospars wrote an explanation on the blog noting that the campaign was often experimenting and that some ideas work and some do not, "but that's the risk of experimenting."[127] The blog post generated a heavy volume of commentary from visitors. Joe Trippi, Dean's campaign manager in 2004, quipped, "The top-down campaign guys need to learn about working with the bottom-up online community."[128]

The Obama campaign also had a noteworthy technological "fail"—their field organizing/get-out-the-vote effort called Houdini. The idea behind Houdini was to give eligible voters who had been targeted by the Obama campaign a four-digit code. Poll volunteers were to dial in that code to the campaign's headquarters to a hotline to indicate who had voted. This, in turn, was supposed to help the campaign identify who still needed to be contacted to vote on Election Day. The system went down in failure, however, when the hotline jammed early. Alternative means of communicating the codes were implemented, but the system never worked as efficiently as the campaign had hoped. According to the *National Journal*, the campaign still was able to identify 1.6 million voters who had voted, cutting the list canvassers had to work through to get people to the polls by 25%.[129] An *ABC News/Washington Post* poll noted that 28% of likely voters had been contacted by the Obama campaign, compared with 22% of voters who had been contacted by the McCain campaign.[130]

The most noteworthy challenge for the controlled interactivity the campaign established emerged around a policy issue. Obama declared in June 2008 that he would support an update to the Foreign Intelligence Surveillance Act called the Protect America Act of 2007. The update would remove a requirement that communication of a suspected terrorist that began or ended in a foreign country would not need to be supervised by a FISA court, which reviews and oversees electronic surveillance. Also included in the updated legislation was a Bush administration amendment that requested retroactive immunity to telecommunications companies that had worked with the federal government.

Obama supporters who were angry at his position on FISA used the MyBo social networking tools to organize a protest against him. The protest group grew to be the largest on the site. At issue was concern about privacy and infringement of civil liberties. Obama in prior years had supported blocking this legislation. As a candidate, he dropped his objections and said he would support the bill, although he would vote against the amendment for retroactive immunity to telecom companies. This reversal led to a vocal outcry by supporters.

Obama and his staff took their case to the liberal blogosphere and even to the official campaign blog to explain and justify his position. Obama had his policy advisors hold a conversation on the blog to respond to the concerns. More importantly, when opponents to the FISA update began organizing against Obama using MyBo, the campaign issued the following statement: "The campaign has an extraordinary group of committed supporters, and we greatly appreciate their willingness to share their time and ideas with us. We believe that an open dialogue is an important part of any campaign, and we are happy that my.barackobama.com has become a vehicle for that conversation."[131] Rather than shutting down the MyBo group or urging them to move elsewhere, the campaign rhetorically embraced the dissent, expressing a philosophy historically grounded in democratic principles of free speech and public deliberation on policy matters.

Yet the rift opened up a challenge, similar to one that the Dean campaign faced in 2004: having opened up the campaign, supporters wanted greater meaningful investment in it—not just to help organize, but also to collaborate on policy and direction for the campaign. At Netroots Nation in the summer of 2008, Steve Hildebrand, Obama's deputy campaign manager, heard a great deal of dissatisfaction from the netroots. Andrew Rasiej, a Democratic strategist, told Hildebrand that the campaign looked too hierarchical, that although there was a perception of bottom-up organizing, the campaign still aimed for tight message discipline.

In effect, Rasiej was accusing Obama of controlled interactivity. Although the rhetoric of agency and the technologies of mobilization were there, the careful message discipline to supporters was used to establish two-step flow—which ultimately benefits the campaign, though not necessarily the netroots.

Conclusion

The 2008 campaigns experimented with controlled interactivity to focus the energy of their supporters to help get the candidate elected. The Obama campaign is credited with developing the most effective strategies and messaging with DCTs. Other campaigns also deserve credit for appreciating the importance of digital media, even though they were unable to harness them to the same degree. McCain, for example, with his Straight Talk Express and his maverick image, which had generated such enthusiasm in 2000, was ineffective in 2008. Ron Paul's supporters drove DCT use but without direction from the campaign, hurting his candidacy. Clinton was constrained by her front-runner image during the surfacing and first voting states, and the campaign lacked the netroots energy and DCT tactics. As her inevitability gave way to uncertainty, the campaign's footing shifted to that of an insurgency campaign, and new activity and energy grew online. Her digital media staff and their strategizing suggested that they recognized the importance of digital media to electoral victory, though ultimately it was not enough.

Although Barack Obama's campaign is heralded for its digital media innovations, several factors need to be recognized about what made possible his success with DCTs. First, Obama's campaign was an insurgency, which so far has proved to be advantageous in the context of digital media. Insurgency campaigns draw more energy and excitement, which can be nicely translated through DCTs into money, volunteers, and visibility. Second, his message resonated with younger voters, who also were more likely living in digital media spaces. Third, his message of agency and change were integrated well with his digital media strategy. That is, his expressions of a commitment to ordinary citizen involvement in politics, that one person can make a difference, and that we are all obligated in a democracy to participate, were underscored by making available a set of DCT tools to help citizens to be involved in his campaign. Fourth, his financial war chest allowed him to innovate with digital media in ways that others, especially McCain, simply could not. Finally, his campaign benefited from the knowledge and expertise of the staff who ran his digital media team. They were at the forefront of experimenting with interactivity in 2004. They understood the challenges as well as the affordances, and thus sought in 2008 to strike the right balance of controlled interactivity and two-step flow, which helped the candidate achieve electoral success.

6

2012: Data-Driven Networked Campaigning

The prior Internet age elections experimented with digital communication technologies (DCTs) to find the best practices to generate contributions, recruit volunteers, and give tools to self-organize super-supporters through controlled interactivity—identifying those who could be mobilized to become activists and evangelists for the campaign. Thus, 2012 was not about further experimentation; instead it was about refining proven practices combined with the most data-driven presidential campaigns in history. Ultimately, these practices helped fuel Barack Obama's successful re-election campaign.

The 2012 presidential election season continued to exhibit the trends of online strategy and practice that had success in 2008. In that campaign, social media, such as Facebook and Twitter, were relatively nascent, but by 2012 had diffused enough to be vital for online campaigning. Researchers boyd and Ellison define social networking sites as enabling users to build a self-created profile, publicly connect with others through lists of connections, as well as browse the profiles of direct connections and other, indirect connections within that site.[1]

Candidates heavily deployed social media and strategic online ad buys, and used their websites as the cornerstones of their campaign practices in the complex, hybrid media environment that Chadwick describes in *The Hybrid Media System*. The way campaigns announced exhibits the nature of campaigning in this complex media system: Republican Tim Pawlenty announced his candidacy on Facebook, the first candidate ever to do so, combined with an announcement speech in Iowa, and a web video that echoed the message in his announcement speech, all of which was reported on cable news and in print and online newspapers; and when Romney announced his creation of an exploratory committee, he tweeted it, and introduced the hashtag #mitt2012,[2] posted on Facebook, and released a video on his website, www.mittromney.com.

Social media offered additional advantages for campaigns, especially by way of two-step flow: targeting and drawing in energized super-supporters who could then be harnessed to talk up the candidate to friends and coworkers and to organize events and fundraisers on behalf of the campaign. Rebecca Donatelli, digital media strategist for the Bachmann campaign, explained to a *New York Times* reporter: "It is about finding people who can amplify your voice to them. It is the old concept of coalitions made new again."[3] Contemplating the digital media practices of campaigns in 2012 through the lens of actor network theory,[4] what I see is that campaigns used DCTs to interact with supporters in a decidedly scripted way—controlled interactivity seemingly perfected.

Yet for all of that carefully scripted work to structure interactivity to greatest advantage for the candidate, a substantial challenge remains: how to manage messaging in the complex, hybrid media environment where gaffes and opposition discourse can be amplified in ways unintended and with unknown consequences for campaigns.

This chapter details the ways that campaigns further perfected controlled interactivity driven by data analytics. First, this chapter describes the background and context that shaped the 2012 campaign, then details the fundraising efforts and innovations by the candidates. As with prior chapters, a close look is offered about the ways candidates constructed their image through DCTs, as well as how they used DCTs for controlled interactivity for citizen involvement. Finally, this chapter looks at how the campaign organizations were structured and some of the noteworthy challenges they encountered.

Background and Strategic Environment

THE POLITICAL CONTEXT

In 2011, when the presidential campaign season began, the top issue facing the nation was the economy. The Great Recession started officially in December 2007 and continued until June 2009. During that time, the US economy retracted, shedding an estimated 7.9 million jobs by 2010.[5] In addition, the US housing bubble that had been growing since the 1990s burst. It was estimated that at the height of the recession 2.8 million homes were in foreclosure, an increase of 120% from 2007.[6] Many who purchased houses after 2003, especially in high-growth areas, such as Las Vegas, Nevada, and Miami, Florida, were "under water," meaning their homes were worth less than the amount owed on the mortgage. One of the major discussion items in 2010 was the costs and benefits to homeowners of simply "walking away" from their debt and their home.[7] Also of concern was the growing wealth gap in the United States. A study by the Pew

Research Center reported that by 2011 those in the middle income tier of wage earners comprised 51% of all adults. By comparison, in 1971, forty years prior, that percentage was 61%. The wealthiest Americans held 46% of the wealth in 2011, up from 29% in 1971.[8]

In the fall of 2008 a banking crisis surfaced, leading to the collapse of financial services company Lehman Brothers and the bankruptcy or near-collapse of several major banks. At the end of the Bush presidency, Congress passed a substantial federal spending program called the Troubled Asset Relief Program (TARP), which provided $475 billion in federal money to bail out major banks, including Bank of America, Citigroup, and Goldman Sachs, in part by buying their "troubled assets" in an effort to stabilize the banking sector. By 2009, the American auto industry also faced collapse, leading to a controversial bailout of General Motors and Chrysler, and provided substantial loans to Ford and other auto makers.

The economic crisis raised questions by observers within and outside of the United States about the stability and functionality of the US government. Major disagreements surfaced between the political parties and across the two houses of Congress about the role of government in regulating banks and industry. Intense cautions were raised about the financial health of the US government, with its dramatically rising deficit impacting long-term debt. In 2011, the US government owed $14 trillion.[9] As a consequence, fear increased that the government could not sustain such debt and that the world's largest economy could collapse. This fear, among other issues, led to policy gridlock around solutions to respond to the weak economy and high jobless rates. The gridlock eventually reached a crisis point when some Republicans in Congress threatened to prevent raising the federal government's debt limit to prevent further long-term economic damage. The stalemate led to the first ever lowering of the US credit rating by Standard & Poor's from AAA to AA+ in 2011. Standard & Poor's directly credited the instability and ineffectiveness of policymakers to enact sound fiscal policy: "The political brinksmanship of recent months highlights what we see as America's governance and policymaking becoming less stable, less effective, and less predictable than what we previously believed."[10]

Thus, President Obama faced a challenging re-election campaign. Having run in 2008 as the candidate of hope and change who promised to be postpartisan by working with Republicans to find solutions to the nation's troubles, the policy gridlock raised questions about his ability to lead. His public opinion approval ratings through most of 2011 were under 50%, indicating a challenging re-election campaign for the incumbent. Moreover, popular wisdom suggested that incumbent presidents do not get re-elected if unemployment rates are over 8%.[11] Thus, throughout the election, the economy was a major focus of discussion and attack by Republican candidates.

Obama also faced challenges on foreign policy. The United States drew down troops, and Obama officially declared an end of operations in Iraq in December 2011. At the same time, the United States put additional military personnel into Afghanistan. Starting in 2009 and continuing through 2010, the United States in partnership with Afghan forces and NATO increased military troops and combat operations to fight the Taliban. On May 2, 2011, President Obama announced that Osama bin Laden, who had orchestrated the terrorist attacks on the United States in September 2001, was killed in his home in Pakistan by US Special Forces.

Although Obama received credit for this success, he soon faced criticism by civil libertarians for killing American citizens that the government had deemed to be terrorists. In September 2011, a drone attack killed American citizen Anwar Awlaki in Yemen, who was deemed a terrorist and enemy of the United States because of his volatile rhetoric and orchestrated attempt to attack the United States. Civil liberties groups decried the killing as unconstitutional and in violation of international law.

Although Obama faced no primary challengers from Democrats, the Republican Party saw an opportunity to unseat Obama. Thus, the primary season was hotly contested within the Republican Party. Nearly a dozen viable candidates threw their hat in or toyed with the idea of running for the presidency on the Republican ticket, including Congressman Ron Paul, businessman Herman Cain, former Speaker of the House Newt Gingrich, Minnesota governor Tim Pawlenty, former senator Rick Santorum, Congresswoman Michele Bachmann, Texas governor Rick Perry, ambassador to China Jon Huntsman, and former Louisiana governor Buddy Roemer. Many of these candidates had moments in which the news media and pundit class viewed the candidate as a viable front runner, creating a dramatic and unpredictable surfacing stage to the campaign. For example, Rick Perry had a meteoric rise in the polls in the late summer of 2007, then misstatements and a decidedly poor debate performance, in which he declared he would cut three government agencies and then could not name the third one, led to his rapid decline. Herman Cain took Perry's place as potential front runner in the fall of 2007. He gained positive media coverage and increased support in public opinion polls when he performed well in debates combined with an economic policy with the catchy slogan of "9-9-9." Within two months, however, he went from front runner to near bottom of the pack when allegations surfaced that he had been accused of sexual harassment while CEO of the National Restaurant Association.

When voting actually began, the polls predicted that former governor Mitt Romney would be the nominee. Thus, when the Iowa caucuses ended up being a virtual tie, with Romney winning by only eight votes over Rick Santorum (both took 25%), the ground shifted, and suddenly the race seemed much more open. In what Mitt Romney's staff described as the "long slog," Gingrich and Santorum attacked Romney during the next set of voting states. Romney eventually emerged as the nominee, but his candidacy was battered, bruised, and broke.

The Democratic convention gave Obama a boost. Pundits judged the convention a greater success than that of the Republicans. Romney's campaign and the party had a set of missteps when they failed to more carefully script the television prime time coverage of Romney's acceptance speech. Instead of airing a compelling biographical film about Romney during prime time, Clint Eastwood, a political independent who had decided to support Romney in this election, extemporaneously talked to an empty chair meant to represent President Obama. The somewhat surreal and convoluted message from Eastwood shattered the typically carefully controlled show that political party conventions have become, and it failed to give Romney the bump he was hoping for.

The general election campaign was intensely contested, with Romney often behind Obama but only by a small margin nationally and in key swing states. Obama began advertising against Romney in key states in the late spring and throughout the summer. Obama's slogan, "Forward," was meant to capture the idea that better times lay ahead. Early in the fall, a video clip was released on the *Mother Jones* website showing Romney declaring that 47% would not vote for him because they were dependent on government, which caused a frenzy of coverage about Romney's attitude and suitability to lead the nation.

The debates, however, especially the first debate, proved vital for Romney's campaign. Although the challenger typically performs better in it, the consensus was that Obama's performance was so poor he lost moderate and independent votes. He gained some of them back when Colin Powell endorsed him, and Obama, having learned his lesson, was better prepared and held his own during the second two debates.

Hurricane Sandy, which brought massive destruction to the coasts of New Jersey and New York, complicated the last week of campaigning for both candidates: Obama did not personally participate in rallies, and the campaign did not collect the usual data on attendees to rallies; Romney turned his events into fundraisers for Sandy, trying to not appear to be campaigning during a national crisis. New Jersey's Republican governor, Chris Christie, who had stumped heavily for Romney in prior months, stepped off the campaign trail to help his state, and praised the president for being responsive during the crisis—much to Romney's and other Republican's chagrin.

Ohio, the critical swing state, was a point of intense focus by both campaigns, but the auto bailout by the Obama administration helped shore up supporters who might otherwise have gone for Romney. Romney's campaign tried to claim that the bailout was actually shipping jobs to China, a claim that was widely refuted. Digital media played a role in each of these events, which are detailed in the rest of this chapter.

DIGITAL MEDIA

Diffusion of the Internet had been relatively flat since 2008, but Web 2.0 engaged architecture applications had grown. Twitter, though heavily used by some campaign staff, was used by a small percentage of US adults on a regular basis (8% in February 2012), according to Pew Internet & American Life data. More adults reported using a social location service, such as Foursquare (17% in January 2011). YouTube and other video services were much more heavily used; 70% of adults, for example, reported watching a video through a streaming video service in May 2011. By 2012, almost half reported using a social networking site, such as LinkedIn or Facebook. Teddy Goff, the 2012 digital director of the Obama campaign who had also worked on the 2008 campaign, was quoted in *The Atlantic* explaining the role of social media in 2008: "Facebook was about one-tenth of the size that it is now. Twitter was a nothing burger for the campaign. It wasn't a core or even a peripheral part of our strategy" and the my.barackobama.com site borrowed the "my" from Myspace, which by 2008 was becoming a fringe social media channel.[12]

By the 2012 election cycle the Pew Internet & American Life project, the premiere source for surveys of digital media and politics, had begun reporting statistics about registered voters rather than Internet users as it had in past election cycles, indicating how pervasive DCTs had become, with 80% of surveyed adults reporting access to the Internet. Thus, survey results suggested that over half of registered voters watched political videos in the 2012 campaign season, with 36% watching political ads online, and 40% watching recordings of candidate speeches, press conferences, or debates.[13] Thirteen percent of adults reported contributing to a candidate, and of those who did, 10% donated via text message.[14] A remarkable 40% of US adults used social networking sites to engage politically in 2012,[15] and of social media users 38% reported sharing or liking (i.e., clicking a "Like" button) political news and commentary, and 20% reported following politicians on social media, such as Facebook. Yet research found that social media use did not affect participation, at least in terms of attending the Republican Iowa caucuses.[16]

One vital affordance of social media is the potential to activate the networked capabilities of social media. That networking potential magnifies the power of two-step flow in remarkable ways, amplifying messages that might not otherwise gain traction, and creating memes, catchy messages (often in visual form) that spread through networks like a virus, thus leading to the phrase "go viral."

Jenkins, in his book *Convergence Culture*, highlights the potential power of viral messaging to create a kind of shared intelligence in which individuals share pieces of information with others in their social network, leading to collective knowledge that we coproduce. Jenkins explains that messages that go viral are those that are the "right idea" in the "right hands" at the "right time."[17] Viral marketing and convergence culture more broadly are concepts that rely on the practice of two-step flow as described by Katz and Lazarsfeld: finding the opinion leaders and giving them a message that resonates, which they in turn communicate with their social network, to greater effect than the original communicator, such as an advertiser, could hope to achieve.[18]

Users of Twitter and Facebook can dynamically manifest two-step flow, especially when combined with links to video sites like YouTube or photo sites like Instagram. Political campaigns in 2012 honed their practices of targeting and mobilizing supporters to engage in two-step flow for the campaign via these communication channels. For example, Teddy Goff, Obama campaign digital director, explained to the *New York Times* the power of Twitter: It "has changed the whole way that politics works. Not just the press element, but the organizing element and the fund-raising element and the relationship building that all campaigns try to do."[19] Because journalists and political elites are heavy Twitter users, campaigns tried to amplify their message by tweeting about it or encouraging supporters to tweet about events or attacks on opponents so as to make a message "trend"—get the attention of journalists and lead to an earned media story, or catch the attention of friends in the network, thereby driving traffic to the website.

Perfecting the Art of Fundraising

Three important shifts happened in 2012 to further push the creative edge of fundraising through DCTs. The first shift was a legal change. In June 2012, as the general election campaign was commencing, the Federal Election Commission allowed contributions by text message. People could text a word, phrase, or number, for example, to the Obama campaign's Short Message Service (SMS) (e.g., 62262, which stood for Obama), and the person would pay for the contribution through a monthly cell phone charge, up to $50. Both general election presidential campaigns deployed contributions by text message. Jim Messina, Obama's campaign manager, explained that "accepting small donations by text message will help us engage even more grassroots supporters who want to play a role by donating whatever they can afford to the campaign."[20]

The second change was an operational shift. Campaigns gave supporters the option to securely store their credit card information. In doing so the supporter could contribute subsequently with one click rather than having to re-enter credit card information. This led to a breakthrough in giving for the campaigns. The one-click donation mechanism, according to news reports, brought in an additional $115 million for the Obama campaign, almost three times what would have come in otherwise according to testing the campaign conducted.[21] This operational change meant that the small, repeat-donor paradigm of contributing was further institutionalized in the ways campaigns fundraised.

The third shift was a technological innovation. Jack Dorsey, the co-creator of Twitter, invented a small credit card reader that could be used with a smart phone enabling easy credit card contributions. Campaigns used the small device and application, called Square at large campaign events organized by the campaign as well as smaller events hosted by supporters. The Romney campaign even gave away Square credit card readers at the Republican National Convention with the hope that people would use them to raise money for Romney.

These innovations, in addition to the data modeling campaigns did to target particular people with specific messages to further produce contributions, led to a record-breaking billion-dollar campaign. According to *Business Week*, the Obama campaign raised $190 million more than in 2008 online.[22] Zac Moffatt, Romney's digital director, reported that the campaign, combined with the Republican National Committee, brought in $65 million in October 2012, the most ever raised for a Republican via DCTs.[23]

Crafting Image in the Age of Social Media

The cadre of Republican primary candidates used DCTs in creative and constructive ways. The greater prevalence of social media, in terms of sheer number of applications as well as the broader diffusion of social media in the lives of ordinary Americans, opened up new opportunities and new challenges for the candidates to make their name, construct their image, and deconstruct their opponents. The Obama and Romney general election campaigns harnessed social media, especially YouTube and Twitter, to hone their image and respond to the tactics of their rival.

IMAGE CONSTRUCTION OF THE ALSO-RANS

Of the Republican primary candidates, two in particular crafted an image as cutting-edge candidates by their heavy use of DCTs: Tim Pawlenty and Newt Gingrich. Pawlenty, known affectionately as T-Paw, established a digital media infrastructure that brought in some of the Republican's top digital media talent. The candidate announced his campaign on Facebook and heavily used a YouTube channel to increase what Patrick Ruffini, his digital media consultant, described as "buzz."[24] The hope was that the buzz on social media would lead to earned coverage in mainstream media as well as sign-ups on the website to volunteer and to contribute. The website design was also novel in that it pushed gamification of online organizing through points and badges. For example, a supporter got ten points for downloading the Pawlenty Facebook application. Ruffini noted that Pawlenty himself was a retail politics sort of candidate, meaning that he liked to and believed in a heavy volume of in-person and small-group conversations with voters, and saw social media as an extension of it.

Gingrich's declaration as the Internet candidate arose out of need. In June 2011 his campaign manager and several top-level staff quit, and the Twitter-verse exploded with the buzz. Gingrich issued a statement via Facebook to assure supporters and to declare to the media that his campaign would continue. He spent heavily on his Internet presence, over $800,000 to launch a new website in the summer of 2011. In public encounters with the press following the shakeup of his campaign, he emphasized that he was running a lean, Internet-based campaign that would be effective at propelling his campaign into the primaries.

Other also-rans used DCTs to help craft their image while responding to the attacks of others, but did not construct themselves as cutting-edge, Internet candidates. Instead they found ways to leverage DCTs to build name recognition and spread viral messaging to capture new attention and support.

In 2008 Ron Paul found himself portrayed as a candidate with a savvy Internet presence primarily because of the energy of his supporters more than something his campaign initially nurtured. By 2012 staff worked to capitalize on Paulites' energy online. For example, when Paul was ahead of other candidates in November polls on the Iowa caucus, his campaign produced an attack ad, "Serial Hypocrisy," against Gingrich that circulated widely through conservative e-mail lists and websites. A second web ad called "Selling Access" attacked Gingrich for his employment as a consultant to industry lobbying groups. These ads were intended to knock Gingrich out of his second place position in polls.

For cash-strapped campaigns, like that of John Huntsman, YouTube was a beneficial way to inexpensively create videos that would be viewed by supporters and, hopefully, shared with others, while also garnering coveted earned media coverage. In Huntsman's case, his YouTube videos were meant to help attract younger voters who were more likely to be sympathetic to his moderate Republican views than those of his rivals. The videos, described as "oddball" in one news report, included one of Huntsman on a dirt bike wearing motocross gear.[25]

Some campaigns used DCTs to generate excitement and fun by playing up a candidate's personality or quirks. Rick Santorum's penchant for sweater vests led to an account for the vest on Twitter: @fearricksvest. The profile read: "I'm @RickSantorum's sweater vest. I've heard Rick say 'sleeves just slow me down!'

Fear me ... and ... hear me! I'm ready to relocate to the White House." A YouTube video was created: "Sleeves Slow Me Down." A website, www.fearricksvest.com, redirected to a Facebook page in support of Santorum. The campaign even sold sweater vests on the Santorum website, generated 100,000 in sales, and $1 million in contributions.[26]

Sometimes attempts at message construction online were less successful. Herman Cain, soon after announcing his 999 tax plan, purchased time on the Rush Limbaugh show for a radio advertisement to air in all Limbaugh's media markets. His campaign also promised a new website: www.999meansjobs.com. The tax plan message was swamped, though, by a controversial video his campaign manager created and posted on YouTube that went viral and garnered substantial, though not necessarily desirable, earned media coverage. The video was meant to energize and mobilize supporters of Cain, but the video featured the manager at the end slowly smoking a cigarette with a message that the Cain campaign will not play by Washington's rules. It generated heavy cable news coverage and was generally read as "bizarre" by political pundits,[27] but it brought in over $3 million in contributions. Huntsman's campaign, seeing an opportunity, capitalized on the notoriety of the Cain video. Huntsman's three oldest daughters, who were heavy Twitter users, created a parody video including fake mustaches, dead-pan stares, and ended with them blowing bubbles. Their parody video in turn generated news coverage and increased visibility for Huntsman.

Rick Perry suffered a similar parody response to his effort at positive image and policy construction. His campaign created a TV and web ad, "Strong," that emphasized Perry's Christian conservatism. In the video he wears a brown work jacket favored by cowboys and stands in a treed field. He explains his Christian values and highlights what he saw as an irony that gays can now serve in the military but children cannot celebrate Christmas or pray in school. The heavily viewed ad was more disliked than liked, according to the buttons viewers clicked, and it generated several web video parodies. One featured Andy Cobb, a political satirist, who explained that he was not ashamed to be an atheist and that there is something wrong with the country if it's "okay to hate on gays and nonbelievers in ads." Some videos highlighted the apparent irony in the Perry ad that the jacket he wore was also the type featured by the characters in the love affair of two male cowboys in the movie *Brokeback Mountain*.

The examples of Cain's and Perry's YouTube "fails" highlight the core tension that candidates have with DCTs: They aim to control the message and control their image by limiting the chances that others can use what they have said against them, while also hoping to use DCTs against others. Yet the interactivity of digital media opens up new interpretations and productions that shift or undermine the candidate's original message. The collective intelligence that

Jenkins writes about can be used to great effect in the political process but in ways that cause consternation for political campaign staff and candidates.[28]

Campaigns struggled in other ways with the complex digital communication environment. Rick Santorum had an especially troubling challenge with Google's search engine. The trouble dated back to 2003 when Santorum explained his opposition to gay marriage, telling the Associated Press that he didn't support gay marriage in the same way he did not support "man on child, man on dog, or whatever the case may be."[29] In 2011 Dan Savage, an editor of Seattle's alternative newspaper, *The Stranger*, created a web page that defined Santorum as the "frothy mixture of lube and fecal matter that is sometimes the by-product of anal sex." The site was heavily linked to by others, which influenced Google's algorithm such that a search on Santorum's name brought up Savage's definition in the top ten search results.[30] Santorum had little recourse for downgrading the search results or pulling Savage's website. The site itself is protected on free speech grounds, and Google's algorithm is a proprietary corporate product that Santorum could not change to remove Savage's site from the search. The complex legal and messaging environment makes message control deeply challenging for campaigns.

Yet, while full message control is impossible, campaigns can use DCTs to manage the chaos by redirecting or changing the messaging in ways that can give the campaign some advantage or at least stem the damage. For example, Perry found himself during a November debate unable to list the third of three agencies he would cut. Not only did journalists report on the gaffe during the debate, they also reported a variety of harsh as well as funny tweets. Perry, in turn, used humor to try to minimize the gaffe he had made. On his website, for example, the campaign invited visitors to e-mail the campaign what federal agency they would like to forget and to email their suggestions to forget-menot@rickperry.org.

Campaigns had the digital affordance of speed at their disposal as a vital way to control the chaos. That is, because DCTs tend to allow communication in real time, campaigns could quickly respond to events in an effort to curtail damage, change the subject, or exploit the event to generate supporters. Cain's campaign, for example, was derailed from his tax message after allegations surfaced of sexual harassment and affairs while running Godfather Pizza and serving with the National Restaurant Association. When one of the accusers came forward, Cain quickly responded to her public allegations by encouraging contributions to his campaign. One of Cain's staff tweeted: "Welcome to the campaign, Gloria Allred [the accuser's attorney]. What took you so long? #Iowafund" and then posted a URL to a website for supporters to give money. A URL link sent people to a CainTruth website that provided a rebuttal to the accusations. Cain's new media director, Michael Johnson, explained, "It is always important to control the message and when there is so much noise online, it is important for us to get in front of it and put our message out there."[31] The campaign paid for ads on Google to return paid search results if people searched for Cain or the accusers. Similarly, the campaign paid for a Twitter advertisement so that if anyone searched for Cain, they got a Twitter message with a disclaimer saying, "Sadly we've seen this movie played out before. Mr. Cain and all Americans deserve better."

Attacking opponents has been done effectively in stump speeches and videos, and in 2012 Twitter became another advantageous channel for lodging attacks. The Romney campaign, for example, used Twitter as a medium of attack against rivals in the primaries, pushing catchy one-line or one-phrase hashtags meant to define the opponents' image. Newt Gingrich, for example, in a Republican primary debate in January talked of having "grandiose ideas." The Romney campaign then started a hash tag #grandiosenewt for illustrious quips of Gingrich's grandiosity, which began to trend on Twitter. Journalists and bloggers, in turn, wrote about it. A *New York Times* reporter described the tactic and its effect this way: "for at least one news cycle, the Romney campaign had stamped a virtual 'grandiose' on Mr. Gingrich's forehead."[32] Thus, campaigns found ingenious ways by 2012 of driving their message home while also attempting to control the chaos of the hybrid media environment.

ONLY DIGITAL: BUDDY ROEMER

Buddy Roemer's candidacy is an intriguing contrast with a candidate like Obama in 2008 or Howard Dean in 2004 because of his efforts to use the Internet to advance his candidacy. Roemer, a former Republican governor of Louisiana and a war veteran, had the credentials to run a credible campaign. Yet, his signature issue, campaign finance reform, positioned him against much of his party. To demonstrate his commitment to ruling out untoward influence of contributors on his campaign, he capped contributions at $100. Without the ability to raise large sums of money, he fell behind other candidates in the surfacing stage. According to Roemer's campaign manager, Carlos Sierra, journalists viewed Roemer as a one-issue candidate who was running simply to make a point about the corrupting influence of money in politics, but Sierra insisted that Roemer was running as a serious challenger against the other Republican candidates.[33]

Campaign staff bet on DCTs as the way they would build support and talk directly to supporters. Roemer was a prolific Twitter user, sending out witty and self-deprecating tweets. He declared in October: "Twitter epitomizes all that is right in America: transparency, dialogue, and an open forum for citizen debate. God bless social media."[34] His campaign website featured Twitter on the front page, inviting supporters to donate one tweet a day to allow the campaign to tweet a message to their networks of followers. This enabled the campaign to reach over 50,000 people.[35] The campaign also hired a staff member from the Twitter strategy and research firm 140elect to manage and tweet through the Roemer campaign Twitter account. Overall, in the primaries, he was the most prolific Republican tweeter.[36] By December 2011, he was the second most retweeted Republican candidate behind Newt Gingrich, another prolific tweeter.[37] Although Roemer was frozen out of all the debates, he held his own debate commentary via Twitter.

Not only did the campaign heavily deploy Twitter, but also their advertising strategy focused on ad buys via Facebook, especially targeting voters in New Hampshire. It heavily relied on YouTube as well to create and disseminate video messages of the campaign. The URL of the website was also broadly disseminated to try and draw people into Roemer's biography and policy positions.

Yet for all that energy on digital media, Roemer's campaign essentially went nowhere. On numbers of followers on Twitter, for example, his were only greater in number than John Huntsman's, who also trailed the other Republicans. Roemer's campaign blamed the news media for completely shutting him out of earned media and the debates, and no matter how much energy the campaign put into generating name recognition and awareness for the candidate through DCTs, it was not enough to launch the campaign.

BELIEVE IN AMERICA: ROMNEY'S VISION

The Romney campaign developed a strategy that aimed to seamlessly integrate DCTs and offline messaging to portray him as a successful, savvy businessman, who through his deep corporate experience would correct the nation's weak economy and put more people to work by stimulating business (See Figure 6.1). Strategically, Obama was most vulnerable on the issue of the economy, and so Romney pushed on that issue throughout the campaign and through all communication channels.

The campaign also aimed to be nimble and responsive to events as they unfolded. For example, when Obama, during a speech in July 2012, explained that "if you were successful, then somebody along the line gave you some help....somebody helped to create this unbelievable American system that we have that allowed you to thrive. Somebody invested in roads and bridges and if you've got a business, well you didn't build that, somebody else made that happen." The Romney campaign pounced on the "you didn't build that" phrase, which taken out of context suggested that Obama dismissed the hard work of business owners. Staff quickly crafted a messaging campaign, with TV ads, a series of web videos, T-shirts, signs, and made it the Republican National Convention theme to attack Obama for not giving business owners credit for

Figure 6.1 Mitt Romney's website

their hard work. The campaign also built an attack website, Obama Isn't Working, that highlighted the ways he failed to grow the economy (See Figure 6.2).

Like the other campaigns, Romney also heavily used web videos to craft his image, hoping that some would go viral. In a well-orchestrated campaign to highlight the economic failures of the Obama administration, Romney created YouTube videos that were meant to reverberate across the complex hypermedia environment that Chadwick describes as the complex interweaving of digital and traditional media.[38] Romney's contrastive "Believe in America" YouTube video, for example, was uploaded before the primaries, and was replayed in New Hampshire on TV news shows and talked about in the blogosphere, on cable news shows, and written about in newspapers and digital news outlets. The message of the ad declared that Obama had failed to steward the economy out of recession and that Romney had a plan for job growth and a balanced economy. Although only 130,000 views of the video happened on Romney's YouTube page by the New Hampshire primary, it disseminated much wider than those 130,000 views and helped spread the Romney economic message.

The Romney campaign used the DCT affordance of speed to advance the message that he had better policy positions for American women. When an Obama campaign advisor, Hilary Rosen, commented that Ann Romney, Mitt

Figure 6.2 The Romney campaign's attack site Obama Isn't Working

Romney's wife, had never worked a day in her life, the Romney campaign had Ann respond on Facebook and Twitter. She tweeted, "I made a choice to stay home and raise five boys. Believe me, it was hard work." Her Twitter account and Facebook page blossomed with supporters. The campaign also created a "Moms for Mitt" Facebook page that attracted over 80,000 followers in a matter of a few weeks, as well as a moms4mitt.com website. The campaign also capitalized on Ann's popularity by putting up a board for her on Pinterest, the social picture sharing site that is used heavily by women. Zac Moffatt, Romney's digital media strategist, described it as a way to touch voters and keep the Romney campaign in their line of sight.[39] The messages disseminated through these channels were crafted to convey two messages: that Mitt Romney was a nurturing and fun father and husband, and that his policies and leadership would be better for moms in the United States.

Yet, for the work they did on that message, it was not enough to inoculate voters on a theme the Democrats were hitting Republicans with: that Republicans were engaging in a "war on women" by trying to curtail access to contraception, abortion, and pulling back on policies aimed to protect women in the workplace and at home. For example, in August 2012, Todd Aiken, running for a House seat in Missouri, said that women who were victims of "legitimate rape" rarely get pregnant. Earlier in the year, a prominent supporter of Rick Santorum was interviewed on MSNBC and said that in his day women put "aspirin between their knees" as contraception. These clips were posted on YouTube, tweeted about, and talked about at length in the blogosphere.

With that as a backdrop, Romney ran into trouble with a statement he made during the second presidential debate. He discussed the work he undertook when elected governor of Massachusetts to promote women into positions of leadership in his administration. He noted that he asked women's groups to help him balance his cabinet, and that they provided him "binders full of women." Within seconds of the statement, Twitter was alight with commentary and quips about the phrase, and it became an instantaneous web meme. Tumblr, Facebook, and a website all featured "Binders full of Women." Humorous reviews on Amazon. com even appeared. One review for three-ring binders read:

> As an intern on the Romney 2012 election campaign, I was tasked with procuring binders for Governor Romney. While these binders are well made, attractive and reasonably priced, and while I'm sure they would make an excellent choice for those wishing to store written or printed documentation in a secure and easily accessible manner, they are unfortunately too small to put women in.

The campaign had little by way of response other than to try and redirect the message back to economy, jobs, and taxes.

Yet as much as the campaign seemed to master DCTs as part of messaging, fundraising, and organizing, there were moments when the challenges of building a digital campaign in a few months showed. A headline on the Huffington Post highlighted three typographical errors on Romney's social media messages in a week, including the widely ridiculed misspelling of America in "A Better Amercia" as part of the "I'm with Mitt" application.[40] The website at times seemed to be in process rather than finished, with the bottom half of the website on one morning in October 2012 simply filled with boxes and white space but no text. It stayed that way almost a day before pictures and text appeared, yet seemingly clickable text had no hyperlinks to "read more." The evening of the first debate, the Romney campaign featured a debate watch, which at times was slow to load, the servers strained by so many page views. After Romney's noteworthy success following the first debate, no mention of the debate was featured on the home page of the website. An online campaign director of a Senate candidate anonymously told a *Politico* reporter that the Romney digital strategy was "not a disaster, but it's all so average and they're going up against Mickey Mantle [referring to Obama]."[41]

As an illustration of the challenges the candidates faced in trying to control the message in the age of inexpensive digital video recording equipment, Romney's campaign was wounded in September 2012 when a video surfaced of him delivering a controversial statement at a May 17 $50,000 a plate fundraiser at the home of a private equity manager. Romney was asked how he would win, and he explained:

There are 47 percent of the people who will vote for the president no matter what. All right, there are 47 percent who are with him, who are dependent upon government, who believe that they are victims, who believe the government has a responsibility to care for them, who believe that they are entitled to health care, to food, to housing, to you-name-it. That that's [sic] an entitlement. And the government should give it to them. And they will vote for this president no matter what... These are people who pay no income tax.[42]

The video of Romney's statement was secretly recorded by a woman identified by *Mother Jones* magazine as Ann Onymous, who had reportedly taken the video because "I saw Romney as dangerous and felt it was my duty to expose him."[43] *Mother Jones* released the video on its website, just as the general election was ramping up. It received massive news media, blogger, and Twitter attention in the weeks afterward. *Mother Jones's* article was tweeted directly from its site over 76,000 times and liked more than 188,000 times. The message was so pervasive that Pew Research found that 67% of registered voters correctly identified Romney as being responsible for the statement, and half of those had a negative reaction.[44] Just as the Obama campaign faced in 2008 a controversial, unauthorized video taken at fundraising events, so too did Romney suffer the same challenge.

FORWARD: INCUMBENT OBAMA'S IMAGE CONSTRUCTION

When Obama ran in 2008, he was the challenger, giving his campaign license to experiment. He was able to generate enthusiasm through a message of change that resonated with voters. In 2012, as the incumbent, the excitement was not palpable; it had to be actively manufactured by the campaign. Given the tough economic situation the country and thus his supporters still were in, Obama had to make a case for why he should be re-elected for another four years. He also recognized that he had lost voters who had supported him in 2008.[45]

His campaign focused on social media as the mechanism through which to generate that enthusiasm. When Obama announced, not only did he do the usual announcement video, relaunched website, and Twitter announcement, the campaign also created an "Are you in?" application that connected people through their Facebook friends to other Obama supporters (and also hijacked the news feed to share the announcement on the Facebook update of those who installed the app). Obama held a town hall meeting with Facebook creator Mark Zuckerberg at Facebook's headquarters and invited supporters to watch a live-stream video of Obama taking questions from viewers. This simultaneous launch online and offline, with the heavy emphasis on social media, served as a harbinger of the Obama campaign's approach to the 2012 election.

Figure 6.3   Obama's campaign website

The campaign also worked to manufacture enthusiasm and bring people back to the campaign through transactional politics. This was done through classic promotions: people were invited to give their e-mail address in exchange for an Obama bumper sticker. If they gave money, they could be entered into a drawing for a chance to win dinner with the Obamas or a night out with a celebratory. One successful promotion was a chance to meet actor George Clooney, an ardent Obama supporter (See Figure 6.3). Data analysts working for the campaign found that it was remarkably successful at driving women in the forty- to forty-nine-year-old demographic to open up their pocketbooks.[46]

The campaign illustrated the benefits of Obama's policies during his first term through an infovideo on the campaign website that featured the life of "Julia." From toddler to senior citizen, the video highlighted how Obama's policies positively affected Julia's life, and illustrated how Romney's policies would have hurt her. The video was meant to encapsulate some of the policies passed during his first term, especially the Affordable Care Act, Obama's signature healthcare legislation, many provisions of which were not set to take effect until 2014. It also was meant to argue against Romney's claims that his administration would be better for women.

Republicans pounced on the Julia infovideo, using the social media affordances of speed and amplification to counterattack. On Twitter the #Julia hashtag was rife with negative quips attacking the president and his policies after the RNC e-mailed supporters urging them to counter the Julia video. Twitter comments, such as "Who the hell is Julia, and why am I paying for her whole life," were replete. Republicans highlighted that the Julia video exemplified what was wrong with the Obama administration and Democrats generally, referring to government as the "nanny" state, or more relevant for this video, the "hubby" state (since Julia seemed not to have a husband, but the government was there to help every step of the way).

The Obama website home page was changed in noteworthy ways for major campaign events, such as the conventions, the debates, and Election Day. Around the debates, the home page featured live fact-checking via Twitter that scrolled on the home page. On Election Day, a live blog updated information about polling places, GOTV (get out the vote) efforts, and the like. The main link at the top of the page was to confirm one's polling place or to "do something" to help the election. The site also featured a fact-check page highlighting Romney and his running mate, Paul Ryan, as the "Go Back" team, versus the Obama slogan of "Forward." It also listed about sixteen issues and critiqued Romney's plans on those issues (education, healthcare, foreign policy, etc.). All of this was shared via social media.

The campaign used DCTs and mass media to underscore a line of argument about Romney meant to undermine his claim that he had the knowledge and experience to get the economy moving again. The Obama campaign created an attack website called Romney Economics (www.romneyeconomics.com) that argued that Bain Capital, a venture capital firm of which Romney had been senior executive, had closed US companies, shifted jobs overseas, and made money for a handful of private investors. In addition to the launch of the website, the campaign purchased airtime around news broadcasts for a two-minute slot to show an ad that highlighted Bain Capital shutting down a steel mill in Kansas City, Missouri. The ad featured unemployed workers, one who called Bain a vampire that had sucked the life out of the employees at the mill. Romney's campaign countered with a web and TV ad that provided a counterstory of a steel mill that Bain saved, and other success stories, like Staples.

The major Obama campaign misstep was his performance in the first debate. The campaign was at a loss how to respond initially to Obama's poor performance, which notably shifted the dynamics of the race with undecided voters finding Romney more likable and presidential. The Obama campaign aimed to shift the commentary about the debate. They latched onto a comment Romney made that he would cut the federal deficit in a number of ways, including cutting funding for public broadcasting. Romney said "I'm sorry Jim. I'm gonna stop the subsidy to PBS. I'm gonna stop other things. I like PBS. I like Big Bird." Within seconds of the statement, someone created a Twitter account called @FireBigBird that gathered nearly 10,000 followers within twenty-four hours. The campaign pushed the message that Romney wanted to fire Big Bird, with Obama integrating an attack line about it in his stump speech. Firing Big Bird quickly became an Internet meme, such as a doctored family photo of the Romney family in front of the family car with Big Bird tied to the top of the vehicle like a dead deer. The kerfuffle was covered on cable and in print.

Thus, candidates in 2012 were faced with a complex, hybrid media environment in which convergence culture had taken full root. In this context, the carefully crafted image construction was launched typically on multiple channels simultaneously in an effort to get the message amplified well beyond the reaches of any single communication channel, to further manifest two-step flow. At the same time, ordinary citizens and political elites could take those carefully crafted images and turn them upside down, shifting them into parodies and then pushing them back through they hybrid media system to echo across the nation. For campaigns, image construction became a task of trying to stay ahead, stay nimble to respond to what might come, and find clever ways to beat the competition. Sometimes it worked; sometimes it did not.

Controlled Interactivity Finely Tuned

The 2012 campaign is a study in how campaigns structured their digital media to channel supporters in ways most conducive to the campaign. Both Romney and Obama faced a challenge in this election, in that neither had the level of enthusiasm and energy of a motivated base. Obama, as the incumbent who also tended to lead in head-to-head polls with Romney, had to focus on energizing supporters and keeping them motivated. Romney, as the challenger, had necessarily more grassroots and organic energy behind his campaign; however, he faced a challenge with the base of his party. Through the surfacing and primary stage of the campaign, he was viewed by the more conservative base as too liberal. He was attacked by Gingrich and Santorum in the primaries as advocating universal healthcare while governor of Massachusetts, and seemed to change positions on abortion and tax policy. Gingrich attacked him for having Swiss bank accounts, and challenged Romney to explain his business practices as a venture capitalist. Those attacks echoed during the general election and dampened enthusiasm for a Romney candidacy among potential super-supporters.

SOCIAL MEDIA IN 2012

The two campaigns' answer to the challenge was the same: social media. They recognized the interconnected media environment and worked to stimulate particular perspectives while also managing the messaging environment from others by aiming for effective ways to shift the narrative or focus it to the advantage of the campaign: what gets tweeted makes its way into earned media stories, which creates user-generated content in the form of a mash-up video, which leads to a fundraising push by the campaign.

In terms of overall effectiveness, the Obama campaign had an advantage in that it already possessed a truly massive social network of people online who could be reactivated as campaigning began. By 2012, it was estimated that the Obama campaign's 34 million Facebook supporters were networked with over 95% of the entire US Facebook community.[47] The campaign used it heavily in the days before and the day of the general election. The staff built a Facebook application that supporters could use. The tool allowed the campaign to identify friends to target, perhaps because they were in a swing state, and then highlighted those friends to Obama supporters and encouraged them to remind those friends to vote. The campaign reported that it reached over 5 million voters in the twenty-nine-and-under age bracket through Facebook[48]—a group that is notoriously hard to contact by phone and so are hard to mobilize. Teddy Goff, a digital staff member for the Obama campaign, described the direct message tool for Facebook as "the most significant new addition to the voter contact arsenal that's come around in years, since the phone call."[49] According to a Pew Internet & American Life study, 30% of registered voters reported that they encouraged friends to vote for Barack Obama. By contrast only 20% of Romney supporters reported the same.[50]

The Obama campaign set up its YouTube page so that organizing could be done directly from the campaign's YouTube landing site. Viewers of a video could send it to their Facebook timeline, and they could also click to donate money or volunteer with the campaign. Stephen Muller, Obama's campaign video director, explained to the New York Times, "One of the biggest challenges with YouTube is giving people a clear action to take after viewing. The goal is to bring our engagement tools to our supporters."[51] The campaign put together a seventeen-minute video called "The Road We've Traveled," which highlighted the challenges that the Obama administration faced immediately after winning office, as the economy collapsed. Tom Hanks narrated the film, which was directed by David Guggenheim, director of Al Gore's climate change movie An Inconvenient Truth, among many other political films. The YouTube video was viewed over 2 million times by the end of the campaign.

It would be a mistake to think the Romney campaign was not aiming for similar results through social media. The Romney campaign, for example, used YouTube in the same ways as the Obama campaign. Moffatt understood that online video was a key messaging channel. He explained that "TV is a kind of a shotgun approach" but with online ads "you're not just blasting it out there and hoping people pay attention."[52] Indeed, research of viewing habits in 2012 suggested that 40% of likely voters preferred to watch TV shows through alternative sources, such as the Interne or digital video recordings (DVR). The same study also found that smartphones were now being used by over half of eligible voters in 2012.[53] Thus, Moffatt's strategy was to record short videos and then tweet and post on Facebook links to them to get talking points to the most mobilized people to effectively work on behalf of Romney offline.

The Romney campaign also created a "Commit to Mitt" application via Facebook. It worked similarly to the application the Obama campaign had built, posting news in the network of friends of a supporter. The application encouraged supporters to privately message or publicly post to friends' timelines the Commit to Mitt application. In one of the many challenges for the campaign on Election Day, it was reported that the application, which was intended to encourage supporters to remind their network of friends to vote, did not function.[54]

Twitter was also a focus for the campaign, as much for monitoring what seemed to be happening out in the broad public as for disseminating messages to rapidly respond to events that unfolded. Summarizing the power of Twitter for campaigns, Moffatt described it as "a leading indicator of what people are thinking about. It's almost like an early warning signal: 'This is what someone's thinking.' "[55] Indeed, during the presidential debates, for example, the campaigns intently followed Twitter looking for signs that their candidate was doing well or poorly. In some ways, Twitter served as a focus group of sorts, letting campaigns float messages to see what resonated, especially with their base.

Romney capitalized on the natural excitement and publicity around the vice-presidential pick through social media. The Mitt VP Facebook app alerted supporters to Romney's pick. The campaign also invited supporters to sign up to receive a cell phone text message about the announcement. The app drove over 2 million people to the website, and 40% through mobile phones.[56] Yet the smartphone app didn't require people to supply personal information of those who subscribed. Moffatt explained that the purpose of the app was to serve as an alternative communication channel to supporters: "We thought it was more important for us that it was a different way for a distribution system. For us, it was an entry point for us to get as many people to download the app as possible. We needed some catalyst."[57] Yet, in a misstep around the VP announcement, the campaign website was slow to reflect the addition of Ryan on the ticket.

Similar to Obama's Dashboard, the Romney campaign had a get-involved tool for people to access voter lists and make phone calls from home. The website also had a fairly elaborate fundraising campaign site, in which supporters could login to the system using their Facebook or Twitter account or by providing their contact information. The MyMitt Member Account allowed subscribers to invite friends, go shopping for Mitt Gear, make calls, and directly donate. Ambitious supporters could create a fundraiser by naming it, set a monetary goal, personalize the page, set an address, and then invite their friends and others via social media or e-mail to attend the fundraiser (similar to an Evite for campaign fundraising).

Yet for all the efforts on behalf of Romney, in terms of sheer volume of liking, friending, and following on social media, Obama had Romney beat. Romney had 12 million Facebook followers, compared with Obama's 34 million, for example. Although the Obama campaign had more followers, in overall activity on Facebook the Romney campaign had parity. Although the Obama Facebook page had more likes, for example, around the Affordable Care Act debate, Moffatt said, "Well, OK, they've got 27.4 million people on Facebook, and we've got 2.6 million people on Facebook. But you look at healthcare; we had 494,000 engagements on healthcare and they had 464,000. So 1.7% of their list thought it was important enough to engage, but 23% of our list did. What's more important, the engagement number or the vanity number? For us, it's engagement every single time, and we're seeing that not just online but offline."[58]

DATA ANALYTICS IN 2012

Both campaigns had a second answer to the challenge of mobilizing their supporters: data analytics. On this front, Obama's campaign had the bigger advantage; they had the "megafile," their massive database of supporters. It was designed as part of project Narwhal, meant to be the white whale of all combined voter and online files. It was built in the time between the two presidential campaigns. The purpose of Narwhal was to solve one of the challenges the Obama campaign's online and field operations faced in 2008, which was the myriad of databases that staff accessed to target potential voters and run analytics.[59] This single, merged datafile could be interfaced by campaign staff to run analyses and pull relevant data about voters to create targeted e-mail messages of weak Obama supporters or walk lists for volunteers in a suburb of Dayton, Ohio. In an article on Slate, for example, reporter Sasha Issenberg profiled a young woman in Ohio who had given the Obama campaign her e-mail address and zip code in 2008 to sign up to receive e-mail updates from the campaign.[60] Through the 2008 election, she received requests to contribute and get involved, but nothing that seemed particularly targeted to her. In January 2012 she received another e-mail, this time asking her to consider the Affordable Care Act's rule requiring full coverage of contraception by insurance companies. The voter remembered being surprised by the e-mail. Its message resonated with her, but she doubted that it would resonate with others in her zip code who likely had more conservative views. That e-mail message had found its intended target thanks to Narwhal. For the Obama campaign, many of the messages that were sent and decisions made about spending were done based on data.

Eventually, Narwhal was used to channel data to volunteers for phone calling and organizing in support of the team-centric approach that was the hallmark of the organizing philosophy of the Obama campaign this election cycle.[61] This was done through an application called Dashboard, which was released in the summer of 2012 as a field organizing tool to help local organizers be more effective and coordinated with the campaign. Dashboard was a homegrown tool that enabled the kind of self-organizing that campaigns since 2000 had been striving for. The tool allowed people to easily find others in their local area to coordinate with, and allowed people to designate themselves as a leader of that group or team, to organize meetings, to make phone calls through the web interface, to quickly contribute by automatically storing credit card information, and by having online discussions with others on their team, creating goals for self and team and tracking when those goals were met. A "fire-it-up section" featured videos specifically for the more active organizers to watch, with the president directly addressing the camera, encouraging and praising the work of these active supporters, as well as videos of fired-up Americans at campaign stops across the country. Dashboard helped organize teams and helped leaders stay in touch with what others in their team were doing, such as number of phone calls made.

The campaign established that enrolling new voters was going to be a critical ingredient to their success; and it was. Staff created a dedicated website for voter registration and polling place information. The site detected by IP address the visitor's state, and provided a lookup to find the polling place. The tool also provided a 1-800 number "voter hotline," and indicated what to bring and when the polling place opened. The field organization declared that the campaign had 60% more voter registrations in 2012 than in 2008, according to Marlon Marshall, deputy national field director.[62] Reports also suggested that in four of the six battleground states, Democrats out-registered Republicans.

The models based on the massive voter database allowed a strategic targeting of voters on Election Day, but also allowed the campaign to engage in careful targeting of audiences of TV watchers. They developed categories of political inclination (i.e., like to vote for Obama to unlikely to vote for Obama) based on the behaviors of voters in their audience's database. Larry Grisolano, who helped create the system of categories, explained, "We were able to create a set of ratings based on a model of our target voters, as opposed to the broader categories that are kind of defined by traditional advertising ratings."[63] They bought ad space on TV Land, for example, a cable station that airs reruns of older TV shows, such as *I Love Lucy*, as well as around late-night comedy shows and ESPN. The campaign pursued undecided voters through these ad purchases, rather than buying around more common spots, such as broadcast TV news and cable news channels. Jim Margolis, a senior advertising strategist, explained to the *New York Times* that the campaign advertised in these uncommon channels to reach people "who may not be as political, may not be deciding until later." He also explained that "a lot of these people are lower-information voters, not necessarily tuned to politics and watching a little more programming that is out of the main lane of what most of us think of."[64] These programs tended not to bring large audiences, but the campaign was not looking for large audiences but the right audiences for its message. In a close election, as 2012 ended up being, those small audiences might make the 2% difference between winning and losing.

The campaign also brought in a team of academic consultants who informed the modeling and message experimentation the Obama campaign conducted.[65] For example, their phone-calling scripts to remind eligible voters to vote included an introductory greeting noting that they had voted in past elections and praising them for voting, which is a form of gentle social pressure encouraging them to continue to emulate their past exemplary behaviors. Later in the calling script, volunteers were instructed to encourage voters to make a plan for when they would vote by asking them about their plan. This message was built on behavioral research that shows people are more likely to follow through on a plan when they have visualized concrete steps to complete it.

Targeted online advertising was a special focus of the Romney campaign. Moffatt explained: "I think our ad team is superior to theirs [Obama's]. It's where we pride ourselves as a campaign to be cutting edge.... We think it's one of our greatest strengths, and it's great that our strength matches up with one of the greatest financial drivers this year."[66] The campaign engaged in careful audience analysis to identify particular types of voters online and then targeted specific ads to them. For example, an ad was created that highlighted Romney's business strengths. They profiled undecided Republican voters who needed a little additional information about Romney in order to be persuaded to support him. Strategists learned through data analysis that Romney supporters tended to have an interest in technology and child care, take quizzes on news and entertainment sites, and share photographs. People who were not supporters included those who visit Christian music websites or who liked video games, bowling, or jazz.[67] Moffatt explained that they did not buy on particular sites; instead they bought for particular audiences: "I'm looking for the audience on any of these sites. I know who I need to talk to in order to be successful, and I don't mind if I find them on Yahoo, Town Hall, Drudge or a local newspaper site. I'm looking for the audience; I'm not looking for the site."[68] Yet by the end of the campaign, according to *Politico*, Romney's campaign had spent $4.7 million on online advertising as compared with $47 million by the Obama campaign.[69] FEC reports suggest that overall the Obama campaign spent $52 million on digital media and advertising compared with $26 million by the Romney campaign.[70]

Related to data analytics was message testing, which both campaigns undertook. Continuing the work started on Kerry's campaign in 2004, both Romney's and Obama's digital media teams engaged in detailed and careful A/B testing, which means creating two different versions of a website splash page, for example, to see which garners the greater click-through rates. They also did message testing to identify the most effective means of connecting with supporters and turning that connection into a benefit for the campaign, through donating or volunteering. Both campaigns continued the careful work of tuning e-mail messaging, shifting their approach to a carefully engineered expression of the campaign. According to reporting in *The Atlantic*, the Obama campaign drafted e-mail messages that were tested with small groups of voters, and response rates to the requested activity, typically fundraising, were monitored. Only the best-performing e-mails were then mass-distributed. Poor performers might net only 15% to 20% of what the best performers were able to bring in in contributions.[71]

Thus, these two presidential campaigns continued to hone a practice of data analysis that political campaigns were only just beginning to practice in the previous decade.[72] Their success in generating money, support, and volunteers suggests that this practice of data-driven campaigning is likely the future of presidential campaigning.

Organizational Opportunities and Challenges

Digital media strategy was integral to all of the presidential campaigns, although they varied with regard to how central digital media strategy was relative to other aspects of the campaign, such as field organizing, events, and TV ads. Cash-strapped campaigns struggled to be prepared when events favored their candidacy. When Santorum barely lost the Iowa caucus to Mitt Romney, creating an immediate increase in interest in his candidacy, his campaign website was unprepared for the onslaught of attention it would receive from visitors and donors. The campaign raised $1 million the day after the caucus, but limped along with a barely functioning website groaning under the strain of so many visitors. The campaign had not strategically positioned itself in the way other campaigns in the past had to capitalize monetarily on the victory (e.g., McCain in 2000). Santorum supporters on Facebook began to post complaints that their calls were going unanswered, and their requests to find ways to get involved in South Carolina were going unfulfilled, suggesting a disorganized ground game for the senator. When Santorum won Minnesota, Missouri, and Colorado, his website servers collapsed under the volume of traffic.

Indeed, traditional organizing, the "ground game," is still vital for campaigns. As Dean learned that lesson in 2004, so too did Gingrich, Santorum, and eventually Romney, who had significantly fewer field offices than Obama, although a top Republican operative in a battleground state scoffed at Obama's field offices as being a waste of money.[73] John Huntsman, commenting on Santorum's unexpectedly close finish behind Romney in Iowa, noted: "You can't Twitter your way to prosperity. You can't Facebook your way to prosperity. You have to be in the state. You have to be felt. You have to be seen."[74]

Organizationally, whoever the Republican nominee was going to be was at a substantial disadvantage compared with Obama. He had the benefit of time— building Narwhal in the interim between the two campaigns. He also had the advantage of a suite of applications to take advantage of social media, so that the campaign could further hone its message and identify accurately potential voters to target. The campaign, in addition to finding new voters to register, spent significant energy on a strategy to identify *persuadables*, those people who were undecided but were potential Obama supporters if they were given the right information. For example, those who unsubscribed from the campaign e-mail list in 2008 were highly likely to reconnect with the campaign after being contacted by them. Experiments were conducted to identify the best way to bring those people back into the campaign (e.g., an impersonal call from someone out of state, versus from someone in their state).[75] The campaign ultimately contacted 150 million people through phone calls and in-person conversations by volunteers.[76] It also scheduled open forum conversations on Reddit, because Reddit's demographic profile was of the type that strategists identified as advantageous. Indeed, as an illustration of the effectiveness of the strategy, when Obama, who typed his own answers into the Reddit chat, dropped in a URL to provide the participants the form to register to vote, 30,000 Redditors did so.[77] Digital media staff even built a tool called Dreamcatcher to do sentiment analysis of social media, which in turn led to further microtargeting.[78]

One of the core strategies of the Obama campaign was to build a local, personal-contact-focused campaign, pushing two-step flow not just digitally but on the ground. Obama, whose identity and campaign philosophy were tied to his early employment as a community organizer, led a campaign that emulated the foundational tenets of such organizing. The campaign opened 45% more field offices in swing states than the Romney campaign. For example, in North Carolina the campaign had fifty field offices and one hundred in Ohio. [79] In targeted states most volunteers lived within ten miles of a local field office. Messina predicted that the combined digital/ground organizing they conducted would add one to two percentage points in key states, like North Carolina.[80]

Philosophically, the Romney campaign reflected the market-driven economic principles that the candidate himself espoused. The campaign ran a lean information technology outfit of around 500 people (as compared with Obama's, which was over 1,000 people).[81] Much of technological work was outsourced to consulting firms and software providers. For example, the campaign used several existing corporate platforms for phone calling (FLS Connect) and for online advertising (Rally.org), and it used Salesforce, a system for tracking contacts. Staff built their own database of voters' online behavior, which they segmented for targeted online advertising. [82] In explaining his approach to running digital media, Moffatt explained that he had to justify the successes of digital media to get more resources because that is "the Gov's viewpoint on the world." In the same interview he lashed out at the Obama campaign, saying: "We have what we need to be successful in November. They [Obama's digital media] are so caught up in their vanity metrics; they're so caught up in all of their 'We're smarter than everyone' hubris. They are convinced that they're smarter than the marketplace." [83] He explained in a different interview that the Romney campaign worked with the company Eventbrite, which is an event-organizing startup company, rather than build something internally to help manage events, because "we would rather go to someone who wakes up every morning and worries about event-ticketing."[84]

The digital component of the overall campaign was not as integrally connected as Obama's. Moffatt's budget, for example, was smaller than other budgets on the campaign and was dwarfed by the Obama campaign's digital media spending. Moffatt noted, "We have to constantly prove what we are doing, but once we do that, we get more resources." He also explained: "Digital is held to a different standard, and yet, we know every single time that the results are coming back to show that it does work. My bigger question to people on the campaign is, why don't the other parts of a campaign have to show what's going on?" [85] At the same time he heralded that he had an equal seat at the table with other senior strategists—something that was not the case for the digital director of the McCain campaign in 2008.

Romney's campaign did build one application internally, a get-out-the-vote application called Orca. It was a web-based application developed to modernize strike lists, the tracking system of who voted in order to focus get-out-the-vote efforts on those who still needed a reminder or a ride on Election Day. It also was intended as a repository of complaints from poll watchers of fraud or vote irregularities so that those could be followed up on later by the campaign if legal challenges were needed. Part of the infrastructure of the system was built to be mobile phone accessible so that poll workers and volunteers in swing states could report turnout of known Romney supporters. Volunteers at Romney's headquarters in Boston could monitor the incoming information through a web-based interface, making calls to Romney supporters who had not yet voted.

It was created by an isolated team of developers under the direction of two political strategists in the campaign, Dan Centinello, the director of voter contact, and Rich Beeson, the political director. Gail Gitcho, communications director, sang the praises of the system to PBS *NewsHour*, claiming that it would beat Obama's ground operation on Election Day. It got its name because orcas hunt and eat narwhals. Moffatt noted in interviews that he had not seen it until its launch on Election Day. In subsequent news interviews, Moffatt highlighted

Orca's successes, including registering 14.3 million voters and identifying over 5,000 ballot issues.[86]

Yet, for all the praise, on Election Day Orca in effect failed. A volunteer with the campaign recounted on a blog that the training phone calls held by Centinello for Romney supporters were more of the slick marketing speech type than helpful training sessions. I had some serious questions—things like 'Has this been stress tested?,' 'Is there redundancy in place?,' and 'What steps have been taken to combat a coordinated DDOS attack or the like?,' among others. These types of questions were brushed aside (truth be told, they never took one of my questions). They assured us that the system had been relentlessly tested and would be a tremendous success.[87]

In actuality, the system had never been beta tested. It was still being built and tuned in the minutes before its launch, never getting the kind of real-life workout needed to determine weaknesses.

To add insult to injury, the campaign did not train users on the system well. The campaign sent out confusing instructions on how to use Orca. The materials referenced using smartphones and the Orca app, but Orca was a web-based application. Volunteers complained of searching Android and Apple app sites for the nonexistent mobile application. News reports of Orca also suggested that it was a smartphone application.[88] Much to the annoyance of some, the campaign sent voter rolls for precincts in which poll workers were to work as large PDF files, as many as seventy pages that volunteers were expected to print out.[89] Finally—less a problem of the technology than one of the user's experience—volunteers were sent incorrect login information, and they could not reset their login credentials even when they tried, effectively shutting them out of the system altogether.

Those who could use Orca swamped the system, causing it to crash for extended periods of time. Comcast, the Romney campaign's Internet host in Boston, at one point believed the traffic coming from Orca was a "denial of service" attack and stopped traffic to the campaign site. News reports noted that campaign workers at headquarters were giddy with this news because they thought it meant that Orca was working so well it was crashing under the weight of all the numbers.

In effect, though, the campaign was "flying blind," according to press reports.[90] Because headquarters was not receiving the data expected, the field offices did not have directives from headquarters on whom to target for get-out-the-vote efforts. One vocal volunteer who took to the blogs to complain about Orca wrote:

> The end result was that 30,000 plus of the most active and fired-up volunteers were wandering around confused and frustrated when they could have been doing anything else to help. The bitter irony of this entire endeavor was that a supposedly small government candidate

gutted the local structure of [get out the vote] efforts of a centralized, faceless organization in a far off place (in this case, their Boston head-quarters). Wrap your head around that.[91]

In the news reports after the disaster around Orca surfaced, the implication was that the Romney campaign was obsessed with beating Obama's techno-logical might. Centinello in a training conference call before Election Day was quoted by Huffington Post as saying: "There's nothing that the Obama data team, there's nothing that the Obama campaign, there's nothing that President Obama himself can do to even come close to what we are putting together here."[92] Yet, in trying to beat Obama's DCT might, some in the Romney campaign seemed to lose sight of the real objective, which is to win. In the end, an analysis of finan-cial records by Ars Technica found that the Obama campaign spent $9 million on technology; by contrast, the Romney campaign spent approximately $3 mil-lion.[93] The net effect of the variety of technologies and tactics the Obama cam-paign used mattered. Romney aides confessed to reporters in the aftermath of the election that voters were coming to polling places to vote for Obama that they did not even know about.[94]

Conclusion

The Narwhal/Orca contest highlights a number of lessons. First, campaigns are pushing toward ever more data-driven decision-making and organizing of political campaigns. This entails new opportunities to control interactivity by carefully targeting messages to receptive audiences, finding ways to move them up the activity ladder from having casual interest to voting to being a precinct captain or team leader. All of the energy is aimed toward situating citizens as weapons in the arsenal or perhaps pawns on the chessboard.

Second, part of the purpose of many of the applications campaigns built for Facebook, YouTube, as well as Orca and Narwhal, were to facilitate two-step flow, and push super-supporters to work on behalf of the campaign, whether it was for GOTV efforts or for helping spread name recognition and excitement about a candidacy, pulling more money to the campaign, or helping manage the chaotic messaging in the hybrid media environment. The Obama campaign, in particu-lar, seems to have found through the team-based approach to on- and offline organizing the magic formula of keeping super-supporters on message to better reflect the current strategies of the campaign, and then ensuring that the message is distributed to the social networks and neighborhoods of the super-supporter. One of the challenges in 2004 and in 2008 was in trying to keep those energized supporters who evangelized for the campaign on message, especially when the message needed to change to reflect a new reality. By 2012, the Obama campaign had found a practice that proved remarkably effective: team-based organizing, mostly done offline, in neighborhoods, especially in swing states, controlling the message in a hierarchical, top-down fashion, orchestrating supporters to move with the campaign as a single entity: citizens enveloped within the campaign, the perfect agents to deploy in service of electing the candidate.

7

Conclusion: Shifting Practices of Political Campaigns and Political Culture

Looking across five cycles of presidential campaigns in the Internet age, this book documents noteworthy and crucial shifts that occurred in the practices of presidential campaigns. Driving visitors to the campaign website, growing name recognition, and engaging supporters was of concern as far back as 1996. Fundraising practices shifted as the legal context shifted. In 1996 there was no incentive to experiment with ways to fundraise through the Internet because of election laws. By 2000, however, that limitation was removed, and John McCain and Bill Bradley both worked to leverage the Internet to fill or refill their campaign coffers, and candidates that followed worked to perfect repeated, small-donor giving. Image building and messaging have grown more complex in the Web 2.0 networked environment, where messages can be amplified through the combined power of YouTube, Facebook, and Twitter, to name a few. Candidates in the position of challenger or insurgent have become much more likely to drum up netroots support that can help create, but does not always guarantee, a strong digital campaign.

This book was written with four goals in mind. First, I aimed to highlight in the prior chapters the stories of the practices of campaigns, not only their uses of digital communication technologies (DCTs), but also other key factors that contribute to success or failure. Looking only at digital practices of political campaigns, we may fail to see that for most campaigns digital media are still only a small part of the overall work, and that even with the best digital media campaigns, some campaigns will falter because of other forces. Thus, the factors identified by Denton that contribute to a successful campaign help scholars better contextualize DCTs.[1]

Second, moving from the practical to the symbolic, my concern is that although affordances of DCTs enable greater visibility and involvement by citizens in political campaigns, even as we have moved from the mass media to the networked media era, there still remains an impulse by campaigns to control and harness citizens as a means to an end. DCTs enable greater interaction to occur between campaign staff and citizens and among citizens, but campaigns have the impulse to limit those interactions and in general turn them toward the work of public relations on behalf of the campaign.

Third, and back to the practical effects of campaigning in the age of the Internet, one consequence of the network of connections people now have in the United States, combined with the complex, hybrid media environment, is that we may see less fragmentation over time. Of much concern, especially since the 1990s, has been the likelihood that people will self-select into information and issue publics. The implication is that the accidental exposure to events, people, and perspectives that helps undergird a healthy democracy is circumvented with the affordance of greater control of exposure to information. As DCTs diffuse, and more people have access to digital media of many types, rather than fragmentation there is a greater likelihood for accidental exposure to diverse views and information.

Fourth, a careful study of the practices is needed, not just of the winners but of a variety of candidates since 1996 who have adopted DCTs as part of their campaign strategy. Although much has been written about the campaigns of Barack Obama and Howard Dean because of their remarkable successes, other candidates, too, have innovated and perfected DCT use in important ways, and those stories also should to be told. The prior chapters were meant to help do that work. In addition, greater reflection is needed on the paradigm shift from mass-mediated campaigning to networked campaigning, and that, as well as the other points, is discussed further in the next sections.

From Mass-Mediated Campaigning to Networked Campaigning: A History

We have witnessed political campaigns shift from a paradigm of mass-mediated politics to networked politics in a hybrid media system. In the era of mass media, most of the energy and money spent by a campaign was in developing an effective messaging strategy to broadcast on TV and through radio and direct mail. The purpose of buying TV ad space was to mass-disseminate a message to a target audience that watched the program. In the networked media environment campaigns must contemplate messaging across more channels, and must take into account the unique affordances of each, while recognizing that groups of people are interconnected across those channels. To put it another way: four decades ago Granovetter contemplated the loose ties that characterize the connections of people who have only weak social connections.[2] Today, those weak ties are easier to build and maintain via DCTs because of personal profiles and linking practices. A true network of interconnections exist between and across groups of people, and the campaigns that understood that important change in the nature of communication online are able to more effectively use DCTs to their advantage. Thus, the methods of persuasion shift in a mass communication environment in important ways from that in a networked communication environment. Targeting becomes especially vital, from identifying typical mass audience characteristics of particular programs to isolating the characteristics of those who would respond to a particular message in a given channel to trigger the desired effect: give money; read more information; pass the message on to a friend.

The 1996 and 2000 campaigns provide excellent cases to see the mass-mediated campaign paradigm at work. The bulk of money and staff focused on television advertising. DCTs, primarily the Web and e-mail, were novelties. The Gore campaign in 2000 was the first to contemplate the power of interactivity and microtargeting through DCTs by creating a chat messaging interface to connect otherwise unconnected supporters. Ben Green, Gore's Internet director, explained,

> The concept was we want to facilitate real-time communication amongst our supporters so they're not relying on the central campaign structure to get their information. We wanted people with common interests, [who were] Gore supporters. But based on what issues you're interested in, we'd like you to connect with other Gore supporters and get them organized.[3]

Although the Gore campaign DCT staff had few resources to build the kind of organizing tools that the Obama campaign eventually did, staff saw the potential of networked interaction. Bush campaign staff in 2000 also saw the potential, not so much for self-organizing supporters as for microtargeting of messaging based on a database of information collected about voters, including their Internet behavior.

The 2004 election marks the shift when campaign practices embraced networked campaigning with zeal. The Howard Dean campaign and the Draft Wesley Clark movement demonstrated that with the right combination of factors a campaign could genuinely open up to supporters, could run a more decentered organization without the hierarchical structure and message discipline of typical political campaigns, and could gain from that openness in the form of support and money. Yet the Dean campaign crashed, ultimately, over the lack of control combined with an absence of the necessary ingredients of successful campaigning, such as field organizing. The Clark campaign is a terrific case study in the clash between the networked campaigning paradigm as exemplified in the Draft Wesley Clark movement and the mass-mediated campaign paradigm exemplified in the Clark for President official campaign. Meanwhile, the Kerry campaign advanced core principles of controlled interactivity, conducting A/B message testing to identify the best messages to drive traffic to its website and convert visitors into contributors and advocates. The Bush campaign continued to build carefully targeted marketing campaigns based on the best data analytics of any presidential campaign up to that point.

If 2004 marked the paradigm shift from mass-mediated to network-mediated campaign, the 2008 and 2012 campaigns exemplify the experimenting and honing of practices that have come to mark this new paradigm of campaigning. Not just Barack Obama's, but all the Democratic and Republican campaigns recognized the changed media landscape and engaged in tactics accordingly. All recognized the importance of DCTs to image construction and message dissemination, and aimed to capitalize on various affordances to get ahead. The Obama campaign rightly deserves credit for figuring out how to really harness controlled interactivity to keep supporters organized in ways that are ultimately beneficial to advancing the candidacy of the politician. Yet that recognition needs to be tempered with understanding the many factors that go into a winning candidacy, which are described more next.

Factors in Winning Campaigns in the Internet Age

In examining what helps to create a winning candidacy in the Internet age, the following must be considered: the organization, the fundraising, the role of the mass media and public opinion polls, the candidates and the image they construct, and the political and social context. Increasingly, as DCTs diffuse, the role of citizens in campaigning has become important. That is, a remarkable shift has occurred over the last three election cycles by campaigns to more actively engage supporters. With each election cycle, campaigns strive to harness the power of two-step flow by having voters not *passively* watching political ads as they would have in the 1980s and earlier, but by getting them out and *actively* talking neighbor to neighbor, calling undecided voters in a nearby state, or sharing on Facebook enthusiasm for a new campaign-generated YouTube video.

The Dean campaign is held up as the forebear in advancing the new paradigm of networked campaigning to involve citizens more deeply in the work of the campaign. It is worth contemplating for a minute why his campaign succeeded using DCTs when another similar sort of campaign did not. A comparison between Dean's campaign and Buddy Roemer's campaign in 2012 provides a helpful contrast. In such analysis, the ingredients that contribute to the success in the Internet age become clear.

Both Dean and Roemer declared themselves Internet candidates and staked their candidacies on digital media to generate attention and translate it into fundraising that would grow the campaign into one deemed viable by political watchers. Dean's campaign grew exponentially in the surfacing stage. Roemer's never got off the ground. What explains the difference?

Dean had a message that resonated with a subset of the Democratic Party base that was angry about the war in Iraq and disgruntled with the Democratic Party. Dean's antiwar message and declaration that he was the "Democratic wing of the Democratic Party," a rebel with a cause, captured the hearts and imaginations of activists within the party who had now found their voice. Roemer's message was focused on cleaning up the political process by limiting the power of special interests, what he called the "money monster" that he saw consuming Washington.[4] In the context of the *Citizens United* Supreme Court decision granting unlimited spending by corporate entities in political campaigns, the message might have resonated in the same way as Dean's, but it did not. The Republican base did not grow inspired and energized by the message, although typically messages about political process rarely do; stronger passions exist around war than about spending in politics. Perhaps that is why journalists dismissed Roemer as a one-issue candidate and the candidacy as a vanity run for the nomination, opting not to cover him. Just like the Draft Wesley Clark supporters who pushed to increase General Clark's name recognition in the surfacing stage of the 2004 campaign, so too did Roemer and his staff work extremely hard to push his name recognition and generate buzz and excitement around the campaign online. Yet, unlike Clark, Roemer never got traction. Without the right message or an ability to fundraise at the level required of contemporary campaigns, Roemer was effectively dead in the water.

For Dean's part, although he found successes on some dimensions, there were also noteworthy failures. He effectively used digital media to amplify his message, gave supporters an easy way to hook into the campaign, and channeled a hopeful message of empowerment to supporters, ascribing the power of the campaign to them. Yet he failed to stay on message, failed to build effective field organizations, and played into media frames of being emotionally unstable (and therefore not suitable to lead the country). Thus, the campaign, while opening up greater interactivity online, did not establish all of the necessary components that create success.

When we look at the Obama campaign, especially in 2008, it seems that it had the right combination of factors. Staff crafted opportunities for controlled interactivity of supporters that channeled enthusiasm into dollars and offline activism for the campaign in ways that translated into votes on Election Day. They also spent nearly $300 million in television advertising (compared with John McCain's $135 million), by far the single largest expenditure of the campaign.[5] That differential, according to public opinion surveys over the course of the general election, translated into support for Obama.[6] In 2008, the staff who had worked on Dean's campaign in 2004 and who founded Blue State Digital (BSD) in the months after the campaign's collapse saw the failings but also the promises of digital media. They could have worked for another candidate and lost. Instead they signed a contract with Barack Obama. Without question the work that BSD did in partnership with other digital media firms to harness DCTs to advance the campaign is commendable, and many campaign professionals I interviewed speculated that the digital campaign made the difference in positioning Obama as a viable candidate against Hillary Clinton. It would be a mistake, though, to underestimate the critical role of the candidate. He or she not only needs to have the raw determination to win,[7] the candidate also needs management skills, fundraising prowess, and the ability to manage the messy, complicated organization that is a political campaign.

The Obama candidacy had something else, something that the successful candidate of the Internet age needs to see and to convey: the idea that citizen supporters are essential to a winning campaign. That entails a philosophical orientation that not only recognizes but also nurtures opportunities for supporter involvement within the campaign. Reflecting on the Obama and Romney campaigns in 2012, both had remarkable fundraising prowess, produced disciplined messaging, and had strong organizations. Their approach to conceiving the role of citizens was remarkably different, however. This is evident in their convention speeches. Romney explained why he was running for president, what his background and biography was, why the country under Obama was fairing so badly, and told listeners that they had a choice to make, and that he was the better choice: "So here we stand. Americans have a choice. A decision." He wrapped up his speech declaring that "America, that united America, can unleash an economy that will put Americans back to work.... That America, that united America, will uphold the constellation of rights that were endowed by our Creator and codified in our Constitution. That united America will care for the poor and the sick, will honor and respect the elderly and will give a helping hand to those in need." By contrast, Obama explained why he was running for a second term, highlighting the successes he saw during his administration, and outlining his plans for another four years. Unlike Romney, he asked listeners to help him: "I'm asking you to rally around a set of goals for your country." On the economy, Obama explained that "we can help big factories and small businesses double their exports.... You can make that happen. You can choose that future."

As he concluded his speech, he explained: "The election four years ago wasn't about me. It was about you. My fellow citizens—you were the change." These quotes illustrate the distinctly different constructions the candidates and their campaigns had about the role of citizens in the political process. Romney spoke of abstract "Americans." Obama spoke of "you," highlighting that they could help the economy, and they were the change that got the Affordable Care Act passed. Obama gave his listeners agency to work for their destiny while Romney spoke of the broad category of Americans, shifting his rhetorical gaze from the members of the audience to the abstract group that is somewhere out there pledging allegiance, fighting in wars, and caring for the poor and sick.

Obama's philosophical orientation, rooted in his first career as a community organizer for the poor and disenfranchised in Chicago, combined with actual organizational practices of the campaign, then further amplified and made more efficient by DCTs, created a synergy between campaign and media environment. The campaign that recognized the potential for interactivity, and could see the paradigm shift from mass media to networked media, had a better chance at success. The campaign that could effectively execute a set of strategies that capitalized on the affordance of interactivity, using digital media to increase name recognition, drive traffic and interest to the website, channel supporters into activism for the campaign, and put digital tools in front of them to harness their ability to evangelize for the campaign, had a real shot at winning.

Yet, in terms of full or genuine interactivity, in which campaigns respond to and promote the messages coming from their supporters, examples are hard to find. Actor network theory provides a method for seeing that a key affordance of digital communication technology is interactivity. In combination with looking at the symbolic uses of that affordance, in the spirit of Edelman's scholarship,[8] it becomes evident that campaigns work to build not a partnership with citizens using DCTs but a transactional relationship in which support is a currency that campaigns aim to grow. Paradoxically, political campaigns, which are the core of a democracy, are decidedly undemocratic affairs.

Controlled Interactivity and its Symbolic Implications

Campaigns ultimately construct and use citizens as objects they need to manage through controlled interactivity in order to reach their objective of winning the election. Political elites, including the candidates, view the Internet, in the words of Browning, as "little more than a big electronic auditorium where millions of people gather to spout off much like high-school kids in a civics class— but nonetheless have little impact on the crafting of policies that govern them."[9]

Such views are in evidence when examining the biographies of prominent political campaign managers. Take, for example, David Plouffe, who headed Obama's 2008 campaign. In describing how Obama would need to win, he writes, "We had to grow the share of the electorate we believed would be the most supportive of Obama. The 2008 caucuses would have to be younger, attended by more minorities... and have a higher percentage of independents and Republicans participating than had historically done so."[10] Citizen support was something to be cultivated, and by implication, harvested on Election Day. Karl Rove, Bush's campaign manager, in his autobiography, describes microtargeting efforts by the 2004 re-election campaign this way: "We spent three years and several million dollars perfecting our microtargeting tools, and it was enormously helpful in focusing volunteer efforts on persuadable voters who needed personal contact to bring them into the Bush camp."[11] They analyzed data about voters and segmented them so that volunteers could focus efforts on evangelizing the Bush campaign to the right people receptive to the right message.

Beyond the stance of campaign managers in thinking about the role of citizens, evidence for how campaigns manage interaction with citizens also can be seen in the nature of the interaction that occurs between campaigns and supporters. In 2000 the e-mail listserv became a primary mechanism for campaign communication. A Majordomo listserv can be configured to allow replies to messages broadcast out to supporters, or that affordance can be closed. Campaigns configured e-mail to close off the opportunity for reply. Campaign staff did this because they felt they could not handle the barrage of messages that could come at them, nor did they want to see such discussion take root as part of the campaign because of the risk of losing control of its message. If spammers, trolls, and critics all took part in the discussion, then what damage could that bring to the candidate's image? In 2004, the campaign blog blossomed as a major communication apparatus that channeled the voice of citizens publicly. The Democratic candidates enabled commenting, a feature like the listserv that can be enabled or disabled. The Republican campaign of George Bush disabled that feature. Yet even the campaigns that enabled it did not actively participate in conversation with citizens who were writing on the blog. In 2008 campaigns began using social media platforms to disseminate their message. Although platforms such as Myspace and Facebook enabled comments and conversation, campaign staff rarely participated in conversations with supporters. One exception was the Obama campaign when confronted by a group organizing itself on the MyBo platform in opposition to Obama's policy position on the Foreign Intelligence Surveillance Act (FISA). In 2012 as social media expanded, a Pew report summed up practices of interactivity: "neither campaign [Obama, Romney] made much use of the social aspect of social media."[12]

Another way to think about the ways that campaigns use DCTs to manifest controlled interactivity is by examining the work of fundraising and spending. Money is essential to political campaigns. In the span of five election cycles spending has gone from $37 million for Clinton-Gore in 1996 to $630 million spent by Obama-Biden 2012. That is a seventeen-fold spending increase. Where does all that money go? The largest share continues to go for advertising, although it no longer means only television.[13] The top firms hired by the Obama campaign, for example, for advertising were companies that combined TV ad design and buying with social media strategy, online ad targeting, and messaging, such as GMMB, Bully Pulpit Interactive, and AOL Advertising. For both the Romney and the Obama campaigns in 2012, television advertising was *half* their total budget. The purpose of advertising is for image construction, not for genuine interaction with the electorate. The next most expensive aspects of campaigns are fundraising and direct mail. Fundraising costs were 10% of each campaign's budget. Direct mail was a larger expenditure for the Romney campaign, at 14% versus 9% for the Obama campaign. Payroll, travel, consultants, and polling also are costs for campaigns.

To pay for the necessities of the presidential campaign, political organizations must fundraise, and to do so they harness controlled interactivity to facilitate that transaction. The Bush campaigns in 2000 and 2004 perfected the art of fundraising through traditional means, incentivizing Republican Party and Bush family loyalists to network with their friends and social networks to work as "bundlers" or fundraisers for the campaign. The checks written through this process were typically closer to the federal limits on contributions of around $2,000. Bush's campaign was so far ahead financially in 2004 that there was no incentive for the campaign to experiment with other online means of fundraising. McCain's 2000 campaign was the first to demonstrate that if a campaign was prepared to capture the energy of a major campaign event, such as a landslide New Hampshire primary win, then many $100 contributions coming in online could re-establish what had been a broke candidacy. The Dean campaign innovation to announce fundraising goals and deadlines on the website and blog to incent contributions further demonstrated that many small contributions could power an otherwise impossible candidacy. The Obama campaign focused on carefully crafting e-mail messages to build a relationship with the recipients before beginning to ask for money. These strategies—being prepared to fundraise online around major events, developing fundraising goals and creating events online to energize giving, and developing a relationship with potential contributors before asking— serve to manufacture a parasocial relationship with supporters, a controlled interactivity, constructing supporters as agents in the campaign, essential actors that will make the campaign possible, if they will just contribute $25, and do so again next month and the month after.

Campaign staff will explain that they do not have time to socialize on digital media platforms on which they are organizing and energizing supporters. They are so busy designing technologies or strategies to generate name recognition, fundraise, or construct the candidate's image or that of the opponent, there is no time to actually interact in an unscripted and spontaneous way with supporters through these digital channels. They will also confess that such conversation may make everyone feel good, but they will not help get the candidate elected. Indeed Joe Trippi, campaign manager for Howard Dean, was derided for seemingly taking his cues from Deaniacs on the blogosphere, and look where that got the campaign. They might suggest third-party platforms— news sites, activist groups, discussion spaces such as Reddit—are where such conversations among citizens should take place; though, ideally, for organizing, campaigns should know who is doing the talking and about what so they can effectively collect data about them for microtargeting in the service of winning the election.[14]

These views highlight clearly how campaigns tend to view citizens. They are unprofessional and unwise about the tactics and strategies of campaigning. Thus, their job is not to provide insight on strategy or on policy. Their job is to take their directives from the candidate and staff to get the candidate elected. The FISA debate in the Obama campaign is a telling case in point. A segment of his supporters who had organized for him, evangelized for him, and gave money to him had a strong policy position opposing an update to the Foreign Intelligence Surveillance Act. They were vehemently opposed to giving telecommunication companies immunity from prosecution for turning over call records to government agencies. They used MyBo, Obama's online organizing tools, against him, becoming the largest group. Although the Obama campaign set up discussions between policy staff and citizens, the move was meant for public relations, not for genuine deliberation. There was no suggestion that Obama would change his position following the discussion.

Yet elections are the cornerstone of a democracy, in which the citizens' voice is unquestionably heard and abided through their vote. The election is the most noteworthy moment in a democracy when the governed give their assent to be so by electing representatives. The political campaign, as the run-up to the vote, serves as a vital opportunity for citizens' voices to be heard in the democracy— an important opportunity for the strong democracy that Barber advocates.[15] Campaigns are important events when Americans are paying at least some attention to politics. Moreover, they are moments in which political participation is advocated and warranted: from public opinion polls that measure the attitudes of the electorate to the visible advocacy work that partisan supporters play when they talk to their neighbors, post political articles to their Facebook wall, make phone calls on behalf of the campaign to undecided voters, and donate money to the candidate who has moved them to act. Thus, political campaigns are espe-cially made for political participation by ordinary citizens.

Yet, in a remarkable paradox, although political campaigns are themselves the touchstones and the mechanisms through which much of that political par-ticipation is enacted, in actuality the prime activity of a campaign is in moving voters to support the candidate when it comes time to vote. The opportunity to deeply engage the public in deliberating on the problems and strengths of the nation and gathering their views and vision on how to provide for a common good, is lost.

The affordances of DCTs, at least to me, magnify that loss. The interactivity inherent in the design of the Internet, which also allows the bridging of geo-graphic distance and the bringing together of people with a diversity of views, could easily be harnessed to empower and further enfranchise the public to enact strong democracy. Campaigns and candidates have it in their power to do so. For practical reasons, they choose not to. The opportunity for an enhanced democracy is lost to the nitty-gritty reality that campaigns are ultimately about winning and losing, not about contemplating the common good of the society by all those with a stake in it.

Challenges of Controlled Interactivity in the Web 2.0 Era

There is one hitch, though, to this view I just sketched. And that is that the con-trolled interactivity that campaigns work so hard to achieve is in some ways harder in the Web 2.0 digital environment to maintain. As campaigns have opened up to blogs and social media and identified ways to carefully script mes-sages that they push to advocates to disseminate out through their social net-works, they are not fully able to control how those messages will disseminate, and they cannot control what might come back at them.

As much of a concern then as today is how to control the messaging environ-ment: the campaign's own and the opponent's. In the early age of the Internet such concerns seemed more apparent: just turn off or do not use such affordances as interactivity in digital media to preclude unruly opponents or unhelpful, though well-meaning, supporters. In the Web 2.0 architecture of participation,[16] part of the complex hybrid media environment in which traditional media and DCTs share news and information and amplify them to a variety of audiences, control becomes challenging in new ways that campaigns must grapple with.

There are a number of examples that attest to the challenges, but 2012 Republican primary candidate Michele Bachmann's candidacy serves as a use-ful example. Her campaign, from its start, worked to build a strong, credible campaign that heavily relied on DCTs. Bachmann was a favorite of the Tea Party, a loosely organized, bottom-up organization of voters who leaned libertarian in their philosophy, advocating limited government power. She also had appeal to Christian conservatives for her strong antiabortion stance.

When she announced her exploratory committee, she already had a cadre of supporters behind her, which the campaign worked through digital media to grow while also converting those supporters into contributors and evangelists. The strategy the campaign had for this was to capitalize on a memorable quote and then disseminate it through a variety of digital media channels to generate money and in turn earned media from traditional news outlets. For example, Bachmann created a web video in which she declared that she needed her supporters to contribute to her campaign to help her "make Barack Obama a one-term president."[17] In a choreographed move, the campaign e-mailed supporters and Bachmann tweeted about the video, aiming to create a money bomb of the sort perfected by Paul's supporters, which had the desired effect. Having started this strategy, she continued to find emotion-arousing phrases to attack the president, which she then mined for contributions. She accused President Obama of having "anti-American views" during a cable news appearance, a claim she also highlighted on her website and in social media. This quickly generated over $1 million in campaign contributions.[18] The campaign also drove traffic to the website by paying for banner ads on the Drudge Report with an appeal for contributions following a debate in June 2011. Her campaign also carefully targeted social conservatives and Tea Party supporters through Facebook.[19] Thus, her campaign quickly generated the money and the support to garner her attention as a viable candidate by the mainstream press.

When she formally announced her candidacy, Bachmann was polling at the top of the Republican pack in Iowa. Yet, in a series of missteps, she lost her momentum. First, she had an image problem, especially with moderate Republicans. Late-night television comedians mocked her as being a wacko,[20] fueled in part by extreme, often inaccurate statements she made. The blog of left-leaning website Think Progress posted "10 of the Craziest Things Michele Bachmann Has Ever Said,"[21] including her declaration that *The Lion King* was propaganda for homosexuality, and that scientists support the theory of intelligent design. The Think Progress list received over 30,000 likes on Facebook and was tweeted over 1,000 times.

Second, she was prone to gaffes, one of which she made during her announcement speech. The gaffe, rather than her announcement, drove news coverage, and she had to explain the gaffe rather than pushing arguments about her abilities as president. The gaffe occurred when she extemporaneously tried to compare herself to actor John Wayne, and his love of country. Unfortunately for her, she attributed Waterloo, Iowa, her hometown and where she made her announcement speech, as the birthplace of Wayne, when in fact it was once where John Wayne Gacy resided (a child predator who killed his victims).[22] Mainstream news media, weblogs, and the pundit sphere on Twitter amplified the gaffe, further overshadowing her announcement.

Her strategy was to try to change the message by demonstrating her credibility and sensibilities to be an effective president through the televised debates with the other Republican candidates. She performed strongly in them, cultivating positive earned media, highlighting her successes in the debates on Twitter, and posting video excerpts of her debate performance, while also showcasing her "Presidential Profile" there.

Yet the news media frame that she was gaffe prone continued to trump the coverage. For example, Bachmann, held an Internet teleconference with supporters that was marred with technical troubles. Michael Shear, writing for the *New York Times* blog, The Caucus, used the trouble as evidence of the challenges her campaign faced in trying to win the Republican Party nomination.

What this tale highlights is that although Bachmann had a savvy digital media campaign, it could not compete with the traditional news media norms that generate simple caricatures of candidates cannot escape from even in the face of alternative frames[23]—caricatures that psychologized Bachmann as gaffe prone and nutty, and that resonated and were then further amplified in the blogosphere, on YouTube, and a variety of corners of cyberspace. Bachmann could not fully control her image and her message off-line or on.

Implications of Fragmentation in the Internet Age

Despite my mostly gloomy outlook on the reality of full democratic participation in political campaigns, there is one outcome of the ways campaigns use DCTs that may be potentially positive for US political culture more broadly. Over the last three decades, we have seen increased political fragmentation and resulting polarization. As I explain next, this ongoing trend in US political culture may be somewhat ameliorated at least during political campaigns by the shift to two-step flow and controlled interactivity.

Much has been written about the increased fragmentation of the electorate. As the Internet was beginning to diffuse in the United States, scholars began to raise concerns about a decidedly negative effect of digital communication. Scholars such as Doheny-Farina, Putnam, and Sunstein fired warning flares that people would use the Internet primarily to interact with those with whom they had something in common, some hobby or political view, and would choose to expose themselves only to information and opinions that they had an interest in or agreed with.[24] The consequence of such was called fragmentation, the "melting pot" society reduced to silos of noninteracting interest and affiliation groups that would rob our society of the value of reciprocity and trust, as we were no longer forced to interact with people who were unlike us.

Indeed, Bimber and Davis conclude in their book analyzing the online campaign practices of Gore and Bush in 2000 that fragmentation was likely to expand.[25] If we assume that most forms of digital communication are based on pull media, such as websites that need to find mechanisms to draw people to the site, then only those who are most interested in politics will seek out or be open to being pulled to a campaign's website. Those with little interest in politics will have little reason to be pulled in or seek a candidate's website. Research conducted by Prior, looking at cable news and Internet news use in the United States, confirms this pattern of behavior.[26] Those with high preference for entertainment opt out of watching news programming on TV of any kind, and as a result they are exposed to less political information. The consequence of this is less knowledge about political actors and events and less likelihood to vote.

Thus, the media environment matters to political fragmentation. Prior argues that in the era of three broadcast TV stations in the 1950s until the 1970s. This had the important consequence of exposing a broad swath of the public to a little bit of political news because those with a preference for entertainment programming had no alternative to watching news when that was broadcast at the same time on all three channels. When cable offered increased choices for entertainment programming, those with little interest in politics or news opted out of news programming. Indeed, Prior argues this is one of the causal mechanisms that led to increased political polarization in the United States. He explains that as those with less interest in politics dropped out of the political process, as they were significantly less likely to vote, then those with a greater interest in politics, as they consumed more news on cable news stations, grew more extreme in their ideological views and increased their strength in their political involvement. Prior notes that Congress grew more polarized, more extreme in members' ideological views after cable news was introduced in the communication environment because those voters who are more ideologically driven were voting at a greater rate for more ideological candidates, overruling more moderate voters' preferences for moderate candidates.

As the Internet has diffused, political participation can be done more quickly and easily online. These modes of political engagement are often referred to as "clicktivism" or, more derogatorily, "slacktivism."[27] Scholars such as Howard take a decidedly skeptical view of such engagement, calling it "thin citizenship" in which the public engages in easy political activities that ultimately have little consequence in the political process.[28] For example, forwarding an e-mail sent from a candidate to a few friends, signing a petition on Change.org, or liking a political group on Facebook is a kind of "five-minute protest," in Howard's words, that entails an impoverished political citizenship.[29]

Perhaps, though, it is not as bad as Howard, Prior, Sunstein, and others fear. One countervailing influence on polarization and thin citizenship is the work of directly contacting voters "where they live," by political activists, candidates, or political parties. Zukin, Keeter, Andolina, Jenkins, and Delli Carpini found in their survey analysis of civic and political participation in the United States that being invited to volunteer or to vote was a significant predictor of involvement.[30] They advise that one way to boost political participation among younger people, who have typically been less involved in the electoral process than older people, would be to ask them more often and more directly to participate. In controlled field experiments of the effects of door-to-door canvassing on voter turnout, Green, Gerber, and Nickerson found that turnout was significantly higher among those who had been canvassed, that is, talked to in person, with a reminder to vote.[31] Moreover, the hybrid media environment can create a hurricane of news on hot topics, as well as move topics that are initially ignored into full view of the public.[32]

In political campaigning in 2012, DCTs were almost fully integrated into the practices of campaigning. In addition, two-step flow and personal communication are increasingly privileged modes for campaigning, especially by volunteers.[33] Finally, DCTs embody the Web 2.0 ethos of the architecture of engagement, in which social connection, user-centered design, and user-generated content are programmed in as core characteristics of software. These characteristics in combination invite the consideration that another shift may be underway in US political culture.

Take, for example, the Obama campaign's 2008 MyBo social media platform or its 2012 upgrade, Dashboard. The logic of that software, just one of many platforms created during and since the 2004 presidential campaigns, is about helping super-supporters organize offline their social networks of friends, neighbors, coworkers, and family members in the spirit of two-step flow. The campaign provides guidance on whom to target and what kinds of activities to hold, but if the rhetoric coming from the Obama campaign is true, the emphasis is on promoting creativity and independence on the part of these super-supporters in activating people in their social networks.[34]

Thus, the implication of these organizing tools as well as the use of social networking sites to disseminate campaign messaging is that a broader swath of the public is being "touched" by political campaigns. They may be contacted directly because a highly interested person gave an e-mail address or connected with the campaign via Facebook, or indirectly because a friend of an interested friend received an Obama announcement on a Facebook newsfeed or the neighbor of an interested supporter was invited to a house party to watch the first presidential debate. Norris found in her research that political interest and media use go hand in hand.[35] As people gain more exposure to political information, they grow more interested, and vice versa, leading to what she calls a "virtuous circle" of political participation. Indeed, a Pew Internet study found that 25% of social media users reported becoming more active on a political issue after reading about it or discussing it on a social network side.[36] Thus, there is a chance that as people gain more exposure to political events and opinions among the contacts in their social network online, they will grow more interested, which in turn will lead to greater attention and perhaps participation.

Another growing concern, brought to light especially in Howard's ethnographic research on political groups in the early 2000s, is the practice of redlining.[37] He observes that political organizations make selective choices about whom they aim to target and activate through a message tailored to reflect the interests and appeal to the emotions of the target. Relatedly, there are people who are identified as undesirable for targeting. Howard explains that typically those who are redlined are "the elderly, poor, and racial minorities" who are "most likely to be victims of imposed political redlining."[38] The implication of the strategic choices campaigns make in whom they actively exclude from contacting potentially deprives our democracy of voices, a kind of soft disenfranchisement.

Although there certainly continues to be political redlining, there also has been new effort in the last two presidential campaign cycles to identify new pools of potential voters who historically are not engaged in political campaigns. The Obama campaign in 2012, for example, used data analytics to identify potential voters who were independent or leaned Democratic, and who likely were relatively politically uninvolved but if contacted with the right message might be motivated enough to vote on Election Day. This is the reason staff purchased ad space on the cable station TV Land, which airs reruns of situation comedies such as *The Golden Girls*. Similarly, the Romney campaign targeted atypical Republican supporters, voters they thought could be persuaded to support the campaign, and voters who lived in zip codes that are in traditionally Democratic districts but had exhibited conservative sympathies either through offline or online behaviors.[39]

Moreover, because of careful data curation processes in the 2012 election cycle, the Obama campaign in particular was able to keep track of potential voters it had touched and gradually try to move them up the ladder of participation. So if a super-supporter were out canvassing in her neighborhood and one of her neighbors expressed that he was undecided but leaning toward Obama, the canvasser would record that information, which would be stored in the voter file. If the super-supporter organized some Obama supporters to canvass the neighborhood again, then they would work on persuading the voter to support Obama. Nearer to Election Day, they would focus on securing his intent to vote.

This expanding reach by campaigns and supporters suggests that fragmentation and polarization may be stemmed by the uses to which DCTs are put by campaigns and their supporters. Research by Holbrook and McClurg suggests that campaign activities, such as campaign appearances and advertising, has little direct effect on voting by partisans but has a significant effect on independent voters.[40] A case study of the 2009 Whole Foods boycott on Facebook suggested that the protest exposed people to the boycott who did not know about it, and also exposed the ideas of the boycott to those who did not support it.[41] If many of these campaign targets are independents, those who had typically dropped out of politics when they could choose to be entertained rather than watch TV news,[42] then the more expansive contacting and targeting of independents with messages tailored to activate them in an effort to win elections may serve as a countering force on polarization in the United States.

Conclusion

Campaign practices have shifted to reflect the communication context within which we live. DCTs have been designed to be ontologically nonhierarchical and to foreground interconnections between people and among groups, and as campaigns use them, they are affected through their use to shift their practices. Like the Web, campaigns have adopted something of the philosophy of Web 2.0 in their daily practices, a nonhierarchical, user-centered approach that may, over time, enable connections across groups, tempering our propensity to selective expose ourselves to people and issues that match our preferences.

Beyond this bright side of a potential mitigation of polarization and fragmentation, what I see most clearly in observing political campaigns as they adapt to and adopt DCTs is this: ultimately, political elites continue to distrust the unruly, flaky, sometimes "unhinged" people that comprise the American electorate.[43] Campaigns wish to mobilize the public in the service of the campaign, but getting too close to them, really listening and empowering them, is dangerous or at least disadvantageous. While I do not dispute that there can be an intensity and an irrationality at times from the public, a healthy democracy enables full participation, which means that political elites contemplate those perspectives and make changes because of them. That is genuine interactivity, and that is what a healthy democracy requires.

Notes

Chapter 1

1. Gary Wolf, "How the Internet invented Howard Dean," *Wired.com*, January 2004, http://sodacity.net/system/files/Gary-Wolf_How-the-Internet-Invented-Howard-Dean.pdf, accessed July 25, 2013.
2. I use digital communication technologies (DCTs) as the covering term to encompass a broad swath of hardware and software that channels communication in digital form, including smartphones, tablets, and computers. The more common term is information and communication technologies (ICTs), but I focus almost exclusively on the communicative affordances of digital technologies and the practices of political campaigns in using them.
3. Stromer-Galley, "Online Interaction and Why Candidates Avoid It."
4. Kreiss, in *Taking Our Country Back*, describes the Dean and Obama campaigns' work of enabling some and closing other channels for interaction as "structured interactivity."
5. Stromer-Galley, "Online Interaction and Why Candidates Avoid It."
6. Individual campaign staff and even the candidate may have aspirations of using DCTs to further democratize the political process. In talking with staff, I observed that they get excited at the idea that their tools and methods of campaigning might bring more people into the political process. At the same time, they also frankly recognize that the entire purpose of a campaign is to get the candidate elected. The tools they build, and the people who are brought into the campaign through those tools, ultimately serve the goal of the campaign: to win.
7. Selnow, *Electronic Whistle-Stop*; Davis, *The Web of Politics*.
8. Bimber and Davis, *Campaigning Online*.
9. Williams and Tedesco, *The Internet Election*.
10. Kreiss, *Taking Our Country Back*.
11. Foot and Schneider, *Web Campaigning*.
12. Throughout, I will refer to *shifting* or *changing* rather than *evolving* as the verbs used to characterize what digital communication technologies are doing over time. I purposely avoid the term *evolve* because it connotes an improvement or a positive advance. I wish to avoid that connotation and prefer to stay neutral, at least with my terminology, on whether the changes are inherently better.
13. Jamieson, *Packaging the Presidency*.
14. See Foot and Schneider, *Web Campaigning*; Kreiss, *Taking Our Country Back*.
15. Denton, "Communication Variables and Dynamics of the 1996 Campaign."
16. Barber, *Strong Democracy*, 132.
17. Edelman, *Constructing the Political Spectacle*; *simulacrum* is used here in the spirit of Jean Baudrillard, *Simulation and Simulacra*.

18. I am not the first to observe this. Howard's aptly titled book *The Managed Citizen*, written over a decade ago, makes a similar argument.
19. Brewin, *Celebrating Democracy*; Jamieson, *Packaging the Presidency*.
20. Bimber, *Information and American Democracy*; Earl and Kimport, *Digitally Enabled Social Change*; Karpf, *The MoveOn Effect*.
21. To declare that DCTs make for more participatory campaigns is a technologically determin-istic argument. It is only through their use that DCTs' affordances are actualized.
22. Stromer-Galley and Baker, "Joy and Sorrow of Interactivity on the Campaign Trail."
23. Abbate, *Inventing the Internet*.
24. Hafner and Lyon, *Where Wizards Stay Up Late*; Mayo and Newcomb, "How the Web Was Won"; Ryan, *A History of the Internet and the Digital Future*.
25. Berners-Lee, *Weaving the Web*.
26. Ryan, *A History of the Internet and the Digital Future*.
27. Andrew Kohut, Carol Bowman, and Margaret Petrella, "Americans Going Online... Explosive Growth, Uncertain Destinations," Pew Internet & American Life Project, October 16, 1995, http://www.people-press.org/files/legacy-pdf/136.pdf, accessed July 20, 2013.
28. Ibid., 3.
29. Farhad Manjoo, "Jurassic Web: The Internet of 1996 Is Almost Unrecognizable Compared with What We Have Today," *Slate*, February 24, 2009, http://www.slate.com/articles/tech-nology/technology/2009/02/jurassic_web.html, accessed July 20, 2013.
30. Andrew Kohut, Robert C. Toth, Kimberly Parker, and Claudia Deane, "One-in-Ten Voters Online for Campaign '96: News Attracts Most Internet Users," December 16, 1996, http://www.people-press.org/files/legacy-pdf/117.pdf, accessed July 20, 2013.
31. "Trend Data (Adults)," Pew Internet & American Life Project, http://pewinternet.org/Trend-Data-%28Adults%29/Online-Activites-Total.aspx, accessed December 7, 2012.
32. Lee Rainie, Aaron Smith, Kay Lehman Schlozman, Henry Brady, and Sidney Verba, "Social Media and Political Engagement," Pew Internet & American Life Project, October 9, 2012, http://pewinternet.org/Reports/2012/Political-engagement.aspx, accessed July 20, 2013.
33. "In Changing News Landscape, Even Television is Vulnerable," Pew Research Center for the People & the Press, September 27, 2012, http://www.people-press.org/2012/09/27/in-changing-news-landscape-even-television-is-vulnerable/, accessed July 20, 2013.
34. Ray Tomlinson, "The First Network Email," http://openmap.bbn.com/~tomlinso/ray/firstemailframe.html, accessed July 3, 2012.
35. Ryan, *A History of the Internet and the Digital Future*.
36. Wiener, *Cybernetics*.
37. See McMillan, "Exploring Models of Interactivity from Multiple Research Traditions," for an overview of the interactivity concept.
38. Rafaeli, "Interactivity," 11.
39. Tim O'Reilly, "Design Patterns and Business Models for the Next Generation of Software," *O'Reilly.com*, September 20, 2005, http://oreilly.com/web2/archive/what-is-web-20.html, accessed July 20, 2013.
40. Landow, *Hypertext*.
41. Trent and Friedenberg, *Political Campaign Communication*.
42. Jamieson, *Packacing the Presidency*.
43. Schudson, *The Good Citizen*, 119–120.
44. Bimber, *Information and American Democracy*; Schudson, *The Good Citizen*, 56.
45. Schudson, *The Good Citizen*, 119.
46. Bimber, *Information and American Democracy*, 51.
47. Ibid., 54.
48. Jamieson, *Packaging the Presidency*, 8–14.
49. Ibid., 9.
50. Schudson, *The Good Citizen*, 133–143.
51. Ibid., 136.

52. Prior, *Post-Broadcast Democracy*.
53. Jamieson, *Packaging the Presidency*.
54. Farnsworth and Lichter, *The Nightly News Nightmare*.
55. Jamieson, *Packaging the Presidency*.
56. Nielsen, *Ground Wars*.
57. Ryan, *History of the Internet*.
58. O'Reilly, "Design Patterns and Business Models for the Next Generation of Software."
59. Trent and Friedenberg, *Political Campaign Communication*.
60. Denton, "Communication Variables and Dynamics of the 1996 Presidential Campaign."
61. Ibid.
62. Ibid.
63. Ibid.
64. Ibid.
65. Nimmo and Savage, *Candidates and Their Images*.
66. Denton, "Communication Variables and Dynamics of the 1996 Presidential Campaign."
67. Ibid.
68. Stromer-Galley, "Online Interaction and Why Candidates Avoid It."
69. Katz and Lazarsfeld, *Personal Influence*.
70. For an excellent analysis of the role of personalized communication in political campaigns see Nielsen, *Ground Wars*.
71. Barber, *Strong Democracy*.
72. For a detailed analysis of the role of media and political pundits in shaping public opinion, see Jacobs and Townsley, *The Space of Opinion*.
73. Delli Carpini and Keeter, *What Americans Know about Politics and Why It Matters*.
74. Ibid.; Neuman, *The Paradox of Mass Politics*.
75. Prior, *Post-Broadcast Democracy*; Putnam, *Bowling Alone*; Zukin et al., *A New Engagement?*
76. Page and Shapiro, *The Rational Public*.
77. Zaller, *The Nature and Origins of Mass Opinion*.
78. Schudson, *The Good Citizen*.
79. Marcus, Neuman, and MacKuen, *Affective Intelligence and Political Judgment*.
80. Arterton, and Orren, *The Electronic Commonwealth*; Barber, *Strong Democracy*, Browning, *Electronic Democracy*; Poster, "Cyberdemocracy."
81. Margolis and Resnick, *Politics as Usual*.
82. Sunstein, *Republic.Com 2.0*.
83. Best and Krueger, "Analyzing the Representativeness of Internet Political Participation"; Hargittai and Walejko, "The Participation Divide"; Nam and Stromer-Galley, "The Democratic Divide in the 2008 U.S. Presidential Election."
84. Latour, "On Recalling ANT"; Latour, *Reassembling the Social*.
85. Marvin, *When Old Technologies Were New*, 5.
86. Ibid.
87. Edelman, *Politics as Symbolic Action; Constructing the Political Spectacle*.
88. Chadwick, *The Hybrid Media System*.
89. Sunstein, *Republic.Com 2.0*.

Chapter 2

1. Foot and Schneider, *Web Campaigning*.
2. Katz and Lazarsfeld, *Personal Influence*.
3. Latour, *Reassembling the Social*.
4. D'Alessio, "Use of the World Wide Web in the 1996 U.S. Election."
5. Ibid.
6. As cited in Kevin Maney, "Cyber-Campaigning: The Future of Politics on the Internet. Potential for Good, or Bad, Still Unknown," *USA Today*, April 15, 1996.

7. See, for example, Klotz, "Positive Spin."
8. Stratford and Stratford, "Computerized and Networked Government Information."
9. Margot Williams, "The Election Year, Candidates Are as Close as Your PC Screen," *Washington Post*, January 8, 1996.
10. Drew and Weaver, "Voter Learning in the 1996 Presidential Election: Did the Media Matter?"
11. De Valasco, *Centrist Rhetoric*.
12. Laura Segal, personal communication, November 25, 1997.
13. Klinenberg and Perrin, "Symbolic Politics in the Information Age."
14. Denton, "Communication Variables and Dynamics of the 1996 Presidential Campaign."
15. Robert Arena, personal communication, November 24, 1997.
16. Andy Sohn, e-mail communication, February 12, 2013.
17. Segal, personal communication, November 25, 1997.
18. Rajiv Chandrasekaran, "Politics Finding a Home on the Net; Post-Election Surveys Show the Web Gains Influence among Voters," *Washington Post*, November 22, 1996.
19. Arena, personal communication, November 24, 1997.
20. Klinenberg and Perrin, "Symbolic Politics in the Information Age," 31.
21. During the vice-presidential debate between Dole, who was Gerald Ford's 1976 running mate, and Walter Mondale, Jimmy Carter's running mate, Dole told Mondale: "I figured it up the other day: If we added up the killed and wounded in Democrat wars in this century, it would be about 1.6 million Americans—enough to fill the city of Detroit." Mondale labeled him a hatchet man in his rebuttal. "NBC Learn K-12," http://archives.nbclearn.com/portal/site/k-12/flatview?cuecard=4671, accessed July 21, 2013. When he ran for president in 1988, Dole placed third in New Hampshire. George H. W. Bush had been asked if he had anything to say to Dole, and he wished Dole well. When the same question was later asked of Dole, he said, "Yeah, stop lying about my record." "1988: 'Thank You, New Hampshire,'" http://www.unionleader.com/apps/pbcs.dll/article?AID=/99999999/NEWS0605/110509961&template=printart, accessed July 21, 2013. Although most Americans did not know much about Bob Dole, the image they likely had of him was as an old guy with an acid tongue.
22. Rob Kubasko, speaking at a panel at the George Washington Institute for Politics, Democracy, and the Internet conference, April 21, 2009.
23. Walter Shapiro, "Prime-Time Battles Never Knockouts," *USA Today*, October 7, 1996.
24. David Maraniss, "With 'Zingers,' Dole Tactic Is Polite Aggression," *Washington Post*, October 7, 1996.
25. As cited in Justin Gillis, "Dole Scores Points with Debaters; but Georgetown University Students Give Alumnus Clinton the Edge," *Washington Post*, October 7, 1996.
26. This example also highlights the challenges the news media faced in trying to become literate with DCTs and the messages through them.
27. Arena, personal communication, November 24, 1997.
28. Segal, personal communication, November 25, 1997.
29. Michael D. Shear, "To GOP, Mark Warner's MTV Web Link Sounds a Sour Note," *Washington Post*, August 3, 1996.
30. Klinenberg and Perrin, "Symbolic Politics in the Information Age."
31. Arena, personal communication, November 24, 1997.
32. Ibid.
33. See Foot and Schneider, *Web Campaigning*, for the practice of informing in campaigns.
34. Segal, personal communication, November 25, 1997.
35. Ibid.
36. Arena, personal communication, November 24, 1997.
37. Ibid.
38. Klinenberg and Perrin, "Symbolic Politics in the Information Age."
39. Bruce Maxwell, "Political Connections; Putting the Party Line on E-Mail," *Washington Post*, February 22, 1996.

40. Foot and Schneider, *Web Campaigning.*
41. Bob Schieffer, "Voters Can Now Surf the Internet to Find Latest Information about Presidential Candidates," *CBS Evening News,* August 3, 1996.
42. Klinenberg and Perrin, "Symbolic Politics in the Information Age"; Stromer-Galley, "Online Interaction and Why Candidates Avoid It."

Chapter 3

1. As quoted in Leslie Wayne, "The 2000 Campaign; the Internet; Regulators Confront Web Role in Politics," *New York Times,* April 21, 2000.
2. As quoted in Tina Kelley, "Candidate on the Stump Is Surely on the Web," *New York Times,* October 19, 1999.
3. Terry M. Neal, "Candidates Hang Hopes on Electronic Hustings," *Washington Post,* April 26, 1999.
4. Janet Kornblum, "Talk Host's TV Show Sparks a Protest Site," *USA Today,* March 2, 2000.
5. Janet Kornblum, "Web Makes Little Impact on Election," USA Today, October 31, 2000.
6. Bimber and Davis, *Information and American Democracy,* 102.
7. Ibid., 105.
8. As quoted in Jim Drinkard, "E-Politics: One Click Can Reach Millions," *USA Today,* August 31, 1999.
9. Max Fose, personal communication, April 21, 2000.
10. Ben Green, personal communication, November 29, 2012.
11. Mike Shannon, personal communication, December 21, 2012.
12. As quoted in Judy Keen, "2000 Candidates Point to Web to Click with Voters," *USA Today,* April 29, 1999.
13. *Inside Politics,* CNN, May 31, 1999.
14. *Moneyline News Hour,* CNN, February 3, 2000.
15. "Internet Fundraising," *USA Today,* January 24, 2000.
16. John Mintz, "McCain Camp Enjoys a Big Net Advantage," *Washington Post,* February 9, 2000.
17. Anthony DePalma, "Responsible Party: Shawn M. Meurer; Meet, Greet, and Collect Online," *New York Times,* April 2, 2000.
18. Ibid.
19. As quoted in Ben White, "Politics; Internet Jackpot Fuels McCain's Gamble," *Washington Post,* February 5, 2000.
20. As broadcast on *World News Tonight,* February 13, 2000.
21. Terry M. Neal, "Politics; Bradley's Fund-Raising Frontier: More Than Half a Million on the Internet," *Washington Post,* September 20, 1999.
22. Lynn Reed, personal communication, April 20, 2000.
23. Verser and Wicks, "Managing Voter Impressions."
24. Bimber and Davis, *Campaigning Online*; Shaw, "How the Bush and Gore Campaigns Conceptualized and Used the Internet in 2000."
25. Bimber and Davis in *Campaigning Online* found a small but important increase in knowledge of the candidate's positions among those who were supporters of the candidate.
26. Ibid.
27. Ibid.; Ku, Kaid, and Pfau, "The Impact of Web Site Campaigning on Traditional News Media and Public Information Processing."
28. As quoted in Ianthe Jeanne Dugan, "Forbes Uses Fund-Raiser to Raise His Profile; GOP Hopeful Stakes Out High-Tech, Family-Friendly Position at New York Bash," *Washington Post,* June 17, 1999.
29. To the best of my knowledge, this was the first attack website by a major-party presidential candidate.
30. Smith and Mansharamani, "Challenger and Incumbent Reversal in the 2000 Election."

31. Jamieson and Waldman, *The Press Effect*.
32. As reported on *Inside Politics,* CNN, November 29, 1999.
33. As reported on the *Sunday Morning Show,* CNN, August 15, 1999.
34. Green, personal communication, November 29, 2012.
35. Ibid.
36. Ibid.
37. Ibid.
38. Wicks and Boubacar, "Going Negative."
39. Crossfire, *CNN,* July 3, 2000.
40. Greta Van Susten, *Burden of Proof,* CNN, November 2, 2000.
41. As reported on *Inside Politics,* CNN, November 29, 1999.
42. "Internet Fundraising," *USA Today,* January 24, 2000.
43. *Cnndotcom,* CNN, January 22, 2000.
44. Tina Kelley, "Candidate on the Stump Is Surely on the Web," *New York Times,* October 19, 1999.
45. As quoted in Ben White, "On Politics; Electrons as Electors? Probably Not Yet," *Washington Post,* April 16, 2000.
46. Ibid.
47. As quoted in Terry M. Neal, "A Web of Bush Tickets," *Washington Post,* May 14, 1999.
48. As quoted in Jill Lawrence, "Bush Team: Web Sites No Clue to Possible No. 2," *USA Today,* May 14, 1999.
49. Rebecca Fairley Raney, "Politics a Hot New Internet Investment," *New York Times,* January 2, 1999.
50. Lloyd Grove and Beth Berselli, "The Reliable Source," *Washington Post,* October 5, 2000.
51. As reported in B. Drummond Ayres, Jr., "Political Briefing," *New York Times,* May 30, 1999.
52. Mintz, "McCain Camp Enjoys a Big Net Advantage."
53. Dan Rather, *60 Minutes II,* CBS, February 1, 2000.
54. Tina Kelley, "Candidate on the Stump Is Surely on the Web," *New York Times,* October 19, 1999.
55. Ibid.
56. Reed, personal communication, April 20, 2000.
57. Howard Kurtz, "Bradley Aides Act Quickly in E-Mail Critique," *Washington Post,* November 11, 1999.
58. Tina Kelley, "Candidate on the Stump Is Surely on the Web."
59. Susan B. Glasser, "Consultants Pursue Promising Web of New Business," *Washington Post,* May 3, 2000.
60. Ibid.
61. Leslie Wayne, "E-Mail Part of the Effort to Turn out the Voters," *New York Times,* November 6, 2000.
62. As quoted in Edward Walsh, "Running on a Tightrope for an Audience of One," *Washington Post,* July 15, 2000.
63. Leslie Wayne, "On Web, Voters Reinvent Grass-Roots Activism," *New York Times,* May 21, 2000.
64. *Inside Politics,* CNN, December 22, 1999.
65. As quoted in Susan B. Glasser, "Consultants Pursue Promising Web of New Business," *Washington Post,* May 3, 2000.
66. AOL and Microsoft had at one point planned to share with Aristotle information about their users, specifically their e-mail addresses; however, they eventually established policies preventing the marriage of their users' information with voter rolls. Ibid.
67. Michael Turk, personal communication, September 12, 2008.
68. Richard Wolf, "Going Online Is Fine, but GOP Sees E-Mail as the Key," *USA Today,* August 3, 2000.

69. Ibid.
70. Ibid.

Chapter 4

1. This term, possibly coined by Jerome Armstrong, a prominent liberal blogger, conveys the idea of political activism through the Internet. Boehlert, *Bloggers on the Bus.*
2. Latour, *Reassembling the Social.*
3. Dan Balz, "Surge of Cash Puts Pressure on Insurgent Dean to Deliver Votes," *Washington Post*, July 2, 2003.
4. "Internet Adoption, 1995–2012," Pew Internet & American Life Project, http://www.pewinternet.org/Static-Pages/Trend-Data-%28Adults%29/Internet-Adoption.aspx, accessed February 16, 2013.
5. Herring et al., "Bridging the Gap."
6. Lawson-Borders and Kirk, "Blogs in Campaign Communication."
7. Kerbel, *Netroots*, 42.
8. Karpf, *The MoveOn Effect.*
9. Lee Rainie, John Horrigan, and Michael Cornfield, "The Internet and Campaign 2004," Pew Internet & American Life Project, March 6, 2005, http://www.pewinternet.org/Reports/2005/The-Internet-and-Campaign-2004.aspx, accessed July 25, 2013.
10. Carol C. Darr, " Internet Donors Can Clean up National Campaign Financing," *USA Today*, July 16, 2003.
11. Trippi, *The Revolution Will Not Be Televised.*
12. Sharon Theimer, "White House Hopefuls Make Final Push for Cash as Second Fund-Raising Period Ends," Associated Press, July 1, 2013.
13. Kreiss, *Taking Our Country Back*; Trippi, *The Revolution Will Not Be Televised.*
14. Mike Glover, "Dean Launches Internet-Driven Turnout Effort," Associated Press, July 2, 2003.
15. "2004 Donor Demographics," Center for Responsive Politics, http://www.opensecrets.org/presidential/donordems.asp, accessed February 10, 2005.
16. Kerry, following Dean, opted out of federal financing in the primary. Kerry did so because he feared he could not effectively compete against Dean in New Hampshire if he were capped by how much he could spend because of federal financing laws.
17. As quoted in Brian Faler, "Campaign Deal: $10 Million for a Quarter," *Washington Post*, September 26, 2003.
18. Sharon Theimer, "Record-Setting Dean Donors Have More Money Left to Give," Associated Press, October 15, 2003.
19. Josh Ross, personal communication, March 5, 2013.
20. Glen Justice, "Bush Still Has More Cash, but Kerry Leads Web Race," *New York Times*, May 21, 2004.
21. Ross, personal communication, March 5, 2013.
22. Glen Justice, "Kerry's Campaign Has Soared from Poorhouse to Penthouse," *New York Times*, June 27, 2004.
23. Glen Justice, "Kerry Kept Money Coming with Internet as His A.T.M.," *New York Times*, November 6, 2004.
24. Peter Daou, personal communication, February 26, 2013.
25. Sharon Theimer, "New Bush Volunteer Fund-Raising Group to Raise $200,000 Each for Campaign," Associated Press, May 22, 2003.
26. Sharon Theimer, "Liberman Raises $5 Million in Second Quarter for Presidential Bid," Associated Press, July 2, 2003.
27. Richard W. Stevenson and Glen Justice, "The 2004 Campaign: Fund-Raising; Bush Took in $130.8 Million in Political Conributions in 2003," *New York Times*, January 8, 2004.

28. Justice, "Kerry Kept Money Coming with Internet as His A.T.M."
29. As quoted in Lois Romano, "Internet Becoming Candidates' Domain; Dean Leads Democrats in Using Web," *Washington Post*, June 29, 2003.
30. Quoted in Laura Bumenfeld, "Empower Play: The Pitch That Works for Dean," *Washington Post*, October 1, 2003.
31. Trippi, *The Revolution Will Not Be Televised*.
32. Gunn, "On Speech and Public Release."
33. As quoted in Will Lester, "Retired General Enjoys the Coverage Candidates Covet," Associated Press, April 11, 2003.
34. John Hlinko, personal communication, February 5, 2013.
35. Lois Romano, "Internet Becoming Candidates' Domain; Dean Leads Democrats in Using Web."
36. As quoted in Todd S. Purdum, "F.B.I. Papers Describe Role of Young Kerry Against War," *New York Times*, May 6, 2004.
37. Kate Zernike and Jim Rutenberg, "The 2004 Campaign: Advertising; Friendly Fire: The Birth of an Attack on Kerry," *New York Times*, August 20, 2004.
38. Michael Cornfield, "Commentary on the Impact of the Internet on the 2004 Election," Pew Internet & American Life Project, March 6, 2005, http://www.pewinternet.org/Reports/2005/Commentary-on-the-impact-of-the-internet-on-the-04-election/Going-Broadband-Getting-Netwise/The-Cyber-Education-of-John-Kerry-and-other-Political-Actors.aspx.
39. Williams, "The Main Frame."
40. As quoted in Jim Rutenberg, "In Politics, the Web Is a Parallel World with Its Own Rules," *New York Times*, February 22, 2004.
41. Wiese and Gronbeck, "Campaign 2004 Developments in Cyberpolitics."
42. Stromer-Galley and Baker, "Joy and Sorrow of Interactivity on the Campaign Trail."
43. As quoted in Lisa Napoli, "Like Online Dating, with a Political Spin," *New York Times*, March 13, 2003.
44. Kreiss, *Taking Our Country Back*.
45. As reported in Ron Fournier, "No Trekkies, These Dean Backers Use Internet Sites to Organize Grass-Roots Campaign," Associated Press, June 5, 2003.
46. As quoted in Lois Romano, "Internet Becoming Candidates' Domain; Dean Leads Democrats in Using Web."
47. Brian Faler, "Dean Leaves Legacy of Online Campaign; Use of Internet to Raise Funds, Organize Rallies May Be Common in Future," *Washington Post*, February 20, 2004.
48. As quoted in Will Lester, "Campaigns Look to Volunteers, Donors from Internet Primary," Associated Press, June 26, 2003.
49. Horton and Wohl, "Mass Communication and Para-Social Interaction," 215.
50. As quoted in Brian Faler, "MoveOn Ads Taken on Bush's Economic Record," *Washington Post*, November 24, 2003.
51. Stromer-Galley and Baker, "Joy and Sorrow of Interactivity on the Campaign Trail."
52. Brian Faler, "After Dean's Vociferous Performance, Bloggers Offer an Earful," *Washington Post*, January 26, 2004.
53. Stromer-Galley and Baker, "Joy and Sorrow of Interactivity on the Campaign Trail."
54. Michael Turk, e-mail communication, February 18, 2012.
55. Ibid.
56. Hlinko, personal communication, February 5, 2013.
57. Ibid.
58. Ibid.
59. Faler, "MoveOn Ads Taken on Bush's Economic Record."
60. Trippi, *The Revolution Will Not Be Televised*, 82.
61. As quoted in Jodi Wilgoren, "You Go, Dean! Babies of Boomers Find a Candidate," *New York Times*, October 7, 2003.

62. As quoted in Elizabeth Rosenthal, "The 2004 Campaign: The Dean Campaign; Political Challenge 2.0: Make a Virtual Army a Reality," *New York Times*, December 21, 2003.

63. Mike Allen, "Bush Turns to Fla. to Set Aggressive Pace; Rally Kicks Off Intensive Grass-Roots Campaign," *Washington Post*, March 21, 2004.

64. Daou, personal communication, February 26, 2013.

65. Ross, personal communication, March 5, 2013.

66. Ibid.

67. Todd S. Purdum and David M. Halbfinger, "The 2004 Campaign: The Massachusetts Senator; with Cry of 'Bring It on,' Kerry Shifted Tack to Regain Footing," *New York Times*, February 1, 2004.

68. Kreiss, "Developing the 'Good Citizen.'"

69. Kreiss, *Taking Our Country Back*.

70. Feld and Wilcox, *Netroots Rising*.

71. Ibid.

72. Kreiss, *Taking Our Country Back*.

73. Howard Kurtz, "Divide and Bicker; the Dean's Campaign's Hip, High-Tech Image Hid a Nasty Civil War," *Washington Post*, February 29, 2004.

74. As quoted in Jodi Wilgoren, "Dean Makes His Exit from the Campaign but Vows, 'We Are Not Going Away,'" *New York Times*, February 19, 2004.

75. Paul Farhi, "Campaign Ads Enrich Advisers, Raise Questions," *Washington Post*, February 10, 2004.

76. Ron Fournier and Mike Glover, "Iowans Besieged by Political Troops, Technology in Get-out-Vote Drives," Associated Press, January 8, 2004.

77. Kreiss, *Taking Our Country Back*.

78. As quoted in Todd S. Purdum, "The 2004 Campaign: The Volunteers; Outside Campaigners Flood Iowa, Sharing Their Candidates' Styles," *New York Times*, January 15, 2004.

79. Farhi, "Campaign Ads Enrich Advisers, Raise Questions."

80. As quoted in Connie Cass, "Washington Today: Dean Faithful Accept Campaign Changes, Wistfully," Associated Press, January 30, 2004.

81. It should be noted that others provided a different picture: that Fowler was disgruntled because he was told he could not run the day-to-day campaign, and that Eli Segal, who worked for Clinton, would be in charge instead. Ron Fournier, "Clark Campaign Manager Quits in Feud over Direction of Presidential Bid," Associated Press, October 7, 2003.

82. Lois Romano, "Clark to Launch Media Blitz in New Hampshire; Ads Aim to Show He Can Take on Dean," *Washington Post*, November 16, 2003.

83. Hlinko, personal communication, February 5, 2013.

84. Ibid.

85. Ibid.

Chapter 5

1. The concept of super-supporters is similar to that of Graham and Wright's "super participants" as described in their article "Discursive Equality and Everyday Online Political Talk: The Impact of 'Super-Participants,'" who are the most involved in online deliberation.

2. Latour, *Reassembling the Social*.

3. See, for example, Abroms and Lefebvre, "Obama's Wired Campaign"; Cogburn and Espinoza-Vasquez,. "From Networked Nominee to Networked Nation"; Kreiss, *Taking Our Country Back*.

4. "Poll: Opposition to Iraq War at All-Time High," September 25, 2006, http://www.cnn.com/2006/POLITICS/08/21/iraq.poll/, accessed July 26, 2013.

5. Joseph Carroll, "Bush Job Approval at 37%," October 10, 2006, http://www.gallup.com/poll/24916/Bush-Job-Approval-37.aspx, accessed July 26, 2013.

6. Joseph Carroll, "Healthcare Edges Up in Public's List of Priorities," February 28, 2007, http://www.gallup.com/poll/26725/Healthcare-Edges-Publics-List-Priorities.aspx, accessed July 26, 2013.

7. Lydia Saad, "Economic Anxiety Surges in Past Year," March 28, 2008, http://www.gallup.com/poll/105802/Economic-Anxiety-Surges-Past-Year.aspx, accessed July 26, 2013.

8. I use *black* to describe Obama's race, rather than *African American*, because Obama typically refers to himself as black.

9. From Pew Internet and American Life Project "Usage Over Time" data, available at http://www.pewinternet.org/Trend-Data-%28Adults%29/Usage-Over-Time.aspx, accessed July 26, 2013.

10. Tim O'Reilly, "Design Patterns and Business Models for the Next Generation of Software," *O'Reilly.com*, September 20, 2005, http://oreilly.com/web2/archive/what-is-web-20.html, accessed July 26, 2013.

11. From Pew Internet & American Life Project, "Usage Over Time" data.

12. Lee Rainie and Aaron Smith, "The Internet and the 2008 Election," June 15, 2008, http://www.pewinternet.org/Reports/2008/The-Internet-and-the-2008-Election.aspx, accessed July 26, 2013.

13. Aaron Smith, "The Internet's Role in Campaign 2008," April 15, 2009, http://www.pewinternet.org/Reports/2009/6--The-Internets-Role-in-Campaign-2008/1--Summary-of-Findings.aspx, accessed July 26, 2013.

14. Nam and Stromer-Galley, "The Democratic Divide in the 2008 U.S. Presidential Election."

15. Baumgartner and Morris, "MyFaceTube Politics."

16. Katie Harbath, personal communication, September 14, 2008.

17. Vincent Harris, personal communication, August 24, 2008.

18. Peter Daou, personal communication, February 26, 2013

19. Justine Lam, personal communication, August 6, 2008.

20. Joe Rospars, speaking on a panel at the University of Southern California Unruh Institute of Politics conference, November 22, 2009.

21. Mark Soohoo, personal communication, November 18, 2008.

22. Jose Antonio Vargas, "Meet the Opos; Online Political Operatives, Such as Mindy Finn and Stephen Smith, Want New Media to Send a New Message," *Washington Post*, May 4, 2007.

23. Ibid.

24. Harbath personal communication, September 14, 2008.

25. Tim Tagaris, personal communication, September 11, 2008.

26. Daou, personal communication, February 26, 2013.

27. Ibid.

28. Leslie Wayne and Aron Pilhofer, "As Coffers Expand and Contract, Strategies Emerge," *New York Times*, October 22, 2007.

29. Adam Nagourney, "Early '08 Fund-Raising Has Clear Blue Tint," *New York Times*, April 5, 2007.

30. Jeff Zeleny and Patrick Healy, "Obama Shows His Strength in a Fund-Raising Feat on Par with Clinton," *New York Times*, April 5, 2007.

31. Chadwick, *The Hybrid Media System*.

32. Jeff Zeleny, "Obama Campaign Raises $32.5 Million," *New York Times*, July 3, 2007.

33. Michael Cooper and Aron Pilhofer, "Democratic Candidates Keep Outraising Republicans," *New York Times*, October 16, 2007.

34. Katharine Q. Seelye, "Maine to Obama; Clinton Replaces Campaign Leader," *New York Times*, February 11, 2008.

35. Michael Luo, "Clinton, Emphasizing Web Presence, Sees Rise in Online Donations," *New York Times*, March 22, 2008.

36. Kenneth P. Vogel, "The Story Behind Clinton's Record Haul," *Politico*, April 26, 2008, http://dyn.politico.com/printstory.cfm?uuid=8C6A167C-3048-5C12-00060790AACE2D82, accessed July 26, 2013.

37. Patrick Healy and Jeff Zeleny, "As Support Fades, Clinton Focuses on Next Contest," *New York Times*, May 8, 2008.
38. David D. Kirkpatrick, "Romney Leads G.O.P. in Money, Tapping Wall St. and Mormons," *New York Times*, April 3, 2007.
39. Sarah Wheaton, "Buying into Web Presence," *New York Times*, July 10, 2007.
40. Soohoo, personal communication, November 18, 2008.
41. Plouffe, *The Audacity to Win*, 326.
42. "John McCain," OpenSecrets.org, http://www.opensecrets.org/pres08/summary.php?cid=N00006424, accessed June 10, 2013.
43. Rick C. Hodgin, "Ron Paul Hauls in $6 Million in One Day Via Internet," December 17, 2007, http://www.tgdaily.com/content/view/35295/118/, accessed July 26, 2013.
44. Leslie Wayne, "Iowa Victories Scramble the Money Game, Too," *New York Times*, January 6, 2008.
45. Sarah Lai Stirland, "Ron Paul Supporters Hack Campaign Finance Law to Send Blimp Aloft," December 10, 2007, http://www.wired.com/politics/law/news/2007/12/paul_blimp, accessed July 26, 2013; Bryce Henderson, "Presidential Candidate Ron Paul Has a Blimp," December 7, 2007, http://www.reuters.com/article/pressRelease/idUS119278+07-Dec-2 007+PRN20071207, accessed July 26, 2013.
46. Bimber and Davis, *Campaigning Online*.
47. Chadwick, *The Hybrid Media System*.
48. Fredreka Schouten, "Paul Campain Fueled by Web Cash and Savvy; While Low in the Polls, He's Tops with Internet Hits," *USA Today*, October 11, 2007.
49. Ibid.
50. Ibid.
51. Sarah Lai Stirland, "CNN-YouTube Debate Producer Doubts the Wisdom of the Crowd," *Wired.com*, November 27, 2007, http://www.wired.com/politics/onlinerights/news/2007/11/cnn_debate, accessed July 26, 2013.
52. Joe Garofoli, "Technology-Savvy Bloggers Hone Candidates' Presence Online; Presidential Hopefuls Recruit Young but Experienced Consultants for Web Strategies," *San Francisco Chronicle*, November 3, 2007.
53. Harris, personal communication, August 24, 2008.
54. CBS Evening News, September 25, 2008.
55. Marc Santora, "A McCain Commercial Turns Romney's Words against Him," *New York Times*, January 2, 2008.
56. Adam Nagourney and Michael Cooper, "McCain's Conservative Model? Roosevelt (Theodore, That Is)," *New York Times*, July 13, 2008.
57. Mark Leibovich, "Hail to the Twitterer, " *New York Times*, August 3, 2008.
58. Michael Cooper, "McCain Laboring to Hit Right Note on the Economy," *New York Times*, September 17, 2008.
59. Jim Rutenberg, "McCain Is Trying to Define Obama as out of Touch, " *New York Times*, July 31, 2008; SooHoo, personal communication, November 18, 2008.
60. Frank Rich, "The Grand Old White Party Confronts Obama," *New York Times*, February 17, 2008.
61. Campbell, "The Discursive Performance of Femininity."
62. Trent, "The Early Presidential Campaign of 2008."
63. Faucheux, "Why Clinton Lost."
64. Patrick Healy, "On Web, Voters Question Clinton Directly," *New York Times*, January 23, 2007.
65. Campbell, "The Discursive Performance of Femininity."
66. Andrew Rasiej and Micah L. Sifry, "A 'Conversation,' and the Real Conversation," *Politico*, February 7, 2007.
67. Stokes, "Clinton, Post-Feminism, and Rhetorical Reception on the Campaign Trail."
68. Alexander, *The Performance of Politics*, 127.

69. As quoted in Jodi Kantor, "Gender Issue Lives on as Clinton's Bid Wanes," *New York Times*, May 19, 2008.

70. Daou, personal communication, February 26, 2013.

71. Andrew Adam Newman, "A Theme Song for Clinton: 'I'm a Believer' vs. 'Cold as Ice,'" *New York Times*, June 4, 2007.

72. Daou, personal communication, February 26, 2013; Faucheux, "Why Clinton Lost."

73. Jamieson, *Packaging the Presidency*.

74. Mike Huckabee had launched a similar type of rebuttal site earlier in 2007, as did Mitt Romney, who also countered negative YouTube videos by flooding the video sharing site with positive videos of Romney.

75. Jim Rutenberg, "Political Freelancers Use Web to Join the Attack," *New York Times*, June 29, 2008.

76. Mike Dorning, "Web Video Maker Unmasked," *Hartford Courant*, March 22, 2007, http://www.courant.com/news/nationworld/chi-0703220173mar22,0,2932972.story, accessed November 1, 2011.

77. David D. Kirkpatrick, "Facebook Free-for-All," *New York Times*, June 12, 2007.

78. Brian Stelter, "The Facebooker Who Friended Obama," *New York Times*, July 7, 2008.

79. Shelly Freierman, "Popular Demand," *New York Times*, April 16, 2007.

80. Dan Siroker, speaking at a May 24, 2009 conference panel at Stanford University, available on YouTube, http://www.youtube.com/watch?v=71bH8z6iqSc, accessed July 26, 2013.

81. Matt Peckham, "Yes We Can, Says Obama, in Video Games Everywhere," October 15, 2008, http://abcnews.go.com/Technology/PCWorld/story?id=6042625, accessed July 26, 2013.

82. In the 2004 campaign, John Edwards's campaign bought digital real estate in the virtual sandbox *Second Life*. Volunteers would hang out there and advocate for Edwards to the curious who wandered in. Visitors could buy digital Edwards paraphernalia, such as shoes and T-shirts, for player avatars.

83. Sweet and McCue-Enser, "Constituting 'the People' as Rhetorical Interruption."

84. Brian Ross and Rehab El-Buri, "Obama's Pastor: God Damn America, U.S. to Blame for 9/11," March 13, 2008, http://abcnews.go.com/Blotter/DemocraticDebate/story?id=4443788&page=1, accessed July 26, 2013.

85. May, "The Preacher and the Press."

86. Rowland and Jones, "One Dream."

87. Larry Rohter and Michael Luo, "Groups Respond to Obama's Call for National Discussion About Race," *New York Times*, March 20, 2008.

88. Brian Stelter, "Finding Political News Online, Young Viewers Pass It Along," *New York Times*, March 27, 2008.

89. Mayhill Fowler, "Obama: No Surprise That Hard-Pressed Pennsylvanians Turn Bitter," April 11, 2008, http://www.huffingtonpost.com/mayhill-fowler/obama-no-surprise-that-ha-ha_b_96188.html, accessed July 26, 2013.

90. Katharine Q. Seelye, "Blogger Is Surprised by Uproar over Obama Story, but Not Bitter," April 14, 2008, http://www.nytimes.com/2008/04/14/us/politics/14web-seelye.html, accessed July 26, 2013.

91. Clinton forcefully responded when the Iowa staff member was identified, declaring that Obama was Christian, and she would not tolerate that kind of attack on Obama in her campaign.

92. Julie Bosman and John M. Broder, "Obama's Campaign Opens a New Web Site to Strike Back at 'Dishonest Smears,'" *New York Times*, June 13, 2008.

93. Chadwick, *The Hybrid Media System*.

94. May, "The Preacher and the Press."

95. See Kreiss, *Taking Our Country Back*, for a description of the organizational shifts in staff from 2004 to 2008.

96. Katz and Lazarsfeld, *Personal Influence*.

97. Lam, personal communication, August 6, 2008.

98. Sarah Lai Stirland, "'Criminal' Botnet Stumps for Ron Paul, Researchers Allege," *Wired.com*, October 31, 2007, http://www.wired.com/politics/security/news/2007/10/paul_bot, accessed July 26, 2013.

99. Germany, "The Online Revolution," 151.

100. Rasiej and Sifry, "A 'Conversation,' and the Real Conversation."

101. Brian Stelter, "The Facebooker Who Friended Obama," *New York Times*, July 7, 2008.

102. Daou, personal communication, February 26, 2013.

103. Josh Ross, personal communication, March 5, 2013.

104. It is interesting to contemplate how her campaign would have fared four years later as social media continued to diffuse and new sites cropped up, like Pinterest, which attracted a female user base.

105. SooHoo, personal communication, November 18, 2008.

106. Ronald Brownstein, "The First 21st-Century Campaign," *National Journal*, April 16, 2008.

107. Rebecca Donatelli, speaking on a panel at the University of Southern California Unruh Institute of Politics conference, November 22, 2009.

108. Dan Gilgoff, "Walking a Fine Line Online," *U.S. News & World Report*, May 21, 2007.

109. Ronald Brownstein, "The First 21st-Century Campaign," *National Journal*, April 16, 2008.

110. Chadwick, *The Hybrid Media System*.

111. Joe Rospars, Presentation at the Personal Democracy Forum 2008, New York, NY, June 23, 2008.

112. Sam Graham-Feisten, personal communication, May 12, 2009.

113. Ibid.

114. Ibid.

115. Horton and Wohl, "Mass Communication and Para-Social Interaction."

116. Kreiss, *Taking Our Country Back*. Indeed, Sam Graham-Feisten at George Washington University's Institute for Politics, Democracy, and the Internet conference panel on April 21, 2009, explained that e-mail "isn't sexy, but it's a key driver for online and offline action." He explained that staff also pushed hard to be authentic in their communication on the blog and through e-mail. Their goal was to tell the stories of the supporters and go beyond "the glib marketing" and focus on "what's going on in their [supporters'] community."

117. As quoted in Ben Adler, "Can McCain Compete with Obama Online?" *Politico*, June 15, 2008, accessed through LexisNexis.

118. As quoted in Jose Antonio Vargas, "Obama's Wide Web; from YouTube to Text Messaging, Candidate's Team Connects to Voters," *Washington Post*, August 20, 2008.

119. Linda Hirshman, "16 Ways of Looking at a Female Voter," *New York Times Magazine*, February 3, 2008.

120. Fernandes et al., "The Writing on the Wall."

121. Trent, "The Early Presidential Campaign of 2008."

122. Michael Whitney, "Barack Obama's One Millionth Supporter on Facebook," *TechPresident*, http://techpresident.com/blog-entry/barack-obamas-one-millionth-supporter-facebook-updated, accessed November 1, 2011.

123. David Schaper, "'Camp Obama' Trains Campaign Volunteers," National Public Radio, June 13, 2007.

124. As quoted in Jose Antonio Vargas, "Text-Friendly Hopefuls Vie for Hearts and Thumbs," *Washington Post*, June 30, 2007.

125. Brian Stelter, "Enticing Text Messagers in a Get-out-the-Vote Push," *New York Times*, August 18, 2008.

126. Ibid.

127. As quoted in Jose Antonio Vargas, "Meet the Opos; Online Political Operatives, Such as Mindy Finn and Stephen Smith, Want New Media to Send a New Message," *Washington Post*, May 4, 2007.

128. As quoted in Dan Gilgoff, "Walking a Fine Line Online," *U.S. News & World Report*, May 21, 2007.

129. David Herbert, "Obama's 'Project Houdini' Revealed," *National Journal*, November 10, 2008, http://www.nationaljournal.com/njonline/no_20081107_4999.php, accessed July 26, 2013.

130. Ibid.

131. As quoted in Noam Cohen, "A Political Agitator Finds a Double-Edged Weapon," *New York Times*, July 6, 2008.

Chapter 6

1. boyd and Ellison, "Social Network Sites."

2. The hashtag allows people to post messages, so that others can search for all posts with it, what Zappavigna refers to as "Ambient Affiliation" leading to searchable talk.

3. Jennifer Preston, "Republicans Shake More Hands Using Social Media," *New York Times*, December 29, 2011.

4. Latour, *Reassembling the Social*.

5. Chris Isidore, "7.9 Million Jobs Lost—Many Forever," *CNN.com*, July 2, 2010, http://money.cnn.com/2010/07/02/news/economy/jobs_gone_forever/index.htm, accessed August 18, 2013.

6. Lynn Adler, "U.S. 2009 Foreclosures Shatter Record Despite Aid," *Reuters.com*, January 14, 2010, http://www.reuters.com/article/2010/01/14/us-usa-housing-foreclosures-idUSTRE60D0LZ20100114.

7. Claire Shipman, "Is It Wrong to Walk Away from a Mortgage Deep Underwater?" *ABCnews.com*, February 11, 2010, http://abcnews.go.com/GMA/mortgage-defaults-borrowers-walk-away-underwater-home/story?id=9802435, accessed July 27, 2013.

8. "The Lost Decade of the Middle Class," Pew Internet & American Life Project, August 22, 2012, http://www.pewsocialtrends.org/12/08/22/the-lost-decade-of-the-middle-class/, accessed July 27, 2013.

9. US Treasury Department, "Historical Debt Outstanding—Annual 2000–2012," http://www.treasurydirect.gov/govt/reports/pd/histdebt/histdebt_histo5.htm, accessed February 25, 2013.

10. Standard & Poor's, "United States of America Long-Term Rating Lowered to 'Aa+' Due to Political Risks, Rising Debt Burden; Outlook Negative," August 5, 2011, http://www.standardandpoors.com/ratings/articles/en/us/?assetID=1245316529563, accessed July 27, 2013.

11. Although analysis by statistician and political observer Nate Silver suggests that there is no correlation between high unemployment rates and electability ("On the Maddeningly Inexact Relationship Between Unemployment and Re-Election," *FiveThirtyEight* [blog] *NYTimes.com*, June 2, 2011, http://fivethirtyeight.blogs.nytimes.com/2011/06/02/on-the-maddeningly-inexact-relationship-between-unemployment-and-re-election/, accessed July 27, 2013).

12. Alexis C. Madrigal, "When the Nerds Go Marching in," *Atlantic.com*, November 16, 2012, http://www.theatlantic.com/technology/archive/2012/11/when-the-nerds-go-marching-in/265325/?single_page=true, accessed July 27, 2013.

13. Aaron Smith and Maeve Duggan, "Online Political Videos and Campaign 2012," Pew Internet & American Life Project, November 2, 2012, http://www.pewinternet.org/Reports/2012/Election-2012-Video.aspx, accessed July 27, 2013.

14. Aaron Smith and Maeve Duggan, "Presidential Campaign Donations in the Digital Age," Pew Internet & American Life Project, October 25, 2012, http://www.pewinternet.org/Reports/2012/Election-2012-Donations/Key-Findings.aspx, accessed July 27, 2013.

15. Lee Rainie, Aaron Smith, Kay Lehman Schlozman, Henry Brady, and Sidney Verba, "Social Media and Political Engagement," Pew Internet & American Life Project, October 19, 2012, http://www.pewinternet.org/Reports/2012/Political-engagement/Summary-of-Findings.aspx, accessed July 27, 2013.

16. Dimitrova and Bystrom, "The Effects of Social Media on Political Participation and Candidate Image Evaluations in the 2012 Iowa Caucuses."

17. Jenkins, *Convergence Culture*, 217.

18. Katz and Lazarsfeld, *Personal Influence*.

19. As quoted in Ashley Parker, "For Campaigns, Twitter Is Both an Early-Warning System and a Weapon," *New York Times*, January 29, 2012.

20. As quoted in Ethan Klapper, "Mitt Romney Campaign Makes Third Spelling Error in a Week," *Huffington Post*, May 4, 2012, http://www.huffingtonpost.com/2012/06/04/mitt-romney-campaign-spelling-errors_n_1569559.html, accessed July 27, 2013.

21. Joshua Green, "Corporations Want Obama's Winning Formula," *BusinessWeek.com*, November 21, 2012, http://www.businessweek.com/printer/articles/83230-corporations-want-obamas-winning-formula, accessed July 27, 2013.

22. Ibid.

23. Zac Moffatt, "Successes of the Romney and Republican Digital Efforts in 2012," In *Targeted Victory*, December 11, 2012, http://www.targetedvictory.com/2012/12/success-of-the-romney-republican-digital-efforts-2012/, accessed July 27, 2013.

24. Patrick Ruffini, personal communication, March 6, 2013.

25. Sandhya Somashekhar and Nia-Malika Henderson, "In N.H., It's Now or Never for Huntsman," *Washington Post*, January 9, 2012.

26. *Erin Burnett out Front*, CNN, January 13, 2012.

27. Martha T. Moore, "Cain Aide's 'Smoking Man' Video Is Smokin' Hot; Clip Goes Viral, Blazes Trail on YouTube," *USA Today*, October 28, 2011.

28. Jenkins, *Convergence Culture*.

29. Noam Cohen, "Dealing with an Identity Hijacked on the Online Highway," *New York Times*, September 26, 2011.

30. Early in the surfacing stage, Savage's definition was displayed above the Santorum campaign's official website link.

31. As quoted in Jennifer Preston, "Cain Camp Turns Google Searches to Its Benefit," *The Caucus* (blog) *NYTimes.com*, November 9, 2011, accessed on Lexis/Nexis.

32. Ashley Parker, "For Campaigns, Twitter Is Both an Early-Warning System and a Weapon," *New York Times*, January 29, 2012.

33. Harvard University Institute for Politics, "Campaign Managers Conference," November 29–30, 2012, http://www.iop.harvard.edu/campaign-managers-conference, accessed December 7, 2012.

34. As quoted in Justin Franz, "GOP Long Shots Take to Social Media," *Daily Dot*, December 19, 2011, http://www.dailydot.com/politics/gop-long-shots-take-social-media/, accessed July 27, 2013.

35. Alex Fitzpatrick, "How the Internet Saved Buddy Roemer's Presidential Campaign," *Mashable.com*, January 5, 2012, http://mashable.com/2012/01/05/buddy-roemer-digital-strategies/, accessed July 27, 2013.

36. Conway, Kenski, and Wang, "Twitter Use by Presidential Primary Candidates During the 2012 Campaign."

37. Franz, "GOP Long Shots Take to Social Media."

38. Chadwick, *The Hybrid Media System*.

39. Martha T. Moore, "Targeting Voters on Pinterest; Political Groups Use Social Media Site to Get Message out to Women," *USA Today*, June 13, 2012.

40. Ethan Klapper, "Mitt Romney Campaign Makes Third Spelling Error in a Week".

41. Steve Friess, "Can Romney Close the Digital Divide," *Politico*, October 25, 2012, http://www.politico.com/news/stories/1012/82870.html, accessed July 27, 2013.

42. David Corn, "Secret Video: Romney Tells Millionaire Donors What He Really Thinks of Obama Voters," *Mother Jones*, September 17, 2012, http://www.motherjones.com/politics/2012/09/secret-video-romney-private-fundraiser, accessed July 27, 2013.

43. As quoted in David Frum, "Who Captured Mitt Romney's 47% Video Clip?" *Daily Beast*, November 14, 2012, http://www.thedailybeast.com/articles/2012/11/14/who-captured-mitt-romney-s-47-video-clip.html, accessed July 27, 2013.

44. "Romney's '47%' Comments Criticized, but Many Also Say Overcovered," Pew Research Center for the People & the Press, October 1, 2012, http://www.people-press.org/2012/10/01/romneys-47-comments-criticized-but-many-also-say-overcovered/, accessed July 27, 2013.

45. Harvard University Institute for Politics, "Campaign Managers Conference."

46. Michael Scherer, "How Obama's Data Crunchers Helped Him Win," *Time*, November 8, 2012, http://www.cnn.com/2012/11/07/tech/web/obama-campaign-tech-team, accessed July 27, 2013.

47. "2012 Obama Campaign Legacy Report," http://secure.assets.bostatic.com/frontend/projects/legacy/legacy-report.pdf, accessed February 28, 2013.

48. Joshua Green, "Corporations Want Obama's Winning Formula,".

49. As quoted in Madrigal, "When the Nerds Go Marching In."

50. Lee Rainie, "Social Media and Voting," Pew Internet & American Life Project, November 6, 2012, http://www.pewinternet.org/Reports/2012/Social-Vote-2012/Key-Findings.aspx, accessed July 27, 2013.

51. Jeremy W. Peters, "With Video, Obama Looks to Expand Campaign's Reach through Social Media," *New York Times*, March 15, 2012.

52. As quoted in Melissa Bell, "Politicians Paying to Get Your Vote," *Washington Post*, October 16, 2011.

53. Charlie Warzel, "2012 Voters Are Going Further 'Off the Grid'; More Aren't Seeing Political Ads on TV," *AdWeek*, August 14, 2012, http://www.adweek.com/news/technology/2012-voters-are-going-further-grid-142709, accessed July 27, 2013.

54. Nick Judd, "For Romney's Digital Campaign, a Second-Place Finish," *TechPresident*, November 7, 2012, http://techpresident.com/news/23106/romneys-digital-campaign-second-place-finish, accessed July 27, 2013.

55. As quoted in Ashley Parker, "For Campaigns, Twitter Is Both an Early-Warning System and a Weapon".

56. Judd, "For Romney's Digital Campaign, a Second-Place Finish."

57. As quoted in Steve Friess, "Can Romney Close the Digital Divide," *Politico*, October 25, 2012, http://www.politico.com/news/stories/1012/82870.html, accessed July 27, 2013.

58. As quoted in Dave Nyczepir, "Movers & Shakers: Zac Moffatt," *Campaigns & Elections*, September 19, 2012, http://www.campaignsandelections.com/magazine/us-edition/328557/movers-and-shakers-zac-moffatt.thtml, accessed August 19, 2013.

59. Sasha Issenberg, "Obama's White Whale: How the Campaign's Top-Secret Project Narwhal Could Change This Race, and Many to Come," *Slate.com*, February 15, 2012, http://www.slate.com/articles/news_and_politics/victory_lab/2012/02/project_narwhal_how_a_top_secret_obama_campaign_program_could_change_the_2012_race_.single.html, accessed August 19, 2013.

60. Ibid.

61. Obama 2012 Campaign, "2012 Obama Campaign Legacy Report."

62. Sarah Lai Stirland, "Obama Campaign Touts Voter Registration Success, Promoted Dashboard," *TechPresident*, October 11, 2012, http://techpresident.com/news/22990/obama-campaign-touts-voter-registration-success-promotes-dashboard, accessed July 27, 2013.

63. As quoted in Jim Rutenberg, "Secret of the Obama Victory? Rerun Watchers, for One Thing," *New York Times*, November 12, 2012, http://www.nytimes.com/2012/11/13/us/politics/obama-data-system-targeted-tv-viewers-for-support.html?ref=politics, accessed July 27, 2013.

64. Ibid.
65. Benedict Carey, "Academic 'Dream Team' Helped Obama's Effort," *New York Times*, November 12, 2012, http://www.nytimes.com/2012/11/13/health/dream-team-of-behavioral-scientists-advised-obama-campaign.html?smid=tw-share, accessed July 27, 2013.
66. Alex Fitzpatrick, "Romney Digital Director: Obama Running Facebook 'Like It's 2008,'" *Mashable*, September 2, 2012, http://mashable.com/2012/09/02/romney-obama-facebook/, accessed July 27, 2013.
67. Jeremy W. Peters, "As TV Viewing Habits Change, Political Ads Follow Would-Be Voters Online," *New York Times*, April 2, 2012.
68. As quoted in Nyczepir, "Movers & Shakers: Zac Moffatt."
69. Steve Friess, "Can Romney Close the Digital Divide," *Politico*, October 25, 2012, http://www.politico.com/news/stories/1012/82870.html, accessed July 27, 2013.
70. Adam Mazmanian, "Republicans Flame Romney's Digital Team," *National Journal*, November 16, 2012, http://mashable.com/2012/11/16/mitt-romney-digital-team/, accessed July 27, 2013.
71. Alexis C. Madrigal, "When the Nerds Go Marching In".
72. Issenberg, "Obama's White Whale."
73. John Dickerson, "How to Run a Killer Campaign," *Slate*, November 15, 2012, http://www.slate.com/articles/news_and_politics/politics/2012/11/jim_messina_offers_his_tips_on_how_barack_obama_s_campaign_team_beat_mitt.single.html, accessed July 27, 2013.
74. As quoted in Holly Ramer, "Huntsman Picks up Boston Globe Endorsement," Associated Press, January 6, 2012, Lexis/Nexis.
75. Michael Scherer, "Inside the Secret World of the Data Crunchers Who Helped Obama Win," *Time*, November 7, 2012, http://swampland.time.com/2012/11/07/inside-the-secret-world-of-quants-and-data-crunchers-who-helped-obama-win/print/, accessed July 27, 2013.
76. "2012 Obama Campaign Legacy Report."
77. Madrigal, "When the Nerds Go Marching In."
78. Sean Gallagher, "Built to Win: Deep inside Obama's Campaign Tech," *Ars Technica*, November 14, 2012, http://arstechnica.com/information-technology/2012/11/built-to-win-deep-inside-obamas-campaign-tech/, accessed July 27, 2013.
79. "2012 Obama Campaign Legacy Report."
80. "Obama Campaign Officials Forum," ABC/Yahoo, September 4, 2012, http://abcnews.go.com/images/Politics/Charlotte%20Yahoo%20Panel%20Transcript.pdf, accessed July 27, 2013.
81. Sean Gallagher, "Romney Campaign Got Its IT from Best Buy, Staples, and Friends," *Ars Technica*, November 18, 2012, http://arstechnica.com/information-technology/2012/11/romney-campaign-got-its-it-from-best-buy-staples-and-friends/, accessed July 27, 2013.
82. Judd, "For Romney's Digital Campaign, a Second-Place Finish."
83. As quoted in Friess, "Can Romney Close the Digital Divide."
84. As quoted in Gregory Ferenstein, "Underdog No More: How Romney's Digital Director, Zac Moffatt, Got Silicon Valley to Power the Campaign," *TechCrunch*, September 7, 2012, http://techcrunch.com/2012/09/07/how-romneys-digital-director-zac-moffatt-got-silicon-valley-brightest-minds-to-work-for-the-campaign/, accessed July 27, 2013.
85. As quoted in Friess, "Can Romney Close the Digital Divide."
86. Steve Mullis, "On Election Day, Romney's Killer Whale 'App' Couldn't Stay Afloat," *NPR.org*, November 10, 2012, http://www.npr.org/blogs/alltechconsidered/2012/11/10/164869691/on-election-day-romneys-killer-whale-couldnt-stay-afloat, accessed July 27, 2013.

87. As quoted in Sean Gallagher, "Inside Team Romney's Whale of an IT Meltdown," *ars Technica*, November 9, 2012, http://arstechnica.com/information-technology/2012/11/inside-team-romneys-whale-of-an-it-meltdown/, accessed July 27, 2013.

88. Amanda Terkel, "Project Orca: Mitt Romney Campaign Plans Massive, State-of-the-Art Poll Monitoring Effort," *Huffington Post*, November 1, 2012, http://www.huffingtonpost.com/2012/11/01/project-orca-mitt-romney_n_2052861.html, accessed July 27, 2013.

89. Gallagher, "Inside Team Romneys' Whale of an IT Meltdown."

90. Maggie Haberman and Alexander Burns, "Romney's Fail Whale: Orca the Vote-Tracker Left Team 'Flying Blind,'" *Politico*, November 8, 2012, http://www.politico.com/blogs/burns-haberman/2012/11/romneys-fail-whale-orca-the-votetracker-149098.html, accessed July 27, 2013.

91. As quoted in Gallagher, "Inside Team Romneys' Whale of an IT Meltdown."

92. Amanda Terkel, "Project Orca."

93. Gallagher, "Romney Campaign Got Its IT from Best Buy, Staples, and Friends."

94. Adam Nagourney, Ashley Parker, Jim Rutenberg, and Jeff Zeleny, "How a Race in the Balance Went to Obama," *New York Times*, November 7, 2012, http://www.nytimes.com/2012/11/08/us/politics/obama-campaign-clawed-back-after-a-dismal-debate.html, accessed July 27, 2013.

Chapter 7

1. Denton, "Communication Variables and Dynamics of the 1996 Presidential Campaign."

2. Granovetter, "The Strength of Weak Ties."

3. Green, personal communication, November 29, 2012.

4. McKay Coppins, "The GOP Longest Long Shot Yet?," *Daily Beast*, March 3, 2011, http://www.thedailybeast.com/articles/2011/03/03/buddy-roemers-long-shot-bid-for-republican-presidential-nomination-in-2012.html, accessed July 29, 2013.

5. "Advertising Money: McCain vs. Obama," *FactCheck.org*, November 3, 2008, http://www.factcheck.org/2008/11/advertising-money-mccain-vs-obama/, accessed July 29, 2013.

6. Kate Kenski, Bruce W. Hardy, and Kathleen Hall Jamieson, *The Obama Victory*.

7. Tagg Romney, Mitt Romney's son, told a *Boston Globe* reporter that his father did not really want to be president: "He wanted to be president less than anyone I've met in my life. He had no desire to . . . run." Tagg Romney explained that his father is a private person and being under the media spotlight he found stressful. He wanted to help his country, but he hated the limelight, as reported by Michael Kranish, "The Story Behind Mitt Romney's Loss in the Presidential Campaign to President Obama," *Boston.com*, December 22, 2012, http://www.boston.com/news/politics/2012/president/2012/12/23/the-story-behind-mitt-romney-loss-the-presidential-campaign-president-obama/2QWkUB9pJgVIi1mAcIhQjL/story.html?utm_medium=referral&utm_source=pulsenews, accessed August 18, 2013.

8. Edelman, *Politics as Symbolic Action*; *Constructing the Political Spectacle*.

9. Browning, *Electronic Democracy*, 12–13.

10. Plouffe, *The Audacity to Win*, 20.

11. Rove, *Courage and Consequence*, 366.

12. "How the Presidential Candidates Use the Web and Social Media," Pew Research Center's Project for Excellent in Journalism, August 15, 2012, http://www.journalism.org/analysis_report/how_presidential_candidates_use_web_and_social_media, accessed July 29, 2013.

13. "2012 Presidential Campaign Finance Explorer," *Washington Post*, December 7, 2012, http://www.washingtonpost.com/wp-srv/special/politics/campaign-finance/, accessed July 29, 2013.

14. Campaign staff I interviewed gave me these sorts of justifications, and I heard such comments from staff and political pundits at conferences, such as Campaigns & Election's CampaignTech and George Washington University's Institute for Politics, Democracy and the Internet.

15. Barber, *Strong Democracy*.
16. O'Reilly, "What is Web 2.0."
17. As quoted in Jackie Kucinich, "Bachmann Appears Poised to Run in 2012; Representative Will Make Announcement in June," *USA Today*, May 27, 2011.
18. Dan Eggen and T. W. Farnam, "Deliver the Sound Bite, Watch Donors Eat It up," *Washington Post*, June 20, 2011.
19. Miranda Neubauer, "A Recent Internet History of Michele Bachmann," *TechPresident*, May 29, 2013, http://techpresident.com/news/23942/recent-internet-history-michele-bachmann, accessed July 29, 2013.
20. Michael D. Shear, "Bachmann Used Debate to Widen Her Appeal," *The Caucus* (blog), *NYTimes.com*, June 14, 2011, accessed in LexisNexis.
21. Accessed June 9, 2013, http://thinkprogress.org/politics/2011/06/16/246618/bachmann-craziest-quotes/?mobile=nc, accessed July 29, 2013.
22. Andrew Malcolm, "Michele Bachmann Confused John Wayne Gacy with The Duke," *Top of the Ticket* (blog), *LATimes.com*, June 27, 2011, http://latimesblogs.latimes.com/washington/2011/06/michele-bachmann-confuses-john-wayne-gacy-with-the-duke.html, accessed July 29, 2013.
23. Jamieson and Waldman, *The Press Effect*.
24. Doheny-Farina, *The Wired Neighborhood*; Putnam, *Bowling Alone*; Sunstein, *Republic. Com 2.0*.
25. Bimber and Davis, *Campaigning Online*.
26. Prior, *Post-Broadcast Democracy*.
27. See Christensen, "Political Activities on the Internet" for a review of the term.
28. Howard, *New Media Campaigns and the Managed Citizen*.
29. Ibid., 185.
30. Zukin et al., *A New Engagement?*
31. Green, Gerber, and Nickerson,. "Getting Out the Vote in Local Elections."
32. Chadwick, *The Hybrid Media System*.
33. Nielsen, *Ground Wars*.
34. Harfoush, *Yes We Did*.
35. Norris, *A Virtuous Circle*.
36. Lee Rainie and Aaron Smith, "Politics on Social Networking Sites," Pew Internet & American Life Project, September 4, 2012. http://www.pewinternet.org/Reports/2012/Politics-on-SNS/Summary-of-Findings.aspx, accessed July 29, 2013.
37. Howard, *New Media Campaigns and the Managed Citizen*.
38. Ibid., 132.
39. Kevin Fogarty, "Election 2012: Who's Winning Big Data Race?," *Information Week*, October 30, 2012, http://www.informationweek.com/big-data/news/big-data-analytics/election-2012-whos-winning-big-data-ra/240012471#, accessed July 29, 2013.
40. Holbrook and McClurg, "The Mobilization of Core Supporters."
41. Kang, "A Volatile Public."
42. Prior, *Post-Broadcast Democracy*.
43. See chapter 4. John Hlinko noted that senior staff in the Wesley Clark campaign viewed the netroots as "unhinged" (personal communication, February 5, 2013).

References

Abbate, Janet. *Inventing the Internet*. Cambridge, MA: MIT Press, 2000.

Abramson, Jeffrey B., F. Christopher Arterton, and Gary R. Orren. *The Electronic Commonwealth: The Impact of New Media Technologies on Democratic Politics*. New York: Basic Books, 1988.

Abroms, Lorien C., and R. Craig Lefebvre. "Obama's Wired Campaign: Lessons for Public Health Communication." *Journal of Health Communication* 14, no. 5 (2009): 415–423. doi: 10.1080/10810730903033000.

Alexander, Jeffrey C. *The Performance of Politics: Obama's Victory and the Democratic Struggle for Power*. New York: Oxford University Press, 2010.

Barber, Benjamin. *Strong Democracy: Participatory Politics for a New Age*. Berkeley: University of California Press, 2004.

Baudrillard, Jean. *Simulacra and Simulation*. Translated by Sheila Faria Glaser. Ann Arbor: University of Michigan Press, 1994.

Baumgartner, Jody C., and Jonathan S. Morris. "MyFaceTube Politics: Social Networking Web Sites and Political Engagement of Young Adults." *Social Science Computer Review* 28, no. 1 (2010): 24–44. doi:10.1177/0894439309334325.

Berners-Lee, Tim. *Weaving the Web: The Original Design and Ultimate Destiny of the World Wide Web*. New York: HarperCollins, 2000.

Best, Samuel J., and Brian S. Krueger. "Analyzing the Representativeness of Internet Political Participation." *Political Behavior* 27, no. 2 (2005): 183–216. doi:10.1007/s11109-005-3242-y.

Bimber, Bruce. *Information and American Democracy: Technology in the Evolution of Political Power*. Cambridge: Cambridge University Press, 2003.

Bimber, Bruce, and Richard Davis. *Campaigning Online: The Internet in U.S. Elections*. New York: Oxford University Press, 2003.

Boehlert, Eric. *Bloggers on the Bus: How the Internet Changes Politics and the Press*. New York: Free Press, 2009.

boyd, danah m., and Nicole B. Ellison. "Social Network Sites: Definition, History, and Scholarship." *Journal of Computer-Mediated Communication* 13, no. 1 (2007): 210–230. doi: 10.1111/j.1083-6101.2007.00393.x.

Brewin, Mark W. *Celebrating Democracy: The Mass-Mediated Ritual of Election Day*. New York: Peter Lang, 2008.

Browning, Graeme. *Electronic Democracy: Using the Internet to Transform American Politics*. 2nd ed. Medford, NJ: Information Today, 2002.

Campbell, Karlyn Kohrs. "The Discursive Performance of Femininity: Hating Hillary." *Rhetoric & Public Affairs* 1, no. 1 (1998): 1–20. doi: 10.1353/rap.2010.0172.

Chadwick, Andrew. *The Hybrid Media System: Politics and Power*. New York: Oxford University Press, 2013.

Christensen, Henrik Serup. "Political Activities on the Internet: Slacktivism or Political Participation by Other Means?" *First Monday* 16, no. 2 (2011). http://firstmonday.org/htbin/cgiwrap/bin/ojs/index.php/fm/article/viewArticle/3336/2767.

Cogburn, Derrick L., and Fatima K. Espinoza-Vasquez. "From Networked Nominee to Networked Nation: Examining the Impact of Web 2.0 and Social Media on Political Participation and Civic Engagement in the 2008 Obama Campaign." *Journal of Political Marketing* 10, nos. 1–2 (2011): 189–213. doi:10.1080/15377857.2011.540224.

Conway, Bethany Anne, Kate Kenski, and Di Wang. "Twitter Use by Presidential Primary Candidates During the 2012 Campaign." *American Behavioral Scientist* (2013). http://abs.sagepub.com/content/early/2013/05/22/0002764213489014. doi: 10.1177/0002764213489014.

D'Alessio, Dave. "Use of the World Wide Web in the 1996 U.S. Election." *Electoral Studies* 16, no. 4 (1997): 489–500. http://dx.doi.org/10.1016/S0261-3794(97)00044-9.

Davis, Richard. *The Web of Politics: The Internet's Impact on the American Political System.* New York: Oxford University Press, 1999.

Delli Carpini, Michael X., and Scott Keeter. *What Americans Know about Politics and Why It Matters.* New Haven, CT: Yale University Press, 1997.

Denton, Robert E., Jr. "Communication Variables and Dynamics of the 1996 Presidential Campaign." In *The 1996 Presidential Campaign: A Communication Perspective*, edited by Robert E. Denton Jr., 1–50. Westport, CT: Praeger, 1998.

de Valasco, Antonio. *Centrist Rhetoric: The Production of Political Transcendence in the Clinton Presidency.* Lanham, MD: Lexington Books, 2010.

Dimitrova, Daniela V., and Dianne Bystrom. "The Effects of Social Media on Political Participation and Candidate Image Evaluations in the 2012 Iowa Caucuses." *American Behavioral Scientist* (2013). doi: 10.1177/0002764213489011.

Doheny-Farina, Stephen. *The Wired Neighborhood.* New Haven, CT: Yale University Press, 1996.

Drew, Dan, and David Weaver. "Voter Learning in the 1996 Presidential Election: Did the Media Matter?" *Journalism & Mass Communication Quarterly* 75, no. 2 (1998): 292–301. doi:10.1177/107769909807500205.

Earl, Jennifer, and Katrina Kimport. *Digitally Enabled Social Change: Activism in the Internet Age.* Cambridge, MA: MIT Press, 2011.

Edelman, Murray. *Politics as Symbolic Action: Mass Arousal and Quiescence.* Chicago: Markham, 1971.

Edelman, Murray. *Constructing the Political Spectacle.* Chicago: University of Chicago Press, 1988.

Farnsworth, Stephen J., and S. Robert Lichter. *The Nightly News Nightmare: Media Coverage of U.S. Presidential Elections, 1988–2008.* 3rd ed. Lanham, MD: Rowman & Littlefield, 2010.

Faucheux, Ronald A. "Why Clinton Lost." In *Campaigning for President 2008: Strategy and Tactics, New Voices and New Techniques*, edited by Dennis W. Johnson, 44–59. New York: Routledge, 2009.

Feld, Lowell, and Nate Wilcox. *Netroots Rising: How a Citizen Army of Bloggers and Online Activists Is Changing American Politics.* Westport, CT: Praeger, 2008.

Fernandes, Juliana, Magda Girucanu, Kevin W. Bowers, and Jeffrey C. Neely. "The Writing on the Wall: A Content Analysis of College Students' Facebook Groups for the 2008 Presidential Election." *Mass Communication and Society* 13, no. 5 (2010): 653–675. doi:10.1080/15205436.2010.516865.

Foot, Kirsten A., and Steven M. Schneider. *Web Campaigning (Acting with Technology).* Cambridge, MA: MIT Press, 2006.

Germany, Julie Barko. "The Online Revolution." In *Campaigning for President 2008: Strategy and Tactics, New Voices and New Techniques*, edited by Dennis W. Johnson, 147–159. New York: Routledge, 2009.

Graham, Todd, and Scott Wright. "Discursive Equality and Everyday Online Political Talk: The Impact of 'Super-Participants.'" *Journal of Computer-Mediated Communication* (2013). doi:10.1111/jcc4.12016.

Granovetter, Mark S. "The Strength of Weak Ties." *American Journal of Sociology* 78, no. 6 (1973): 1360–1380.

Green, Donald P., Alan S. Gerber, and D. W. Nickerson. "Getting Out the Vote in Local Elections: Results from Six Door-to-Door Canvassing Experiments." *Journal of Politics* 65, no. 4 (2003): 1083–1096. doi:10.1111/1468-2508.t01-1-00126.

Gunn, Joshua. "On Speech and Public Release." *Rhetoric & Public Affairs* 13, no. 2 (2010): 175–215. doi:10.1353/rap.0.0146.

Hafner, Katie, and Matthew Lyon. *Where Wizards Stay Up Late: The Origins of the Internet.* New York: Touchstone, 1996.

Harfoush, Rahaf. *Yes We Did: An Inside Look at How Social Media Built the Obama Brand.* Berkeley, CA: New Riders, 2009.

Hargittai, Eszter, and Gina Walejko. "The Participation Divide: Content Creation and Sharing in the Digital Age." *Information, Communication & Society* 11, no. 2 (2008): 239–256. http://www.webuse.org/the-participation-divide-content-creation-and-sharing-in-the-digital-age/index.html.

Herring, Susan C, Lois A. Scheidt, S. Bonus, and E. Wright. 2004. "Bridging the Gap: A Genre Analysis of Weblogs." In *Proceedings of the Thirty-Seventh Hawaii International Conference on System Sciences (HICSS-37).* Los Alamitos, CA: IEEE Press. http://ieeexplore.ieee.org/xpl/articleDetails.jsp?arnumber=1265271&searchWithin%3DHerring%26sortType%3Dasc_p_Sequence%26filter%3DAND%28p_IS_Number%3A28293%29. doi: 10.1109/HICSS.2004.1265271.

Hobbes, Thomas. Leviathan: With Selected Variants from the Latin Edition of 1668. Edited by Edwin Curley. Indianpolis, IN: Hackett, 1994.

Holbrook, Thomas M., and Scott D. McClurg. "The Mobilization of Core Supporters: Campaigns, Turnout, and Electoral Composition in United States Presidential Elections." *American Journal of Political Science* 49, no. 4 (2005): 689–703. doi:10.1111/j.1540-5907.2005.00149.x.

Horton, Donald, and R. Richard Wohl. "Mass Communication and Para-Social Interaction: Observations on Intimacy at a Distance." *Psychiatry* 19, no. 3 (1956): 215–229.

Howard, Philip N. *New Media Campaigns and the Managed Citizen.* New York: Cambridge University Press, 2006.

Jacobs, Ronald N., and Eleanor Townsley. *The Space of Opinion: Medial Intellectuals and the Public Sphere.* New York: Oxford University Press, 2011.

Jamieson, Kathleen Hall. *Packaging the Presidency: A History and Criticism of Presidential Campaign Advertising.* 3rd ed. New York: Oxford University Press, 1996.

Jamieson, Kathleen Hall, and Paul Waldman. *The Press Effect: Politicians, Journalists, and the Stories That Shape the Political World.* New York: Oxford University Press, 2004.

Jenkins, Henry. *Convergence Culture: Where Old and New Media Collide.* New York: New York University Press, 2006.

Kang, Jiyeon. "A Volatile Public: The 2009 Whole Foods Boycott on Facebook." *Journal of Broadcasting & Electronic Media* 56, no. 4 (2012): 562–577. doi: 10.1080/08838151.2012.732142.

Karpf, David. *The MoveOn Effect: The Unexpected Transformation of American Political Advocacy.* New York: Oxford University Press, 2012.

Katz, Elihu, and Paul F. Lazarsfeld. *Personal Influence: The Part Played by People in the Flow of Mass Communication.* New York: Free Press, 1955.

Kenski, Kate, Bruce W. Hardy, and Kathleen Hall Jamieson. *The Obama Victory: How Media, Money, and Message Shaped the 2008 Election.* New York: Oxford University Press.

Kerbel, Matthew R. *Netroots: Online Progressives and the Transformation of American Politics.* Boulder, CO: Paradigm, 2009.

Klinenberg, Eric, and Andrew Perrin. "Symbolic Politics in the Information Age: The 1996 Republican Presidential Campaigns in Cyberspace." *Information, Communication & Society* 3, no. 1 (2000): 17–38. doi: 10.1080/136911800359.

Klotz, Robert. "Positive Spin: Senate Campaigning on the Web." *PS: Political Science and Politics* 30, no. 3 (1997): 482–486. http://www.jstor.org/stable/420127.

Kreiss, Daniel. "Developing the 'Good Citizen': Digital Artifacts, Peer Networks, and Formal Organization During the 2003–2004 Howard Dean Campaign." *Journal of Information Technology & Politics* 6, nos. 3–4 (2009): 281–297. doi:10.1080/19331680903035441.

Kreiss, Daniel. *Taking Our Country Back: The Crafting of Networked Politics from Howard Dean to Barack Obama.* New York: Oxford University Press, 2012.

Ku, Gyotae, Lynda Lee Kaid, and Michael Pfau. "The Impact of Web Site Campaigning on Traditional News Media and Public Information Processing." *Journalism and Mass Communication Quarterly* 80, no. 3 (2003): 528–547. doi:10.1177/107769900308000304.

Landow, George P. *Hypertext: The Convergence of Contemporary Critical Theory and Technology.* Baltimore, MD: Johns Hopkins University Press, 1992.

Latour, Bruno. "On Recalling ANT." In *Actor Network Theory and After,* edited by John Law and John Hassard, 15–26. Oxford: Blackwell, 1999.

Latour, Bruno. *Reassembling the Social: An Introduction to Actor-Network-Theory.* New York: Oxford University Press, 2007.

Lawson-Borders, Gracie, and Rita Kirk. "Blogs in Campaign Communication." *American Behavioral Scientist* 49, no. 4 (2005): 548–559. doi:10.117/0002764205279425.

Locke, John. *Locke: Two Treatises of Government.* Edited by Peter Laslett. Cambridge: Cambridge University Press, 1988.

Marcus, George E., W. Russell Neuman, and Michael MacKuen. *Affective Intelligence and Political Judgment.* Chicago: University of Chicago Press, 2000.

Margolis, Michael, and David Resnick. *Politics as Usual: The Cyberspace "Revolution".* Thousand Oaks, CA: Sage, 2000.

Marvin, Carolyn. *When Old Technologies Were New: Thinking about Electric Communication in the Late Nineteenth Century.* New York: Oxford University Press, 1988.

May, Albert L. "The Preacher and the Press: How the Jeremiah Wright Story Became the First Feeding Frenzy in the Digital Age." In *Campaigning for President, 2008: Strategy and Tactics, New Voices and New Techniques,* edited by Dennis W. Johnson, 78–101. New York: Routledge, 2009.

Mayo, Keenan, and Peter Newcomb. "How the Web Was Won." *Vanity Fair,* July 2, 2012. http://www.vanityfair.com/culture/features/2008/07/internet200807 2008.

McMillan, Sally J. "Exploring Models of Interactivity from Multiple Research Traditions: Users, Documents and Systems." In *Handbook of New Media,* edited by Leah Lieverouw and Sonia Livingstone, 163–182. Thousand Oaks, CA: Sage, 2002.

Nam, Taewoo, and Jennifer Stromer-Galley. "The Democratic Divide in the 2008 U.S. Presidential Election." *Journal of Information Technology & Politics* 9, no. 2 (2012): 133–149. doi:10.1080/19331681.2011.579858.

Neuman, W. Russell. *The Paradox of Mass Politics: Knowledge and Opinion in the American Electorate.* Cambridge, MA: Harvard University Press, 1986.

Nielsen, Rasmus Kleis. *Ground Wars: Personalized Communication in Political Campaigns.* Princeton, NJ: Princeton University Press, 2012.

Nimmo, Dan, and Robert L. Savage. *Candidates and Their Images: Concepts, Methods, and Findings.* Pacific Palisades, CA: Goodyear, 1976.

Norris, Pippa. *A Virtuous Circle: Political Communications in Postindustrial Societies.* Cambridge: Cambridge University Press, 2000.

Page, Benjamin I., and Robert Y. Shapiro. *The Rational Public: Fifty Years of Trends in Americans' Policy Preferences.* Chicago: University of Chicago Press, 1992.

Plato. *The Republic.* Translated by Benjamin Jowett. New York: Heritage Press, 1972.

Plouffe, David. *The Audacity to Win: The Inside Story and Lessons of Barack Obama's Historic Victory.* New York: Viking Press, 2009.

Poster, Mark. "Cyberdemocracy: The Internet and the Public Sphere." In *Reading Digital Culture,* edited by David Trend, 259–271. Malden, MA: Blackwell, 2001.

Prior, Markus. *Post-Broadcast Democracy: How Media Choice Increases Inequality in Political Involvement and Polarizes Elections.* New York: Cambridge University Press, 2007.

Putnam, Robert D. *Bowling Alone: The Collapse and Revival of American Community.* New York: Simon & Schuster, 2000.

Rafaeli, Sheizaf. "Interactivity: From New Media to Communication." In *Advancing Communication Science: Merging Mass and Interpersonal Processes*, edited by Robert P. Hawkins, John M. Wiemann and Suzanne Pingree, 110–134. Thousand Oaks, CA: Sage, 1988.

Rove, Karl. *Courage and Consequence: My Life as a Conservative in the Fight.* New York: Simon & Schuster, 2010.

Rowland, Robert C., and John M. Jones. "One Dream: Barack Obama, Race, and the American Dream." *Rhetoric & Public Affairs* 14, no. 1 (2011): 125–154. doi:10.1353/rap.2011.0007.

Ryan, Johnny. *A History of the Internet and the Digital Future.* London: Reaktion Books, 2010.

Schudson, Michael. *The Good Citizen: A History of American Civic Life.* Cambridge, MA: Harvard University Press, 1998.

Selnow, Gary W. *Electronic Whistle-Stops: The Impact of the Internet on American Politics.* Westport, CT: Praeger, 1998.

Shaw, Daron R. "How the Bush and Gore Campaigns Conceptualized and Used the Internet in 2000." *Journal of Political Marketing* 1, no. 1 (2002): 39–65. doi:10.1300/J199v01n01_04.

Smith, Craig Allen, and Neil Mansharamani. "Challenger and Incumbent Reversal in the 2000 Election." In *The 2000 Presidential Campaign: A Communication Perspective*, edited by Robert E. Denton Jr., 91–116. Westport, CT: Praeger, 2002.

Stokes, Ashli Quesinberry. "Clinton, Post-Feminism, and Rhetorical Reception on the Campaign Trail." In *The 2008 Presidential Campaign: A Communication Perspective*, edited by Robert E. Denton, Jr., 127–147. Lanham, MD: Rowman & Littlefield, 2009.

Stratford, Jean Slemmons, and Juri Stratford. "Computerized and Networked Government Information." *Journal of Government Information* 23, no. 3 (1996): 359–364.

Stromer-Galley, Jennifer. "Online Interaction and Why Candidates Avoid It." *Journal of Communication* 50, no. 4 (2000): 111–132. doi:10.1111/j.1460-2466.2000.tb02865.x.

Stromer-Galley, Jennifer. "Interactivity as Process and Interactivity as Product." *Information Society* 20, no. 5 (2004): 391–394. http://dx.doi.org/10.1080/01972240490508081.

Stromer-Galley, Jennifer, and Andrea Baker. "Joy and Sorrow of Interactivity on the Campaign Trail: Blogs in the Primary Campaign of Howard Dean." In *The Internet Election: Perspectives on the Web in Campaign 2004*, edited by Andrew Paul Williams and John C. Tedesco, 111–31. Lanham, MD: Rowman & Littlefield, 2006.

Sunstein, Cass R. *Republic.Com 2.0.* Princeton, NJ: Princeton University Press, 2009.

Sweet, Derek, and Margret McCue-Enser. "Constituting 'the People' as Rhetorical Interruption: Barack Obama and the Unfinished Hopes of an Imperfect People." *Communication Studies* 61, no. 5 (2010): 602–622. doi:10.1080/10510974.2010.514679.

Trent, Judith S. "The Early Presidential Campaign of 2008: The Good, the Historical, but Rarely the Bad." In *The 2008 Presidential Campaign: A Communication Perspective*, edited by Robert E. Denton Jr., 1–17. Lanham, MD: Rowman & Littlefield, 2009.

Trent, Judith S., and Robert V. Friedenberg. *Political Campaign Communication.* 5th ed. Westport, CT: Praeger, 2004.

Trippi, Joe. *The Revolution Will Not Be Televised.* Rev. ed. New York: HarperCollins, 2004.

Verser, Rebecca, and Robert H. Wicks. "Managing Voter Impressions: The Use of Images on Presidential Candidate Web Sites During the 2000 Campaign." *Journal of Communication* 56 (2006): 178–197. doi:10.1111/j.1460-2466.2006.00009.x.

Wicks, Robert H., and Souley Boubacar. "Going Negative: Candidate Usage of Internet Web Sites During the 2000 Presidential Campaign." *Journalism & Mass Communication Quarterly* 80, no. 1 (2003): 128–144. doi:10.1177/107769900308000109.

Wiener, Robert. *Cybernetics: Or, Control and Communication in the Animal and the Machine.* Cambridge, MA: MIT Press, 1948.

Wiese, Danielle R., and Bruce E. Gronbeck. "Campaign 2004 Developments in Cyberpolitics." In *The 2004 Presidential Campaign: A Communication Perspective*, edited by Robert E. Denton Jr., 217–240. Lanham, MD: Rowman & Littlefield, 2005.

Williams, Andrew Paul. "The Main Frame: Assessing the Role of the Internet in the 2004 U.S. Presidential Contest." In *The 2004 Presidential Campaign: A Communication Perspective*, edited by Robert E. Denton Jr., 241–254. Lanham, MD: Rowman & Littlefield, 2005.

Williams, Andrew Paul, and John C. Tedesco, eds. *The Internet Election: Perspectives on the Web in Campaign 2004*. Lanham, MD: Rowman & Littlefield, 2006.

Zaller, John R. *The Nature and Origins of Mass Opinion*. New York: Cambridge University Press, 1992.

Zappavigna, Michele. 2011. "Ambient Affiliation: A Linguistic Perspective on Twitter." *New Media & Society* 13, no. 5 (2011): 788–806. doi:10.1177/1461444810385097.

Zukin, Cliff, Scott Keeter, Molly Andolina, Krista Jenkins, and Michael X. Delli Carpini. *A New Engagement? Political Participation, Civic Life, and the Changing American Citizen*. New York: Oxford University Press, 2006.

Index